WOULD YOU BELIEVE!
My Life In Television

By

Andrew J. Selig

DEDICATION

This book is dedicated to my wife, Marie. She never complained about the long hours I spent at the studios. Marie kept telling me to write this book, and she inspired me to do it. My only regret is that I didn't start it sooner so she would have been able to read it. She passed away in June, 2015.

ANDREW J. SELIG

CONTENTS

1 The Early Years   1

2 Television   17

3 The $64,000 Question   31

4 Transitions   58

5 California   69

6 Marie   82

7 Moving On   99

8 World Events, Sports & Weddings   112

9 Every Day Is Different   131

10 A New Job   158

11 SOAP   182

12 The Eighties   208

13 What's Happening Now   225

14 End of an Era   251

15 After Television   257

16 Challenges   281

17 Saying Goodbye   297

   Acknowledgements   309

   Appendix A & B   312

   About the Author   322

PROLOGUE

These are stories of my life in television 1956 to 1992. When I started out, all shows were done LIVE! —which meant you only had one chance to do it. And there was only one way to do it: RIGHT. In live television, you work with whatever happens, you improvise when things don't go as planned, you solve problems on the fly, and you live with the results. This has been a good description not only of my work, but of my life.

CHAPTER 1
THE EARLY YEARS

I am a child of New York City. I was born in 1938. I joined my mother, Ceil, my dad, Milton, and my brother Steve, who was five years older, in an apartment at 86th Street & Madison Avenue. I have early memories of the bustle of transportation. From busses to trolleys, elevated railways to subways, you had options on how to get around the City. Back then, five cents got you on. If you had to get across town, there were cross-town busses, and if you were transferring from one of the Avenue busses to cross-town, you would ask for a free transfer from the bus driver. If you were on the 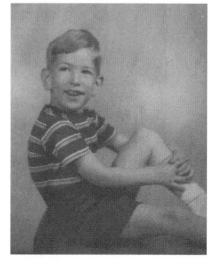 subway and needed to get from the East Side to the West Side or vice versa, you got off at 42nd Street and walked over to the shuttle, which was free. My mother took me to see the Empire State Building, and an elevator whooshed us up to the observation deck on the 86th floor. My ears popped in the elevator on the trip back down. We also went to Central Park, where they had a playground at 85th Street.

From l-r: Irv, Helen, Sam, my mother Ceil, Mac, Mae, and Dave

New York was a fascinating place that had the Natural History Museum and the Hayden Planetarium right next door. It had the Central Park Zoo and The Cloisters, a museum and garden which was part of the Metropolitan Museum of Art. It also had pigeons. One day, when I was about five years old, while walking home from Central Park on Fifth Avenue, a flock of pigeons startled overhead and pooped all over me. I shook my finger up at them and scolded, "Don't do that!!" My mother couldn't wait to get back to the apartment and put me in the tub.

Once, when I was about five years old, my mother, Steve and I were invited to visit the home of Harry Wurman in Pottstown, Pennsylvania for the day. Wurman was the president of Bayuk Brothers Cigars, the makers of the popular "Phillies" cigars. The brand of cigars later made an appearance in Edward Hopper's iconic painting "Nighthawks." Wurman was also patented a method of treating raw tobacco for cigars. We were excited about the invitation but, because my mother couldn't drive and my Steve was only ten years old, we could only get there by train. We went to Pennsylvania Station, and after Mom bought the tickets and found out what track from which it would depart, we went and stood in a line. Mom kept asking everyone around us if we were in the right line for Pottstown. My brother kept telling her that we were on the right line. She wouldn't trust him and would ask someone else. Steve was getting more and more impatient.

We were, in fact, on the right line, and took it all the way to Pottstown and back without a problem.

When we returned home, Steve remembered that we had a book by Robert Benchley, called *Pluck and Luck*. It was a collection of short stories, including one that was titled, "Ask That Man," which reminded Steve of Mom. In it, Benchley is tired of his wife pushing him to ask for directions, even though he knew the way. He devised a scheme where he pretended to ask for directions and then intentionally took the wrong path. After ten days of relying on wrong information, his wife finally ceded navigation to her husband. Steve handed this story to Mom, and she agreed it sounded just like her.

Later, when my brother married, he took the book with him. But I was able to find another copy at a used book store years later that cost me $2.00.

My brother Steve and I were never close, but we both attended P.S. 6, which was at Madison Avenue & 85th Street. There was a playground area, with an entrance on 86th Street, and most of the time that's how we entered the School. During recess at school my friends and I would play dodge ball or stoopball, where we would hit a rubber ball against the curb of the building. The object was not to have someone catch it. If they did, then it was their turn to hit the curb.

One of my best friends was Peter Berkman who lived across the street from us. I could see his apartment from ours. We would play cowboys using cap guns. At that time, one of the hit radio shows was *Gunsmoke*, and we would take turns being Marshall Dillon, the other relegated to being the bad guy. We played this on 86th Street because there were more places to hide. Marshall Dillon usually won.

The first time I went to Peter's apartment, I found out that his father, Aaron Berkman, was an accomplished artist who had come to New York during the Depression. He had been appointed by the Works Progress Administration as a Director of Federal Art Project's Contemporary Art Center in New York City. During this period, Aaron helped establish the first artist cooperative gallery in New York City. Our parents became friends and at Christmas we would exchange gifts. Aaron usually gave us one of his paintings, which

I still have.

My dad was had his own painting and decorating business in the city, and had both commercial and private clients. One of his contracts was with the Woolworth stores, which he could only paint after they closed at 6:00 p.m. He also painted Elizabeth Arden's residence. I was fascinated by her. She was also into Horse Racing, and won the Kentucky Derby in 1947, with her horse Jet Pilot, which made a big impression on me. Dad put a $10 bet on her horse.

When I was young, we would go to my Uncle Irv and Aunt Gert's home for Thanksgiving to celebrate their wedding anniversary. Uncle Irv, whose name was Irving Feinson, was a member of the Society of American Magicians. The Society, founded in 1902 Martinka's famous magic shop in New York City, was one of the oldest and most prestigious societies in the world. In fact, Harry Houdini had been president from 1903 until his untimely death in 1926. Uncle Irv served as a reporter for the Society's magazine, the *Conjurer*.

When we visited their house, my Uncle Irv would perform magic tricks after dinner. I was fascinated, and wondered if I could ever be a magician. I think Uncle Irv sensed that I was captivated by it.

A few years later, Uncle Irv invited me to the convention of the Society of American Magicians at the Barbizon Plaza Hotel in New York City. Luckily, my parents agreed to take me. There, Uncle Irv introduced me to some of his fellow magicians and I got a first-hand look at the entertainment business—dazzling lights, magicians in front of sets draped in red velvet. When the show started, some of the magicians did hand tricks, like pulling a rabbit out of a black hat, or doing card tricks, asking people from the audience to participate.

Sometimes, the magicians would ask for volunteers from the audience and my uncle told me to raise my hand. I was chosen to assist with the trick. I never knew what they were going to do because they wanted authentic reactions. One time I had to unbutton my sports jacket so he could pull a stuffed animal from the back of my shirt. I was captivated. I learned at an early age the magic of illusion, and how marvelous entertainment could be. Even then, I wanted to be involved in show business. Could I be a professional magician? Could I help entertain people?

Uncle Irv suggested that I start off with card tricks, and sent me to a man named Louis Tannen who owned Tannen's Magic Shop, the

oldest magic shop in New York. Lou took the time to show me how to do them. I went go home and practiced until I could perform them. A couple of months later I went back and Lou showed me how to do other tricks, including one called the "finger guillotine." It was a miniature guillotine device, with a finger-sized opening. I took my trick to my dad's office to try it. Mr. Fasler, my dad's estimator, agreed to be my guinea pig. I almost cut his finger on the first time, but then I remember what Lou taught me, and it . . . worked!

I also had a love of Broadway, a benefit of growing up in New York City. Dad would take us to see Broadway shows for our birthdays. Steve always wanted to see dramas, and I always picked a musical or a comedy. We usually went to a matinee and then to a restaurant for dinner. It was a highlight of the year for me.

I was about nine years old when I saw *Brigadoon,* my first show. This was following by *Finnian's Rainbow,* and *Along Fifth Avenue.* In those days, there were no microphones so the actors had to project their voices so everyone could hear them.

I did, however, have other opportunities. Around the same time as my introduction to magic, my dad started taking me on jobs with him, and to meet his painters. As I got older, I would work for my dad during school vacations, and get paid $25.00. Dad was also an officer with the Painting & Decorating Contractors, and I would go with him to have lunch in their dining room occasionally. I felt like my dad was training me to work with him, and so I took my responsibilities seriously.

Some of my chores were to brand his name on the paint brushes his men would use, and if they got terminated they had to return their brushes before they got their final pay. I grew into more and more responsibility. I would ride the Third Avenue Trolley under the elevated subway, or use the subway to go to various jobs and give the men their pay. In those days, we always paid with cash. Margaret, the bookkeeper, would call the bank to let them know what amount she needed in twenties, tens, fives and ones. Steve or I would pick up the cash from the bank. One time, my dad couldn't find a parking space and circled the block while Steve went inside to pick up the cash. Steve came out of the bank and started running to catch up with the car. Dad thought for sure that someone would think he had robbed the bank.

Back at the office, Margaret would put each employee's pay into an envelope. On school breaks, I would travel around New York City sometimes with hundreds of dollars in cash in my pocket. I guess no one expected that a 10-year-old boy would have any money.

One of Dad's clients was Benjamin Sonnenberg, considered the father of public relations. His clients included some of the most important businessmen and famous personalities of the 1930's and 40's. Mr. Sonnenberg had purchased just the historic townhomes at 19-20 Gramercy Park, and took out the walls to create a larger home. The result was a 37-room-plus mansion, which Sonnenberg planned to use to through extravagant, celebrity filled gatherings. To this day, although with different owners, it is still considered one of the finest mansions in New York City.

My father was hired to do the painting for the renovation project. One Friday, I went by the house to pay my father's workers. Mrs. Sonnenberg happened to be home, and noticed me. I was apparently the same age as her son, Ben, and she asked me if I would help her choose the colors for Ben's room.

I was so nervous. Here I was, an 11-year-old boy, representing my father's business to one of the wealthiest families in New York. What if I made a mistake? What if she disapproved? Nevertheless, I followed her through the large home. The floors were laid in intricate parquet patterns, and had beautiful carved wooden paneling on many of the walls. We climbed a staircase with ornate balusters to get to Ben's bedroom, which was enormous and lofty, so different from my little bedroom in our apartment on 86th street. The ceilings were 18 feet tall. But I had listened carefully to my father over the years. What colors would work for this space?

I thought for a minute, and suggested dark brown for the ceiling, and light gray for the walls. I told her that Dad would probably do a sample for her and her husband to look at. She thought that sounded like an excellent idea. I left the mansion, trying not to let my nervousness show.

When I got back to the office, Dad saw that I was a little shaky, and I explained what had happened at the Sonnenberg's house. He told me I did a good job, and that he would talk to them. He made up paint samples for them, and they ended up choosing the colors I suggested. I'm not sure if this was the key event or not, but I decided that I would like to work full time for my dad after I finished high school.

I liked spending time with my dad. He also belonged to the Circle Riding Club at Durland Riding Academy at 7 West 66th Street in New York. The Academy had horses to rent and an arena to ride in. These men had been friends for a long time and enjoyed getting together once a week. Most of them had their own McClellan saddles which had been used by the Army Cavalry. On Thursday nights, they would meet at the stables, and for about forty-five minutes would do different drills. Steve and I would sit in the stands and watch, but after that we would get a horse and join them to play basketball with a deflated ball. They would pass the ball around and, eventually, someone would take a shot at the basket. Since I was the shortest player, it was too hard for me to dismount, so I never had to retrieve the ball. Then, after putting the horses

and saddles away, we would go out and get dessert and coffee. I had milk or a Dr. Brown's Cream Soda.

I started taking riding lessons. Although my brother and I both rode, we weren't close. Steve loved picking on me, and found ways to torment me whenever he could. I finally got my revenge when I got a new pair of riding boots. I asked him to see if they looked too big. While he on his knees checking out my left foot, I cocked my right foot and kicked him in the knee. I broke it, and he never picked on me again.

Although we worked hard during the year, my parents decided that we needed to have a different experience during our summer vacation, and decided to send us to Camp Zakelo in Harrison, Maine. We would order the camp's t-shirts, shorts and sweatshirts, which we packed into small trunks along with tennis racquets and other personal items. There was enough room left over in my trunk that I took my magic tricks. We boarded the sleeper train from Grand Central Station, well-fortified with my Aunt Mae's Tollhouse cookies. We'd arrive in Portland, Maine the following morning, and take a chartered bus to camp.

We were assigned to cabins with boys our own ages. We had lots of group activities to choose from, including arts and crafts, canoeing, printing, baseball, soccer, and—my favorite—horseback riding. At three o'clock each day we would go back to the cabins, change into our swimming trunks and go to Long Lake for a swim. In the evenings, we had movies or some other kind of entertainment. One of the counselors, Mal, did magic, and I showed him the tricks I had brought to camp.

At the end of the first four weeks, parents were invited to visit and see us perform. Our parents came again at the end of eight weeks and stayed in Harrison for a few days. The last night of camp, after dinner, the counselors gave out awards for best baseball player, swimmer, tennis player and overall camper. Steve won the second year we were there. There were also reunions in New York City, held at the Croyden Hotel, across the street from where we lived. We attended this camp for three years. The last year when Mom and Dad picked us up, we could tell that something was wrong. When we finally got home, they told us they were getting divorced. I was twelve years old.

Everything changed. My father moved into a hotel and I stayed with my Mother. Steve stayed with her too, but at seventeen years old was almost out of the house anyway. Suddenly it was just me and my mother.

I had a premonition that my father was having an affair, but I wasn't sure. My first meeting of the other woman took place when I went to visit my dad at his hotel. I knocked on the door and she greeted me wearing a bra and half-slip. Her name was Hermine and they got married about three months later.

Hermine seemed to take over all aspects of my father's life, and I was no longer sure if I still had a place in it. I found out about a year later. One evening, while I was taking his wife home from a job, she informed me that I would not be welcomed into the business. Suddenly my plan of joining my father in the family business was over. I was devastated. Now what? I had no idea what I wanted to do with my future.

I was never a good student, as opposed to my brother Steve, and I never felt I could compete with him. Steve went to the High School of Science in the Bronx, and after graduating went to Williams College, where he was valedictorian of his class and Phi Beta Kappa. He had his future mapped out. He went on to Columbia Law School and had his pick of job offers after graduation. He settled on Baer, Marks, Freidman, a firm that specialized in advising companies on the stock exchange.

I attended Walden School at 88th Street in New York City. The school was very popular with intellectual families from New York's Upper West Side and with families based in Greenwich Village. It was based on a progressive ideal, that education was a vehicle for individual transformation, emphasizing creative expression and self-directed learning. Competition between students was minimized. No exams were required for admission. Students called teachers by their first names. It was a good fit for me.

There were only 23 students in my class, and I found myself interested in theater set design and lighting. I got involved with building new lights for the stage in the Auditorium, and I volunteered to do the lighting for our production of Gilbert & Sullivan's *Trial by Jury*. They needed a backdrop for the scenery, which we didn't have. I asked Ray John for permission to contact Broadway shows that were closing, to see if I could get some of their scenery. Usually, when a Broadway show closes, its scenery is usually destroyed so no one else could use it. Still, I contacted about five shows I knew were shutting down, and told them I needed six backdrop flats, which are usually about fifteen feet high. I finally found one that agreed to give them to me. They even offered to deliver them for free. All we had to do was paint them. They worked perfectly.

Ray John was the faculty advisor for the show, and he complemented me for doing a great job. The senior class was impressed, and they asked me to do the lighting for their Senior Class Show of 1954. I happily agreed.

After the success of the that show, the Senior class asked if I would help them out with their graduation. They wanted to hold the ceremony on the roof of the building, but wanted to know if I could figure out how to set up lights on the roof. I was intrigued by the project. This was exactly the kind of self-directed challenge the Walden

School encouraged.

I went to the Bill, the Shop teacher, Bill, who helped me decide on the lighting design and the equipment we would need. The Walden School gave us permission to do it. We took the lights we made for the school's auditorium and installed them on the roof, running the cables back to the auditorium from the roof. I was surprised that everything worked perfectly. That's when I got the idea that I wanted to become a Lighting Designer for Broadway. It combined so many things I enjoyed: theater, the magic of show business, but from the back-stage part of the business. It was both creative and practical, entertaining but useful. It seemed like a perfect combination of everything I'd thought I'd do for a living.

I needed a job for the summer of 1954, and I overheard Sam Nash, the Director of the Walden High School talking about a camp that he was going to be working at in Beacon, New York. I asked if there was a possibility that I could work there, too. He talked to the owners, learned that they were still interviewing, and gave me the information. I had a good meeting with owners, who were husband and wife, and was hired to work with the handyman on staff. I wouldn't receive any salary, but that was fine with me. My dad and brother drove me to the camp.

The handyman was very easy to work with, and his wife was the nurse at the infirmary. I only made one mistake. We were doing so work in the rafters of the infirmary, and I thought the ceiling could hold my weight if I stepped onto it. I was wrong, and I went through the plasterboard. Luckily it was only a small hole that had to be replaced. At the end of the summer, I thanked Sam for the experience, and would see him back at Walden in September.

At around the same time, my mother was talking to one of her friends, and mentioned that we had a spare bedroom. My brother Steve had moved out. About two weeks later we had dinner at our apartment with Mom's friends, the Marx's, and they brought along a young woman named Sally Shair to meet us. What was surprising was that she brought her luggage. And, yes she decided to stay. Sally was working at Ohrbach's Department Store as a buyer for women's underwear. After a little while I started calling her my "sister," a position she has maintained in my life.

One day, Sally told me she had a friend that knew Jo Mielziner, who was a set and lighting designer for Broadway. And not just any designer. Jo was considered the most successful set designer in the golden era of Broadway, having produced sets for, among other shows, *Carousel, South Pacific, Guys and Dolls, The King and I, A Streetcar Named Desire, Death of a Salesman, Cat on a Hot Tin Roof, Gypsy*, and *The Prime of Miss Jean Brodie*. At the time, he was the production designer for the show *Picnic*, for which he later won an Academy Award.

Sally's friend gave me Jo's information, and I called to make an appointment for a job interview. I went to see him. I nervously sat down in the chair across Mr. Mielziner, a somewhat stocky man with slicked back hair, wearing a natty vest and bow tie. He was a huge presence in the room. His first question to me was if I had graduated from Yale or Carnegie Tech with a degree in Set Design. My answer was no. He was very kind to me, but told me that I would not be able to work in the industry. That was the end of the conversation and, I thought, my career as a set designer. I was devastated. I had no idea where to turn next.

CHAPTER 2
TELEVISION

M y visions of being a Broadway set designer dashed, I still wanted to find a way to work in entertainment. I was intrigued by television. Back then, television was quickly eclipsing radio in popularity. People looked forward to their favorite TV shows, just as they had scheduled their time around radio programing. Most people had black and white television sets, and people watched Huntley & Brinkley on NBC, and Walter Cronkite on CBS.

So television was the next big thing. The question was, what could I do? In January of 1956, I ran into Ron Dubin, a friend of my brother who working in television production company called Entertainment Productions Inc. I mentioned that I was looking for a job in the entertainment industry, and thought he might have some ideas. He told me there was an opening at E.P.I. for a new runner.

Entertainment Productions Inc. was the new name for Louis G. Cowan Productions, founded by Louis G. Cowan. Cowan was a big name in show business in both radio and television. In 1941, Cowan had created *The Quiz Kids* for radio, and it was a huge hit. I remember listening to it when I was a boy. The show featured a panel of bright children, none older than 16 years old, who answered questions sent in by listeners. He also created *Take It Or Leave It,* which debuted on radio on April 21, 1940. The contestant was asked questions arranged by difficulty. The first question was worth $1.00 and then it would be doubled. The final question was worth $64.00. After each correct answer, the contestant would be asked if he or she wanted to go on, or take the money they had won or leave it. This was the precursor to *$64,000 Question.*

Cowan had recently sold his production company and gone to work for CBS, which precipitated the name change. At that time, E.P.I. produced the *$64,000 Question, Down You Go, The Big Surprise,* and *Stop the Music.* The concept for the shows, the set design, staffing, and direction for the shows was done by EPI, who then sold the show to advertisers, who then bought time on one of the three networks, ABC, CBS, or NBC. For example, the *$64,000 Question* was sold to Revlon, who in turn bought broadcast time on CBS, where Mr. Cowan was now Vice President.

I called and was fortunate enough to get an interview. I had no idea what to expect, since this was the first interview I ever had. I was nervous. The meeting would be with the treasurer of the company, Kyle Faber. On the following Monday, I took the Madison Avenue bus to 57th Street, and crossed the street to 575 Madison Avenue. Their offices were in the penthouse. I took the elevator to the 25th floor, and walked up the stairs to the offices. I arrived fifteen minutes before my appointment, and the receptionist informed Mr. Faber's office that I was there. His secretary Millie came out, and escorted me to his office. I had no idea what to expect. Mr. Faber looked to be about forty, with a crew cut. He put me at ease, and I thought the interview went well, and I would know by the end of the week.

On Friday, I received the call, and I was hired. I called Ron that evening, and thanked him. He suggested that I may want to go to the School of Radio Technique, where they also teach about television production. I took his advice, and enrolled. I was fortunate that the classes were in the evening, and would last for three months. Because I was working on *Down You Go*, which aired on Thursday evenings, I missed those classes, but it didn't affect my studies.

During the third month, the instructor asked what we would each like to do in the studio. Most wanted to be camera people, some wanted to be boom operators. He said he needed someone to be an audio mixer, and I raised my hand.

For our final exam, we produced a show, and they invited people in the television business to sit in the bleachers and observe us for possible hires. Since I was the audio mixer for this show, I went to Sam Goody, a record store, and bought Gordon Jenkin's "Manhattan Tower," which I thought would work for the opening and closing. The instructor liked it, and he showed me how to use a grease pencil to mark the cues on it, which could be removed after we were done. Audio mixing ended up being a good path for me to work my way into the industry.

But that was all to come. I started out as a runner at EPI, and made

$75 per week. My desk was up another flight of stairs from the executive offices, along with our Art Department. I worked next to Bill Watt & Ken Dorman, who prepared the art work for *Down You Go*, *$64,000 Question* and *The Big Surprise*, and they also worked in the studios. Our floor also held the were cubicles where prospective contestants were interviewed, and a mimeo room where we run off the scripts each week. My job duties included opening the telephone switchboard from 8:30 a.m. until 9:00 a.m. when Charlotte, the receptionist, arrived and took over, going to the bank, getting lunch for the executives, or running other errands. In those days, you always wore a shirt, tie and jacket.

One of my first errands was to CBS Headquarters at 485 Madison Avenue, which was five blocks from our office. I had to go see Mr. Louis Cowan and have him sign some papers. I had never met Mr. Cowan in person, but he had a tremendous reputation, and I knew *about* him. He was a giant in the entertainment industry, and was known for creating shows with an intellectual slant for mainstream audiences. He was also a very decent human being. During World War II, he had been influential in creating positive portraits of African-Americans and military personnel in his popular radio programs.

I arrived at his office and his secretary, Elaine, said it would be a few minutes. I sat down and waited, wondering what it would be like to meet this great man. Would he be gruff? Impatient? Would he even look up from his desk to greet me? After I had waited a half hour, Mr. Cowan came out personally. He shook my hand and apologized for keeping me waiting. One of the most powerful men in television was apologizing to a teenaged runner in his company! I was astounded. He invited me into his office, signed the papers I had brought and just chatted with me for a while. I guess I made a good impression, because I was asked to go there at least twice a week. I looked forward to going to his office, because he would spend quality time with me, and was interested in what I wanted to aspire to. I felt he was truly interested in me, and his example would influence the way I worked with other people throughout my career. Lesson number one: treat people the way you would like to be treated.

Although my salary was small, there were perks that came with working at the Studio. I started out instructing the audience when to applaud, and eventually I moved up to being a stand-in for the Emcee during rehearsals. For this, I was paid an extra $15.00 per show. I tried to get as many of these opportunities as I could.

My first show was *Down You Go*. It was produced by E.P.I. and aired by ABC. At the ABC Studio, which was located next door to the famous Sardis Restaurant, a hangout for celebrities and newspaper columnists, I found out that Mr. Cowan's wife Polly had created the show. The premise of the show was like the game of Hangman, in which a panel of four celebrities would try to solve phrases sent in by viewers. The emcee, Dr. Bergen Evans, would ask the panelist to guess a letter in the phrase. If the guess was incorrect, the Emcee would say "Down You Go," and he or she would be eliminated for the rest of that round. The viewer who had sent in the phrase would get a cash award.

Part of my job was to take the phrases being used for that week's show to a photographer to make slides for the game board, bring them back to the office, and them bring them to the studio on Thursdays.

It was aired in primetime (which was from 8:00 p.m. to 11:00 p.m.) and the show was, of course, performed live. On the day the show aired, the emcee and staff would rehearse three one-minute commercials for an hour, and then we would rehearse the show itself for a half-hour to make sure everything was working. During these rehearsals, our staff would sit in for the celebrities.

During the hour break before doing the actual show, I learned that there were two poker games regularly held off stage. One was with the ABC personnel, where the stakes were high, and the other with our *Down You Go* staff, where we could bet up to ten cents a hand. Usually after about twenty minutes, some of the ABC people would join our game.

Then the audience would come in and be warmed-up by a comedian. Part of his routine was to tell the audience what would happen if they didn't laugh or applaud. He brought out a board on stage that had a printed layout of all the seats on it with wires coming out the back. He would randomly hit the button marking one of the seats, and the stooge sitting in that seat would jump up and leave rubbing his backside.

Then we went on LIVE! The show went on no matter what.

For example, before Valentine's Day one year, FTD (Floral Telegraph Delivery) bought one of the three live Commercial spots on the show. After the commercial, the FTD spokesperson took one of the long-stemmed roses, and put in his mouth, forgetting that there were thorns attached. You can picture what happened next.

Also challenging was that ABC used four General Electric cameras at this studio. Each had an electric turret with four different focal lengths, depending on what the director wanted. The director would switch to another camera while the focal length was changed, and then switch back. At least once a month a turret would jam, and we would be down to three cameras for the rest of the half hour. The director was very upset, and tried to get these cameras replaced, but to no avail. We came up with our own names for ABC, such as Amateur Broadcasting Company, Almost Broadcasting Company, Ass-Backward Corporation, Always Buy Cheap.

The next day after the shows aired, we would receive a sixteen-inch audio recording of the show, so if there were any problems, we would have a way of checking. For example, sometimes a contestant would object that they had given a different answer on air, and these recordings were backup for what had occurred. This was done for all our shows.

We also produced *Stop the Music*, emceed by Bert Parks. Bert would play a song, and after it was played, he would call a home viewer would be called and ask them to correctly name the song he had just aired. If the viewer was correct, he or show won a prize, as well as a chance to identify a short clip from the Mystery Melody for more prizes. If the viewer missed the first song, he or she would get a consolation prize, and members of the audience would be asked to identify the song. Some of the secretaries from the office would make these phone calls to the viewers.

I finally felt like I was becoming an adult. Although I was still living at home with my mother, I was much more independent. Our company used a broker to get theater tickets, and I called them to treat my mother to Broadway plays. All of this kept me busy. I worked six days a week in order to be available for all the preparation as well as the actually airing of the shows. I got Sundays off.

Steve had recently graduated from Columbia Law School, and found a job at Baer, Marks & Friedman, located in the financial district. He invited me to have lunch with him one day, and he introduced me to one of the partners, Mr. Friedman. I found out that his daughter had also attended Walden High School, and graduated a year before I did. We then walked over to the Fulton Fish Market for lunch.

Since Steve and I were both employed, we had dinner with our Dad, who was divorced from our Mother, on a weekly basis. The plan was to take turns picking up the bill. I felt very lucky to have just gotten a Diners' Club credit card, and I enjoyed showing it off. Yet it seemed odd that my brother never managed to pick up the bill. So, the next time we got together I said to Dad, follow my lead after dinner. At which time I said I needed to go to the rest room, and Dad said he had to go also. As we left the rest room, I said let's go outside, and stare through the window at Steve, sitting there with the bill. He ended up paying the bill, but he didn't like it.

On the bus line to my home, it would stop right in front of the Madison Delicatessen. A couple of times a weeks I would get off and pick-up a sandwich and Dr. Brown Cream Soda, and then walk across the street to our apartment building

After a while, my boss, Mr. Faber, informed me that I would also start working on a show called *The Big Surprise*. This was done at NBC, at 30 Rockefeller Plaza, in Studio 6A. The show aired at 8:00 pm on Saturdays from October 8, 1955 until June 9, 1956, and then on  Tuesdays from September 18, 1956 until April 2, 1957, and the show was telecast in color. Those early RCA cameras were big and bulky, and we had four on the set.

If contestants decided to stop early in the contest, they were shown a passbook—just like the one you would get from the bank—listing the amount of money they would win at that point. Part of my job would be to mount the various passbooks on blue cards. We made up new passbooks every week, because they were dated, and the amounts would change.

The producer of *The Big Surprise* was Merrill Heatter, the nephew of Gabriel Heatter, who was a well-known radio journalist. Merrill made a name on his own as both a screenwriter and a producer. Merrill liked me because I would run some personal errands for him, like getting his cleaning, theater tickets, or lunch, and not tell anyone about it. Once he invited a few of the people from the office to a birthday party at his apartment. After dinner, he sat down and started playing the piano. After he finished playing, his wife said, "I didn't know you played!"

The contestants on *The Big Surprise* played for a grand prize of $100,000. They could select easy or hard questions, which were worth different amounts of money. Two models, Sue Oakland and Mary Gardner, would hand the questions to the Emcee. In rehearsals, the models were kidded about being "easy and hard." James Colvin from *Encyclopedia Britannica* was there to authenticate the answers. One of the contestants on the show in 1957 was Errol Flynn and his category was "Ships and the Sea".

The control room was in a small space behind the audience. The director, associate director, video engineer, audio engineer, the NBC unit manager, and the producer all squeezed into the space.

When I started, the emcee was Jack Barry. Part my job was to hold up cue cards for him when a contestant answered a question. Depending on if the answer was right or wrong, Jack had different cue cards for him to read. Even though all this information was on the tele-prompters, the operator couldn't scroll down fast enough and the cue cards were a quicker source. Jack was not easy to work with. He would complain that I took too long getting the cue cards up for him. Then in March of 1956, Barry was dismissed as emcee, and replaced by Mike Wallace. Mike understood how the show worked, and didn't need the cue cards. He could remember what he had to do with the contestants, and this made my job a lot easier.

Mike had been a successful radio announcer, but this was television. You would never have known that this was Mike's first game show.

NBC decided to change the day we aired, and moved us to Saturday nights at 7:30 p.m. This introduced a recurring problem. Every two weeks at the end of the show, Bill Danhauser, the NBC Unit Manager assigned to the *The Big Surprise*, would get a phone call in the control room from the NBC Kinescope Department, telling him that they forgot to record the first two minutes of the show. Because the West coast market was on a time delay, it never got to see the opening of the show.

On another occasion the director told the cameraman to dolly in, or move the camera closer. He forgot to tell him to stop, and the cameraman put a hole in the curtain covering the back wall.

Live television offered lots of opportunities for things to go wrong. Harry Fleischman, the new President of EPI, also owned a music business called Tree Publishing in Nashville. One of its biggest hits was "Heartbreak Hotel" by Elvis Presley. This one particular Saturday, Fleischman asked me to go with him to the studio where *Your Hit Parade*, a television show played the most popular songs of the week, was rehearsing to see if they could use the song on their show that night. He brought along a copy of *Billboard & Variety* to show them the song was number one. The producers of *Your Hit Parade* didn't have any plans to do the song, but after seeing it was number one, they did add it to the show. The only problem was that Snooky Lanson sang it. It just wasn't the same without Elvis. The performance was a disaster.

Sometime in 1957, the Screen Directors Guild, which represented the television directors, went on strike. They walked out on a Wednesday, but we didn't have a show until Saturday. The company had found a director who would cross the picket line for us. I talked with someone who was also doing a show at NBC, whose director also crossed the picket line. I asked him to show me how this was done. I met him at Fifth Avenue and 50th Street. We went into a building, and walked down a flight of stairs to a concourse, which would take us to the basement of 30 Rockefeller Plaza and the NBC Studios. On Saturday, I met the director at the same location, and took him to

Studio 6A. We started rehearsing, and at 6:30 p.m. we heard that the strike and been settled, and the real director would be there by 7:00 p.m.

I kept up my regular contact with Mr. Cowan. I guess I really impressed Mr. Cowan, because he asked me to bring the 16mm projector from the office to his home for his children's birthday parties. The movies were either comedies or musicals the Cowans had procured, and they were waiting for me when I arrived. That's when I met his wife Polly for the first time. Polly was a remarkable person. She was as kind and honorable as her husband. The children were well behaved and she put me at ease. Plus, she always made sure I got a piece of birthday cake.

Mr. Cowan also called me at the office to see if I would help put together news footage for John F. Kennedy's presidential campaign. I jumped at the chance. He sent me to Movietone News to find newsreel footage. It took about a week to review all the footage and get it all together. When I called to let him know that the reel was ready, he said he would let me know when the people who needed it would be available. Two days later, he told me they were coming. I had no idea who "they" were. Into the viewing room walked Eleanor Roosevelt, the former first lady, and Thomas K. Finletter, a public servant in Truman's administration, and most recently Secretary of the Air Force. Talk about being nervous! They were very cordial, however, and listened politely when I explained where I had found the footage. After playing the reel for them, they seemed pleased with it, and took with them.

Things were going well for me. After all my childhood daydreaming, here I was, working in television. In less than a year I had moved from unknown runner to an employee with decent pay, some responsibility, and the respect of people I admired. I was 19 years old, and television was in its infancy. We were both growing up.

In 1957, I was given a new opportunity. I was asked to start working on the *$64,000 Question*, a show that would make television, and national, history.

CHAPTER 3

THE $64,000 QUESTION

The *$64,000 Question*. This show was one of the biggest spectacles on television. It had started out as a radio program called *Take It or Leave It* in 1940, and then in 1950 became the *$64 Question*, in which the prize money topped out at $64. It had been successful as it was, but Lou Cowan, the producer, decided to add three zeroes to the program's top prize to make the *$64,000 Question*. Back then, $64,000 was a fortune. Remember, I was making $75 per week, or about $4,000 per year.

Having developed the idea for the show, Louis B. Cowan had to find a commercial sponsor. In those days, the sponsor owned the time slot, paid for the production costs, had live commercials included in the program, and had ultimate control of the show. Cowan approached several companies—Helena B. Rubenstein, Chrysler, among others, and was turned down.

Then he found Revlon. Revlon had founded during the Great Depression by Charles Revson and his brother Joseph along with a chemist, Charles Lachman, who contributed the "L" in the Revlon name. Revlon at that time was deep into the "lipstick wars" with Hazel Bishop, a Barnard educated chemist who invented the first kiss-proof lipstick ("it stays on you . . . not on him"). Charles Revson knew that Hazel Bishop's company had taken over 25% of the lipstick sales, in part due to her successful advertising on the show *This Is Your Life*. Revson decided to give television advertising a try.

The show used contestants who were average people, not celebrities. Another feature was to stretch the drama of the competition out over a five-week period. The show was hosted by Hal March, and his assistant, a woman named Lynn Dollar.

The premise was straightforward. A contestant's name was announced by Bill Rogers. Lynn Dollar would escort them down to the stage and Hal March would interview them. He would tell them to look at the Question Board and pick their subject (such as "World History" or "Baseball" or "Opera"). Lynn would then press the subject number on the IBM machine, and the first four questions would come out. Only one contestant would be on stage at a time to answer questions. The contestant would attempt to answer questions only in that category, earning money for each right question. The winnings started at $64 for the first question, then doubled with each right answer and the questions became more difficult. The amount was $64.00 for the first question and then it would double to $128, and then triple to $256, then quadruple to $512. The winnings went from $64 to $128, to $256, to $512, then $1,000, to $2,000 to $4,000, and so on.

Once a player answered the $1,000 question, Hal would walk them over to Ben Feit from New York Manufacturer's Trust Bank for the $2,000 and $4,000 questions, which were pulled from a vault watched by two guards. If they opted to continue, they were placed in the Revlon-branded isolation booth for the $8,000 questions, and all subsequent questions. . This was done so the Revlon and Chrysler Air Temp Air Conditioner logos would be seen. The contestant would then be asked to return the following week, when they would be given the option of quitting or to keep going for the $64,000 price. If, however, they decided to go for the top prize and gave an incorrect answer, they went home with a Cadillac convertible as a consolation prize. In those days, there were fees paid to the production company for showing corporate logos, such as IBM, Chrysler Air Temp Air Conditioners, American Airlines. Cadillac gave us credit for its cars, and they would apply them if a contestant lost the game, but won the car.

The show was a phenomenal success, and gained a #1 rating on Neilson's. This was at a time when television was becoming the dominant form of entertainment. A PBS film on the show stated that

No program in the short history of television had ever attracted so many viewers so quickly -- 47 million in ten weeks. Audiences loved the idea of watching people like themselves compete for huge sums of money by answering tough questions. "The common man as genius," one writer called it. . . . At the times these shows aired, the crime rate and movie theatre attendance actually dropped.[1]

---

[1] The Quiz Show Scandal," *The American Experience*, Public Broadcasting Service, 1999, Television.

Phil Cuoco, the CBS set decorator assigned to our show, once told us that when he was in Texas on vacation, and had gone into a bar. At 9:50 p.m., the bartender told everyone to get their drinks because at 10 p.m. the bar closed until 10:30 p.m., so they could watch the show uninterrupted. They really looked forward to Tuesday nights.

The first big winner was a Marine Richard McCuthen whose category was cooking. Part of the genius of the show was to find contestants who were ordinary people from traditional fields of work, but who had expertise in an unexpected feel. Another contestant was Dr. Joyce Brothers, a previously unknown psychologist, whose category was boxing. She had memorized over 20 volumes of material, and was fortunate enough to win the $64,000.

Another interesting contestant was Billy Pearson, who was a race horse jockey. In his lifetime, he won 826 races around the world. His category was Art. Billy got interested in Art after a riding accident.

One of Billy's question dealt with the order in which horses finished in a race. I created a Plexiglas panel that had six horses attached by wire. Billy would tell Hal, the host, the order and Hal would arrange the six horse figures in order.

Billy went on to win $64,000. The next day he went to Dunhill's

Tobacco Shop, and bought the staff gold lighters. Since I didn't smoke, I gave it to my Mother, who did.

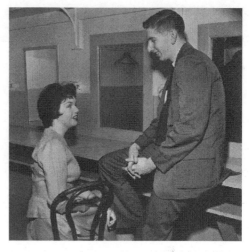

Another contestant was Barbara Hall. Her category was Shakespeare. She did very well, and won the $64,000. You probably do not recognize the name because she changed it to Barbara Feldon, and went on to become Don Adam's partner on "Get Smart".

Of course, the show was broadcast live every Tuesday at 10:00 p.m., so we had a lot of behind the scenes work to do to make it run smoothly. I would finish filming *Big Surprise* on Tuesday at 8:00 p.m., and then I'd rush over to CBS Studio 52, which was between Broadway and Eighth Avenue on 52nd Street, about four blocks away. The studio had previously been used as a theatre for Broadway productions before being converted for television. It could hold an audience of about 700 people.

Rehearsals for *$64,000* Question would start at 8:30 p.m. The show has a 12-piece orchestra, conducted by Norm Leydon, who also composed the theme music. Leydon had also been one of the arrangers for Glenn Miller's Air Force Bank. Bill Taylor, the audio engineer would begin rehearsal by balancing the sounds of all the orchestra instruments. We would sometimes stand in front of the orchestra while they were tuning and suck lemons. You wouldn't believe how bad the horn musicians sounded when we did that.

Hal March would arrive at the Studio at 8:30 p.m., and meet with the producers, and go over the interviews, and any questions that required visual props, like the race horse question, or how to operate a Geiger counter, or any other device.

Revlon aired three one-minute commercials during the show, so we always rehearsed these ads with actress Barbara Britton, Revlon's spokesperson, before our camera rehearsal.

Dr. Bergen Evans, a Professor at Northwestern University, was used to authenticate the questions used on the show. He would make the trip to New York every week. He would prepare the questions ahead of time and then meet with Mert Koplin, the producer to review and edit them.

At the end of each broadcast, the credits would be superimposed. It was part of my responsibility to make sure to have any new cards made. They were printed on 11 x 14-inch art cards, with white lettering on a black background. I would deliver them to the stage manager and he would instruct the prop man where to insert it. The director would cue the stage manager, who in turn would tap the prop man on the shoulder to pull the pin for the next card, and the cameraman would have to check focus for each one.

Since I was the new person on the show, I would go up to the balcony ten minutes before going on the air, and when Bill Rogers, the announcer/warm-up person, would ask the audience to applaud so the audio engineer could have some idea how loud they were going to be.

I would raise my hands and lead the applause. They were also asked to be quiet during the commercials.

I finally graduated from leading the applause in the balcony to doing it on the stage level. I was also given the opportunity to stand-in for contestants or show the cameraman, Hal Clausen, if the contestants had any family members in the audience, and where they were seated.

One evening, the executive producer, Steve Carlin, was trying to get to the control room before the show started. I told him that he would have to wait until after the opening because the doorway would be partially blocked by the audio boom after the opening of the show. Steve just froze in the doorway, and was hit by the back of the boom. He said he was alright, and then proceeded to the control room with a slight headache.

Gay Taylor was approached by the CBS publicity department, to recommend someone for the article that the *New York World Telegram & Sun* newspaper was going to do called "Big Picture Looks Clear in TV Production Jobs." They interviewed me about what I did on the show, and submitted pictures of me at the Studio. The article was in the June 7,

1957 issue. They had a picture of me talking to the director Seymour Robbie, who took over when Joe Gates left as director.

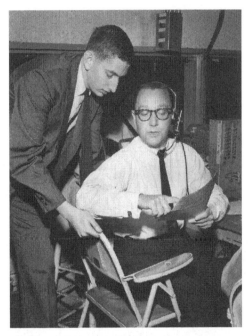

Seymour would come into the office on Tuesday afternoons, and meet with the producers to go over the new contestants, and any visuals that would be used on the show that night.

One night, two brothers were going to be, and in the rehearsal staff played the brothers. Someone mentioned that the brothers had a sister, and that she changed her name to Hazel Bishop, Revlon's main competitor. Unknown to us, Charles & Martin Revson, who owned Revlon, were in the audience at the time. The next day, Harry Fleishman, the president of EPI, got a letter stating that it wasn't funny. We never did anything like that again.

One of the most surprising things happened after a Contestant won $32,000 on the show. She went to the Manufacturers Trust Bank and cashed her check. The following day she was back in the office asking for another one. It seems she went to the race track, and lost it all. And, no she didn't get another one.

One week, I mentioned to CBS that we would be using a Geiger counter in two weeks. This was used for detecting some metals that were part of the questions. The night we were going to use it, I was informed that the stage crew, and the engineers were fighting over who had jurisdiction of plugging it in. CBS had forgotten to talk to the union stewards. Since we had no back-up plan, I got the head electrician and the technical director together. We all went over to the wall, and had both plug it in together. I told them they could file a grievance the next day. Fortunately, they didn't.

Just before the summer of 1957, Hal asked if he could get away for a few weeks. The producers granted his request, and brought in celebrities to fill in. The first week was Ed Sullivan, who had his own show, *Toast of the Town*, a variety show on CBS. Ed didn't really understand how the show worked, and he just barely made it through the half hour. The next guest emcee was Charlton Heston, and he understood what he had to do. When he had finished rehearsing, I noticed that he wore a small chain link belt, and I asked about it. He told me you never know who might want to start a fight, so I am prepared if that happens.

Because the *$64,000 Question* was the #1 show, I would get calls occasionally from the movie studios wanting VIP tickets, and in return I would be invited to sneak previews of their movies, and the cocktail parties afterwards.

There were other perks. The show used the Encyclopedia Britannia to authenticate its answers, and they asked if Hal, the emcee, would pose for some publicity pictures. In return they offered Hal a set of Encyclopedias or the *54 Books of the Western World*. Hal took the

Encyclopedias, and because I helped to set it up, Encyclopedia Britannia gave me the *54 Books of the Western World.*

This worked out well for me. At that time, my brother Steve was engaged to be married to a woman named Judy Harris. The set would make a perfect engagement present.

My brother Steve asked me to be his Best Man. On Friday, September 6, 1957, his friends and I held a stag party for Steve. He and I left the party about midnight, and took a cab to our apartment on 86th Street. As we were leaving the cab, Steve kissed the bald head of the driver. The driver wanted to belt him, but I was able to convince him not to, because he was getting married. I gave the driver a generous tip, and proceeded to the apartment.

On Saturday, Steve told me to pick-up the suitcases from Judy's apartment and take them with his to the St. Regis Hotel. After arriving there, I confirmed their reservation, and went to the florist shop to get rose petals that he wanted me to strew around the room.

From there I went to J. Press to pick-up the tuxedos for Steve, myself, and the ushers. The wedding was held at the Warwick Hotel at 69 West 54th Street, where Judy's aunt and uncle lived. At noon, Steve showed up, and was surprised that I had everything there, and asked if I had any problems at the St. Regis. I told him everything was taken care of.

The ceremony started at 1:00 p.m., and Rabbi David Putterman, from the Park Avenue Synagogue where we were members, performed the wedding ceremony. Everything was perfect. At the reception, when it was time to give the Toast, I said "Here's to my little brother and his

Bride." I was six-foot-three, and Steve was five-nine. He and Judy went on their honeymoon to Europe and moved to an apartment at Abingdon Square near Greenwich Village. Life was moving ahead. I was a single man, living in the city, with a great job in television. Things were looking up.

I guess I was doing a good job, because Kyle Faber, the treasurer for EPI, asked if I would be interested in learning what a Production Supervisor's job was, I jumped at the opportunity to learn more.

I shared an office with Joe Stahl, who was the production supervisor for E.P.I. While Kyle Farber, the treasurer, was in charge of "Above the Line" costs—including the director, producers, talent, writers, office and their overhead charges, the production supervisor was in charge of the "Below the Line" costs. Joe was responsible for budgeting for stagehands, technical crews, wardrobe, makeup and hairdressers, and ushers all of which were provided by the studio, which in this case was CBS. Joe gathered the costs from CBS and incorporated them into the budget.

Joe was a very gracious mentor, and was always willing to teach me parts of his job. He showed me the various rate cards from ABC and NBC and other things. I think that's when I decided this is what I wanted to do.

Joe was also a prankster. One time we took the pins out of Executive Producer Steve Carlin's door, and just propped it back in place. Steve had been at a difficult meeting, and when he came back he was furious. He went into his office, and slammed the door. It just fell over. Joe and I high-tailed it out of the office, and came back an hour later when things had calmed down.

Another time, Joe and I snuck into Producer Mert Koplin's office and we removed his desk and chair, leaving him with his phone, pad and pen, and a cushion on the floor to sit on. Mert didn't think that it was funny, and he wanted everything back by the time he got back from lunch. It was. That was the last time we tried anything.

During this time, we hired two new runners, one of whom was Stu Billet, who would become a friend of mine. These two were very creative. They turned the mimeo room into a little commissary, and were selling sandwiches and sodas to the employees. Everything was going well, until they decided one day to cook some fish. The aroma is what did them in.

One Wednesday, after *$64,000 Question* aired, Harry Fleishman, E.P.I.'s president, asked Joe to come see him about a problem that occurred the previous night. When Joe came back to our office, he was in tears. He told me he had just resigned, and packed up his belongings and left. Soon after, Kyle Farber told me that I would now replace Joe. I never learned what had happened. All I knew what that I was now a Production Supervisor on the *$64,000 Question*.

A few weeks later, I handed a check for a Contestant to Ben Feit, the vice president from Manufactures Trust Bank. Two checks accidentally stuck together, probably because of the humidity in the studio. The following morning I was summoned to Harry's office to tell him what happened. I gave him the explanation, and he asked why I wasn't crying like Joe had. I explained that it was an accident, and that I was sorry. He accepted it.

Harry decided that he was missing too many important phone calls while he was in the men's room shaving in the morning, so he had a phone installed in there. There were tiles all over the room, and when the phone rang, the sound just echoed off the walls. Some of the time after he shaved, he would come out with tissues over his cuts. The phone lasted three months.

Based on the success of the $64,000 Question, E.P.I. decided to produce a sequel to it, called the *$64,000 Challenge*. The premise was to get previous winners from the *$64,000 Question* who won at least $8,000. They would get questions starting at $1,000 each. When they reached the $4,000 plateau both contestants entered two isolation booths. They each got the same questions, until one of them missed.

Shirley Bernstein was hired as the producer for the *$64,000 Challenge*. I found out after a few weeks that she was Leonard Bernstein's sister. She would ask me to pick up reference materials for possible questions. I would pick up two copies of the books, so we would have pictures for the contestants, and pictures for the home audience. For musical questions, I would get the records, and Shirley would mark them, and I would then go and have it dubbed off.

E.P.I. made a great spectacle of preserving the honesty of the show. All of the questions used for each show were sealed in an attaché case that I would take to Chase Manhattan Bank on Friday afternoons at 2:00 p.m. so they could put a wire around it and put a seal on it so it could not be opened. I then took the case back to the office. On Sunday, I would go to the office to take the case to the studio in a taxicab. The case was then unsealed on the set by 9:30 p.m. on Sunday evening, just prior to the show. What the Bank didn't know was that the producers often wanted to change the questions at the last minute. They found that they could slip the wire off, put the revised questions inside, and slip the wire back around.

For the *$64,000 Challenge* Revlon wanted to share the cost of the show this time, and got Kent cigarettes to go in with them. Revlon rehearsed their commercials in the same studio where the show was done, but, in order to keep cigarette smoke out of the studio, Kent had to rehearse theirs in a satellite studio on East 58th Street. A half hour before we would go live, the technical director would check in with satellite studio, and CBS Broadcast Operations Control, because their commercials had to be fed to our studio, and then go on the air.

I usually got to the Studio at about 3:00 p.m. on Sunday, and after checking that everything was working, I would go next door to Studio 50, and watch part of the rehearsal for the *Ed Sullivan Show*.

Shirley occasionally asked me to deliver things to her brother, Leonard, and I jumped at the chance. I had gone to see his production of *West Side Story*, and was a big fan. After doing this a few times, she offered me house seats, and they were usually in the fifth-row, center section. The only problem was that the perspiration from the dancers would come off their hands and into the audience where I was sitting. Still, as a boy who grew up in New York City loving Broadway, I felt was getting the true essence of a Broadway show.

Sonny Fox was the first Emcee of *$64,000 Challenge*. On our first show the opening was the tympani drum. On the first show, the Executive Producer Steve Carlin was running to the control room and tripped on a camera cable. He fell into the drum to stop his fall. A snare drum just didn't have the same effect.

After a few months, Sonny was replaced with Ralph Story. Ralph had a bald spot on his head, and the make-up artist used a spray to hide it. When he went home, all he had to do was shower it off. We would talk after rehearsals, and he found out that I lived close to where he was renting an apartment. After a couple of weeks he offered me a ride home.

One Sunday we were going to have Vincent Price and Edward G. Robinson on, and their category was Art. I was asked to go to see Mr. Robinson at his hotel, and go over his interview with him. Although the producers had done a lot of research on Robinson, I was sent to make sure everything was accurate. When I entered his room,

there was no place walk; he had art books covering almost the entire the floor. He gave me ten minutes, and ushered me out, so he could back to studying.

We had another contestant whose category was Skeet Shooting, and many of her questions involved live coverage of the contestant shooting. We located a skeet shooting range in New Jersey to use. This was going to be my first location shoot. After doing the survey at the location, we decided that we would need three pieces of Plexiglas about an inch thick to protect the camera lenses and cameramen. I ordered the Plexiglas and had it delivered to CBS Production Facilities on West 57th Street. The Plexiglas was put on the technical truck along with the lighting equipment used on site. There was a second remote truck, which held the cameras and the dollies and had an antenna to get the signal back to CBS. This was our mobile control room, where the technical director, audio engineer, director and associate director, and I sat.

On the Sunday the skeet shooting segment aired, Hal, the lighting director, said he would pick me up and drive me to the location. I put a mystery box in his trunk, and didn't explain what was in it. When we went to set-up the remote truck, the weather was cloudy. By 4:00 p.m., it started to drizzle. Luckily there was a sporting goods store about a mile away, and we went and bought all the rain gear they had for everyone. We had set-up the Plexiglas for the cameras, but because of the rain, the Cameramen couldn't see the contestant shooting skeet.

The compromise was to turn the Plexiglas sideways, so that the Cameramen were protected. We then wanted to make sure that the skeet shooter could see the clay pigeons. We let her practice beforehand, and she was able to. We let Shirley Bernstein know that we would be able to do it. If it didn't work, they had a standby contestant in the studio. I was grateful we had no problems getting the signal back to studio.

After a successful show, and after everything was packed up in the Remote Truck, I asked Hal to open his trunk so I could retrieve the box. Inside was liquor for the crew, and Hal. I only asked that they take it home, and not drink it on the spot. They were very thankful.

I was getting more skilled at my job, and soon became curious about how they figured the total costs for the shows, not just the ones I was responsible for. I asked Grace Viverito, the bookkeeper, if I could see the entire budget. She asked Kyle Farber for permission to divulge the information, and he said yes. The *$64,000 Question*, cost us $20,000 to produce, and we sold it to Revlon for $40,000. In addition, Revlon put money into the prize account.

One day I was talking to Grace, and mentioned that I was a big fan of Broadway Musicals, and collected all the recordings. Grace told me that her sister owned a record store, and suggested I buy them from her. My collection really grew.

In addition to the $64,000 Questions and $64,000 Challenge, I helped worked on several other shows.

On *Giant Step* our Emcee was Bert Parks, and this was a children's show. Students from the age of seven to seventeen picked a topic, and they were asked eight questions about that topic over eight weeks. If they were successful answering all the questions, they received a grand prize of a free college education, and after completing college, were given an all-expense paid vacation anywhere in Europe.

CBS had given us a 7:30 p.m. time slot on Wednesdays. Bert was happy that we were on earlier so he would be able to get to Grand Central Station and be home in Connecticut before his children went to sleep.

To make it easier for Bert to interview the kids, we had an elevator installed in the basement, which he able to control so he could be at the same level with them. When the show was over, the stagehands put a disk to cover the hole in the floor. Parks was at eye level, which made the kids less nervous. After the  interviews, they would move to a giant game board with eight squares. If they gave the correct answers they kept moving to the next square. If they could finish all squares they would win a college scholarship.

Our sponsor would rehearse the commercials before we did our camera blocking. The cameramen didn't like their director, and they finally had had it with him. They had about six set-ups for each commercial, and this day they followed his instructions, and all three cameras were tied together, because he hadn't done his blocking correctly. I had to sell the advertising agency fifteen minutes of my rehearsal time so they could make the corrections. When they were through, the cameramen went to the control room to relax before we rehearsed. The director came out of the control room and confronted them, and started swearing at them. They hit him, and the technical director was asked to put them on report. He said he saw nothing. The next week there was a new director hired for the commercials.

Top Dollar was a word game where contestants vied for cash. The Emcee was Toby Reed, and Merrill Heatter produced it. The show involved three contestants playing a word game. They were given the first three letters. For every letter added after that, $100 was added to the jackpot. The goal was not to give the last letter to complete the word. If you did, you were eliminated. Play would continue until only one player remained, and that player won the pot.

At the end of the show, they took the first eight letters of the longest word and, using a telephone dial, would convert the first eight letters into digits on a dollar bill. Viewers watching at home inspected their dollars, and sent the matching dollars to our office. The owners of the matching dollar bills were announced the following week and would split a $5,000 prize.

CBS Special Effects Department was asked to build a game board for the show. It was huge, and very heavy. There were twenty-six rows across for the entire alphabet, plus eight rows that went from zero to nine for the dollar bill numbers. I made the answer strips for each show, so that the operator knew what the answers were.

Then, in the summer of 1958, trouble came to the game show industry. CBS had a daytime show called *Dotto*, sponsored by Colgate-Palmolive. The game was a combination of a general knowledge quiz and a "connect the dots" game. It became the highest rated daytime program in television history at that time. In an odd arrangement, an evening version of the show was also aired on CBS's competitor, NBC on Tuesday nights. Then, at the height of the show's popularity, the show was abruptly cancelled. A scandal broke when backup contestant, Edward Hilgemeier, Jr., found the notebook of contestant Marie Winn containing the future questions and answers to be used during her appearance. The Hilgemeier tore the pages from the notebook and shared them with Winn's opponent, Yaffe Kimball. He was later paid $1,500 to keep quiet.

Hilgemeier finally decided to let Colgate-Palmolive what he found, who then informed CBS. Thomas Fisher, CBS's executive vice president, reviewed films of the show as well as the pages that Hilgemeier had. CBS also interviewed Frank Cooper, *Dotto's* creator, about the potential for rigging. Finally, CBS informed NBC about what they had learned. Both networks cancelled *Dotto* abruptly.

CBS suddenly had a daytime slot to fill. The only show it had available was *Top Dollar*. It quickly added a daytime version with Warren Hull as the host. At 11:30 a.m., viewers expecting to see *Dotto* heard an announcer say, "*Dotto*, the program which normally airs at this time, will no longer be seen. Instead . . . welcome to *Top Dollar*."

All was not well with the *Top Dollar*, however. Grace, the bookkeeper at EPI, called me into her office and showed me that some of the dollar bills had the numbers rearranged to match the winning numbers. What these people forgot was that the picture on the back of the bill would be askew. I called the US Treasury office and made an appointment to go see them. I showed them what people had done, and they told me that they had defaced the U. S. Currency, which was against the law. I asked them what the show could do, and they gave me a form letter we could mail to the offenders to let these people know that they had committed a crime, which could be punishable.

They asked us to make announcements on the show, letting the viewers know about defacing the U.S. currency, and that it was a Federal Crime. It didn't happen again.

Jack Narz eventually replaced Warren Hull as emcee. Along with cash winnings, the show offered other prizes supplied by Stanford & Associates. One of my jobs was to find out what the prizes were for the following week and make sure they were at Walton Warehouse for delivery to the studio.

Another one of my responsibilities gave me an opportunity to start my own business. Our sponsor, Colgate-Palmolive, aired their commercials on our show. The advertising agency for Colgate sent over the copy they wanted Jack to say before each commercial. CBS informed us that we were responsible for making the cue cards for these lead-ins. We didn't have anyone to handle this task, so I formed

a company to handle this work. I got the information from Ted Bates Advertising Agency, paid for the cue-card stock, and printed them. I earned $5.00 for every lead-in.

The model on the *Top Dollar* was Joanne Copeland. Once, she mentioned that she was dating Johnny Carson, and that she was having a hard time deciding whether to marry him. Bill Egan, the CBS Production Supervisor, and I took her to lunch a few times to discuss it, and she finally decided to marry him.

Another day, a shop steward for the stagehands visited, and admired an interesting battery-operated toy that we were giving away on the show. I told him I could probably get one for him. The crew steward overheard the conversation, and asked me to do him a favor and give it to the shop steward on stage. A couple of days later I called the steward, he came to the stage, I gave him the toy, and he left. I later heard that they accused him of taking a bribe. I never saw him again. The crew didn't like the steward, and used this as an opportunity to get rid of him.

The gameshow business was booming, and we at E.P.I. kept developing more and more shows. Not all were equally successful. We had another show *How Do You Rate?*, a CBS daytime show. It had a short life span. It premiered on March 31st and ended on June 28th. In it, male and female contestants competed in aptitude tests. Still, it offered me new challenges. Some of the questions had to be on slides. I had heard that Polaroid had just come out with a new *opaque* film, 3 inches by 4 inches, and Polaroid had slide holders for it. I contacted the company, and bought the camera, which was new to the market. They lent us the stand for making the slides, and the projector to use in the studio. CBS allowed us to give them credit at the end of show.

We had hired a new Runner who was a son of a Vice President at CBS. One of his first tasks was to go the bank and cash a check for eleven hundred dollars for Harry Fleischman. He was told to come back with eleven new ones. I guess he forgot to look at the check, and came back with eleven new one dollar bills. I got a call from Grace, who asked if I would go to the bank and get it resolved. I found out who the teller was and met with her. She was very embarrassed, and asked if anyone else knew at the bank. I told her no. I got the eleven hundred. Another time the same runner had to go to CBS at 52nd & Madison. This was five blocks from our office, yet he took a cab both ways. He was gone by that Friday.

What's It For? was a show where four celebrities each week try to figure out what the invention was used for after seeing a demonstration. The producer received weekly updates from the U.S. Patent Office, and he would choose from these to pick the ones to feature on the show. Some of the celebrities that appeared were: Cornelia Otis Skinner, Betsy Palmer and Hans Conreid, and Abe Burrows. Like the other game shows, it was broadcast live. Abe Burrows, who was a rather short, stocky man, wore elevator shoes to make him look taller. One day, just as we began to air, Abe was late coming out of his dressing room, and ran across the stage to get to his seat. He somehow tripped on a camera cable. Lucky for him there were two big stagehands there who caught him before he hit the wall. Many years later I would meet his son Jim Burrows, who directed Cheers.

CBS also brought back *Quiz Kids* and put it on at 10:00 p.m. on Thursday nights. Because of the late hour, we had to get a permit for the children from Society for the Prevention of Cruelty to Children. Once a month I would visit the Society to get the permits. We also had to provide the children dressing rooms with beds in them so they could rest before the show. The SPCC only came to one show to make sure we were following the rules. Clifton "Kip" Fadiman was the emcee.

One night as we were getting ready to go on the air, the father of one of the children had a heart attack in the studio. We called 911, and the ambulance came right away took him to the hospital. We called the boy's mother, who immediately came to the studio to let him know that his dad would be alright. I told her that the company would take care of everything, and not to worry.

Stu Billet, who I originally met when he was a new runner, heard that there was a job opening for Production Assistant on a show called *Who Do You Trust*. Johnny Carson was the host, and Ed McMahon was the announcer. This was the first time Johnny and Ed had worked together. In this show, three couples competed on each show, nearly always a man and a woman chosen for their unique backgrounds. Ed would introduce couples one at a time, and then Carson spent more time interviewing the contestants than quizzing them.

In the quiz portion, Carson would tell the male contestant the category of the upcoming question; the man would then have to decide whether to answer the question himself or "trust" the woman to do so.

Stu went for the interview and got the job. Stu invited me to see how his show worked.

The couple of times I went, it was interesting what Johnny would do to Ed. Ed would get the copy for the opening of the show only 10 seconds before going live. Johnny would go over and take out a lighter, and start to burn all four corners of the script. Luckily Ed was a quick reader. Another time Johnny started undressing Ed, who kept right on going. Because of Johnny's pranks, you can see why he chose Ed to be his announcer and side-kick on *The Tonight Show*.

Stu later moved to Los Angeles, California, and teamed up with Ralph Edwards to create *The People's Court*, which was the forerunner of all judicial shows.

These were exciting times. Television was immensely popular, and game shows were primarily what people watched. There were dozens of shows on television then. I felt I had found the work I wanted to do. I had challenging tasks, made decent money, and got to participate in the entertainment business. Things couldn't have been brighter.

Then, following closely after the cancellation of *Dotto*, the game show scandal exploded. *Dotto's* cancellation, which disappointing to viewers, was still a mystery. The reason was not made public. That was about to change. It would become too big to hide.

At the core of the scandal was the basic structure of how the shows were funded. Remember, sponsors owned the time slot and had tremendous sway in how the show was run. Companies like Revlon started to notice that their sales went up when certain contestants were winning, contestants like golden-boy and university professor, Charles Van Doren. Sponsors asked producers to rig the games to ensure that popular contestants stayed on the air longer.

I knew nothing about the rigging until one day in 1958 I overheard a conversation about getting rid of an unpopular contestant. It was not surprising to me to hear executives discuss the popularity of a show or a contestant. This was, after all, entertainment. I had no idea they would resort to cheating to make it happen.

The first public awareness of the rigging started with the game *Twenty-One*. Contestant James Snodgrass proved that the show was rigged. He documented every answer that he was coached on by sending himself a series of registered letters prior to the taping of the shows.

Although in theory, none of what the shows were doing was *illegal*—most producers argued that they were just providing entertainment. Still, the public was horrified, and the luster on the game show business was gone. There was soon talk of criminal charges and congressional investigations. Charles Van Doren went from being the golden child to a public piranha. The game show industry tanked.

In October of 1959, I was working on *Top Dollar*. We shared a studio with *The Big Payoff*. All I remember is that after we went off the air at 12:00 noon, the producer from *The Big Payoff* received a call from CBS Daytime, saying their show would not air again. Soon after, we were also told that we off the air, and would be replaced by re-runs of *December Bride*. I was suddenly out of a job and, as I saw it, a future.

Closing the office was very hard. I helped pack the folders and pictures from *$64,000 Question*. In hindsight, I should have asked for a souvenir. I continued to work for Kyle Farber for free. He had taken very good care of me at E.P.I., and I stayed on to support him.

After everything was ready for storage, Kyle asked me if I wanted anything I asked if I could have Mert Koplin's desk. It was a regular desk, nothing particularly fancy. But it was ell-shaped, with space to work with my typewriter and calculator. It reminded me of the few excellent years I had spent at E.P.I. Kyle said yes, and I arranged to have it moved to my Mom's apartment, where I was living.

From 1959 to 1960 there was very little work for me in the industry.

I collected unemployment benefits, which required that I go in every Friday to show proof that I was trying to find work. My friends and I would meet for lunch at Nedick's, or as we called it the "Orange Room." where for thirty cents you could get two hot dogs and an orange drink. On Fridays, we would splurge and get a hamburger, fries and a coke at Hamburg Heaven.

When my unemployment ran out, my Mother called my cousin Bert, who had taken over the running of my Uncle Mac's business, a soap dispenser company called the American Soap Dispenser. I went to the office, and Bert said that I would work on the production line, putting four screws into a piece of metal. I did this for a week, and had to tell Bert that I was losing it. He understood, and offered me the job of addressing envelopes to companies interested in buying the dispensers. I could do this, and I could do this from home.

So here I was, 20 years old, living with my mother and doing mind-numbing work at home. Once again, I wasn't sure where my life was going.

CHAPTER 4
TRANSITIONS

Throughout my enforced leave from television, I followed the quiz show scandals in the news. Congress launched an investigation in 1959. Dan Enright was revealed to have rigged *Twenty-One*. Eventually, Charles Van Doren came clean with what he had done. President Eisenhower even weighed in, saying that the fixing was "a terrible thing to do to the American people." Plainly, the television advanced so quickly laws and regulations meant to monitor them couldn't keep up.

In 1960, Congress amended the Communications Act of 1934, prohibiting the fixing of quiz shows, something that had not previously been illegal. Most networks imposed a limit on winnings.

In 1960, CBS decided to give quiz shows another try. I had kept in touch with the producer of *Top Dollar*, Merrill Heatter, and he told me that he and his partner Bob Quigley got the approval from CBS to do a show. However, they wanted the show to be tested before doing any rehearsals or a pilot. Merrill asked if I was interested in working with them. The show was called *Video Village*, and was a game played on a life-sized game board. Two contestants played the role of tokens on a human-size game board with three streets: Money Street, Bridge Street and Magic Mile. Players advanced according to the roll of a large six-sided die, rolled on the sidelines by a partner, who was usually a spouse or boyfriend/girlfriend. Merrill had hired artist Bob Synes to make a smaller scale model of the set. After CBS executives saw the completed model, they wanted to see how much a contestant could win on the show.

I was asked to play the game 500 times, and keep a record of everything. They wanted to test how much money or how many prizes a contestant could potentially win, and to make sure that the game worked the way they intended.. After they reviewed my records, they gave us the go-ahead to make up a full-size cardboard version of the set, and we did some rehearsals for them at the Hotel Beacon on Broadway.

Keith Quigley, Bob's wife, was in charge of screening contestants. We finally got the green light to film a pilot show. Merrill found office space, and asked Bob Synes, the artist, to paint a TV studio on the blank white wall. Bob did a beautiful job using black paint only. Gary Smith was brought on as art director to design the set. (Years later, Gary teamed up with Dwight Hemion to form a very successful production company.). CBS had some directors under contract at that time, and suggested interviewing a man called Jerry Shaw. He had never done a game show, but was interested in the challenge. CBS assigned Bill Egan as our production supervisor, and he would do the budget for the studio costs. After he had the numbers, we met and he gave me a copy of it, and said I had to present it to Merrill and Bob.

The budget for the show personnel was done by Merrill and Bob, and then both budgets were given to Walter Shier, their attorney, to negotiate the package deal with CBS. The final budget was $11,250 per week for the daytime version. This was high due to the fact that the stagehands were being paid overtime from 6:00 a.m. to 1:00 p.m. They usually worked from 1:00 p.m. to 10:00 p.m.

Bill and I became very good friends. CBS put the show in Stage 52, which was the stage that had been used for *$64,000 Question*. This made my life easier since I already knew the stage crew. My head prop man was Joe Mullens, who was in his nineties.

We had a few problems doing the pilot. We found out that the bridge for the contestants to get to the Magic Mile wasn't built to hold a lot of weight. We had two brothers on the stage Crew who together weighed about 500 pounds. When they walked across the bridge together, they went through the floor. Luckily, neither man was hurt, and I thanked them for testing it. The next day it was fixed.

The next problem was that we had to use wireless microphones on the Contestants, and we had trouble with the placement of the antennas, due to the fact that Consolidated Edison Company had a power plant next door. After much trial and error, we hung three antennas on pipes over the set, and it worked.

We started filming. The partner would roll the six-sided die on the sidelines. The Town Crier would call out the number that was rolled, and the contestant would go that number of squares on the game board. The object was to be the first to go through the village. They would start out on Money Street, that had squares that offered cash, then move on to Bridge Street, where they would answer questions. There were also some setbacks, such as Lose a Turn, and Go to Jail. Finally, they reached Magic Mile where there were stores with merchandise as prizes, and some setbacks, such as Exchange Places.

I would let the electrician know when to flash the signs on the Magic Mile, and let the prop man know what prize cards to use.

Whoever won the game then faced another contestant. Jack Narz was the Emcee, and he was quick to understand how the game worked. Joanne Copeland was the hostess, and Ken Williams was the Announcer and Town Crier.

CBS bought the show, and started out on nighttime on July 1, 1960 LIVE!. The daytime show started ten days later, and our time slot was at 9:30 a.m. Monday through Friday.

We also hired Stanford & Associates to handle the prizes for the show. They supplied the 11x14 artwork for the stores on Magic Mile. After the show, Stanford's representative, Anita, got the contestant's information and had the prizes delivered.

Every day, the set would arrive from the warehouse at 6:00 a.m. We would rehearse from 8:00 a.m. to 9:00 a.m. Bob Quigley would warm up the audience by telling them funny stories. To prevent the contestants from getting hurt while playing the game, they were outfitted with sneakers. CBS informed us that we would be responsible for making the cue cards for the lead-ins to the commercials. Since I had formed a company to do this when I was doing *Top Dollar*, I just continued billing the advertisers, as I had done before.

When the weather turned cold and it snowed in New York, the only people that would come watch the show were homeless people. We had coffee and sweet rolls, so they could come in and warm themselves for an hour. Our saving grace was that CBS had a McKenzie machine that would make it sound like we had a larger, live audience. These machines added laughter and applause. The music for the show was performed life by an organist named Arlo Hults. Arlo had invented a machine that could simulate drums, piano, and other instruments, a very early prototype of a synthesizer. He also brought his pet monkey to the studio, who sat by Arlo. Arlo game the monkey peanuts in the shell, and it was fun to watch him open them.

Andre St. Laurent, was the associate director assigned to the show by CBS. He went by "Andy." He kept time of the show, and let the director know when it was time to put in the commercials. Andy also had to keep a log of what the commercials were. After the first week, he asked me if I could do that for him, because he was too busy. Andy said that I would need a stop watch to put the times on the log. Fortunately, Steve had given me one for being his Best Man at his wedding. That first week I listened for his countdown to start the show, and I then I started the watch. After the show, I gave Andy the log, and he said it was perfect, and I continued doing it.

Before Producer Bob Quigley came back to the States, he was a radio disc jockey in Johannesburg, South Africa. He still wanted to do his radio show for South Africa from a distance. My office was the only one that had some soundproofing in it, and we recorded the show there on audio tape, leaving space for where they would play the 45 rpm records. I acted as his audio engineer, and Bob kept me in stitches with his stories about the songs. He received letters from people in South Africa, asking how he could stay current on the current hits in another country. All he did was read *Billboard*, *Cash Box*, and *Variety* to know.

For doing these shows Bob, was paid all of $6.00, and it cost him a lot more that to ship the music. In those days they used 45 rpm records. After a few months, Bob quit.

One of CBS's sponsors, French's Bird Seed, wanted to do a live commercial. The advertising agency for French's was in Philadelphia, Pa., and Alice, the account executive, said she would bring the parakeet to be used in the commercial with her.

When Alice arrived, she was in tears. I asked what was wrong. The weather was cold on the train, so she had put a heating pad in the bottom of the parakeet's cage, and left the cover over it. The bird suffocated. We all expressed our sorrow over her tragedy, and I asked her why she brought the parakeet with her, and her answer really surprised me. She said that she thought that when you goes on location, you must bring the props you need with you. I mentioned there was a pet store around the corner from the Studio, where she could rent one, which she did. The commercial was a success.

Bill Egan also did *Person to Person* with Ed Murrow, who would interview celebrities in their homes from a comfortable chair in his New York studio. One Friday, Bill invited me to watch the live telecast. I usually watched it at home, and I was blown away by the simplicity of the set. One of the arms of Ed's chair was a little higher than the other so he could rest his elbow while holding his cigarette. He also had a fan facing him on low, to keep the smoke from the cigarette away from his face. I also thought that he watched the celebrities on a big screen, but I was surprised to see that he was watching a 19-inch TV. The home viewer saw what the control room had overlaid on the big screen. One of the guests that night was Mae West, and she invited Ed to see her bedroom. Ed noticed that she had mirrors on the ceiling, and he asked her why. She said she liked to see how she was doing at all times. Remember, this was live.

CBS eventually decided to replace the aging head Carpenter and his assistant with younger men. At the time, one would arrive at 6:00 a.m., and the other at 11:00 a.m. They would alternate. I was also informed that I was paying for both starting at 6:00 a.m. I went to the crew steward and told him I wasn't happy with this arrangement. At the same time, he wasn't pleased that the two carpenters were being let go, and told me who to talk to at CBS. I called the person, and said I wasn't happy with paying for someone who doesn't show up until 11:00 a.m. He said that was the deal they made with them and didn't want to change it. I told Bill Egan that I didn't want him to get involved until I called Larry White, who was the Vice President of Daytime, and relayed what was happening. I received a credit for the extra money we'd paid and from then on, both men showed up at 6:00 a.m.

The popularity of the show was catching on, and a few communities in Long Island & New Jersey were closing off streets, building the sets on site and playing the game. Also Milton Bradley came out with a board game that was selling very well.

Bill Egan called me, and told me that he was being assigned to a new show for CBS called *You're in the Picture*, with Jackie Gleason as host. Bill asked if I would be interested in doing the cue cards for him. He put me in touch with Steve Carlin, the producer, with whom I had worked with at E.P.I. I told Steve that I would charge $25 a show, and he agreed. I arrived at the Studio, and met with Seymour Robbie, the director, with whom I had worked on *$64,000 Question*. He told me where I could stand so I would not be in the way of the cameras. I also found out that the show had been created by Don Lipp and Bob Synes, who had worked on *Video Village*.

The premise of the *You're In The Picture* was that four celebrities— Pat Harrington Jr., Pat Carroll, Jan Sterling and Arthur Treacher— placed their heads in a life-sized illustration of a famous scene or song lyric, and took turns asking yes or no questions of Jackie to try to figure out what picture they represented. The show debut on January 20, 1961, at 9:30 p.m., the same evening of President John F. Kennedy's Inauguration Ball. The show received terrible reviews because the premise just didn't work. Jackie decided to apologize in a serious way. During the second airing, he stood alone on an empty stage. I was notified that my services would not be needed for this show, but what interested to see what Jackie was going to do, I tuned into the broadcast. Jackie had a bare stage, with all the stagehands sitting in chairs facing the back wall in silhouette. He then went on to apologize for the flop that had been aired the previous week.

In January 1961, Jack Narz said he would be leaving *Video Village*, because commuting from Los Angeles to New York every week was creating a problem in his marriage. Bill Cullen, Jack's brother in law,

65

tried to convince him to stay. We were all sorry to see him leave.

Monty Hall was brought in to take over for Jack Narz. It was also then that CBS installed Video Tape Machines, and wanted us to use them, allowing us to tape the show ahead of time and broadcast it later. This was a monumental shift in television, giving us unprecedented flexibility. We taped two shows a day for three days a week. Our contract with CBS was for doing five shows a week, and we were making a profit for not using the studio for 2 days.

I also received a call from CBS, asking us to split the cost for transmitting the show to the West Coast. This was a different ball game. Our shows were broadcast live. CBS installed the videotape machines at Grand Central Studios, where master control was located, and wanted us to use them, so the show could be taped and then rebroadcast three hours later on the West Coast.

Our agreement with CBS only stated that we had to deliver a live show to them. How they got it to the West Coast was their problem, not ours.

I called Walter Schier, our attorney, and explained what CBS wanted, and he said he would take care of it. CBS wasn't happy, and suggested that we should think about moving the show to Los Angeles. Looking for alternatives, I explored the idea of switching the show to the ABC studios in New York. When CBS heard about this, they told the producers that we could choose either to move the show from New York City or be cancelled.

Heatter-Quigley decided to approach CBS with another show, *Double Exposure*. CBS bought the new show and Heatter-Quigly

Productions agreed to make the move. Merrill & Bob made a trip to Los Angeles to meet with CBS executives there, and to talk to the art director, Robert Tyler Lee, about designing the set for *Double Exposure*, and to look for office space.

We started taping additional shows of *Video Village* in New York so that we would have enough to air while we moved sets and personnel to California.. We worked quickly, and we could finish taping two shows before noon. Jerry, Bill and I would often go around the corner to the China Song Restaurant after taping.

About the middle of February, Bill told me that the owner of the China Song had died, and asked if I wanted to attend the wake. We went with three other CBS employees, and it was very interesting. After entering the chapel, and signing the guest book, you then paid your respects to the family, and as you left there were two golden urns. One with a piece of sweet candy wrapped in foil, to remind you of the sweet thing in life, and the other was a quarter, also wrapped in foil so you could buy more. His widow thanked us for coming.

I found out that Walter Schier, the attorney for Heatter-Quigley Productions, and Jerry Shaw would be flying First Class, while I was in Coach. I mentioned to Merrill that it might be beneficial if I flew in First Class with them so we could conduct strategy for the meeting at CBS the next morning. CBS agreed to pay the upgrade.

On February 28, 1961, after doing our final taping in New York City for *Video Village*, the set, props, wardrobe and Arlo's band were packed up and put into an 18-wheeler to be trucked to California.

I saw that everything was loaded on the truck, and I said my goodbyes to the stage crew. I had enjoyed working with them for years, and it was strange to be leaving now. CBS had arranged to have a limo take Jerry to JFK airport, and he invited me to go with him for the flight to Los Angeles. We sat in the limo and stared at the city that we were leaving. After living my entire life in New York City, my life was about to change dramatically. I was heading to California.

CHAPTER 5
CALIFORNIA

We landed in California, and Jerry gave me a ride to Hollywood, where I would be staying. The first thing I noticed were all the palm trees, and how warm it was. I saw the iconic Hollywood sign on the Hollywood hills, and I felt worlds away from New York City.

CBS agreed to give us relocation money for two weeks so we could find places to live. My Mother contacted her friend Nellie about putting me up for a few days, so I could find an apartment. I was fortunate to find one on Holloway Drive, which was 10 minutes from the office on Beverly Boulevard.

On our first day, Jerry picked me up about a half an hour before our meeting with CBS. He drove us to Hollywood Boulevard to showed me Grauman's Chinese Theater, where movie premiers were held, and the sidewalks with the hand prints of movie stars.

As part of my compensation, I was to have a car. Merrill had arranged for a rental with Hav-A-Car on Sunset Boulevard. I arrived and I was shown to an old—and I mean *old*—Ford station wagon. I was also given a company gas card.

At our first California production meeting at CBS, they had people representing every department. Charles Cappleman, Director of Design & Production Services conducted the meeting. Harry Zipper oversaw putting the budget together. He used a very old type of adding machine, which I had never seen before, and he just kept inputting the information he got from Walter, Jerry, me, and the various departments. He kept moving this cylinder up and down. His assistant Ray Savoy made sure he didn't miss any department. By the time we finished the meeting, the budget was finished, and Harry told us that Cappy (Charles Cappleman's nickname) would get copies to us. Jerry asked if he could have the same associate director and stage manager for both shows. CBS said they would let us know.

Charles Cappleman told us that they had a Prize Department at Television City, and that I could let them know what we needed for our shows. I was also told that they would take care of doing the cue cards for both shows. All I had to do was bill the advertisers, as I had done in New York. I continued billing and advertising agencies, and had the checks sent to my mother in New York. She would then mail them to me in Los Angeles.

Jerry, Walter and I then went to the Heatter-Quigley production offices at 8170 Beverly Boulevard, which was five blocks from CBS. I think that meeting helped Jerry and I become friends. The rest of the staff was there. Bob Cheechi oversaw getting the photos for *Double Exposure*, and getting them to CBS to mount for the game boards. Lil Sperling was the bookkeeper. We also hired was Lloyd Haynes for the runner's position.

To fill out our stable of shows, CBS also moved the soap opera *The Brighter Day*, and bought another game show, called *Your Surprise Package*.

One night Jerry and I went to the Valley for dinner, that's when we found out my station wagon really didn't have any pep. We were stopped by the police for going too slowly over Laurel Canyon Boulevard, and for driving without a California license. The following morning, I told Merrill about the incident, and he arranged for me to get a Chevrolet Impala coupe. I mentioned to Jerry that I was going to go to the DMV to get my license, and asked if he wanted to come along and get his at the same time. Jerry went first at the DMV, and then it was my turn. I really didn't have much time to practice with the Chevy Impala, and the inspector gave me a second chance. I passed.

The following Monday we started rehearsals for *Double Exposure* with Steve Dunn as Emcee, and Ken Williams as the announcer. Robert Tyler Lee designed the set. I also learned that he had been the art director on *Playhouse 90*.

The show would share the studio with *Video Village*. *Double Exposure* would tape Monday and Tuesday's mornings, and *Video Village* would tape Tuesday afternoon and Wednesday's. The producers decided to speed up the time it took the *Video Village* contestants to get from the Finish Line back to the start of the game by using a golf cart. CBS was pleased with the move, because they were saving $5,000 in studio costs every week. At Television City, everything was stored there, and that also saved them money.

I kept going to the loading dock to see if the truck had arrived from

71

New York. We had packed Arlo Hult's music machine, and we needed it for the show. Fortunately for me, it arrived at 11:00 a.m., and luckily it was one of the last things put on the truck, I was relieved that it arrived safely.

Double Exposure involved two contestants. Each would be shown pictures puzzles of celebrities that were covered with different numbered pieces. They couldn't see what each one had uncovered to get an upper hand on the answer. One would call out which segment they wanted uncovered by our stage models, June Palmer and Betty Andrews. They played for cash and prizes.

Our Emcee, Steve, really didn't understand the game, and Ken, the announcer, became known as Mr. Rules. He would interrupt Steve, and remind him what the rules were.

Joanne Copeland of *Video Village* didn't make the trip with us to Los Angeles, because she was going to marry Johnny Carson. She was replaced by Eileen Barton.

One day, Bob Synes, Lil Sperling, Lloyd, and I decided to go to Canters' Delicatessen on Fairfax for lunch. Lloyd was an African American, and you wouldn't believe the stares we got from other patrons as we were seated. This was the first time I had witnessed racism up close. I had never encountered anything like this in New York City. Lloyd wanted to leave, but we insisted he stay. This was 1961. We hadn't expected that kind of reaction, but we weren't about to back down. I think it helped Lloyd enjoy his meal. We also found out that Lloyd attended acting classes at the Film Industries Workshop. He appeared in the second *Star Trek* pilot. But his most memorable role was Mr. Pete Dixon on the series *Room 222*. The rest of the cast was Denise Nicholas, Michael Constantine and Karen Valentine. The show ran for five seasons on ABC, from 1969 to 1974. Sadly, Lloyd passed away at the age 52 from lung cancer.

One of the sponsors wanted some personalized commercials with Monty Hall, who had replaced Jack Narz on *Video Village*. The commercials were only supposed to be broadcast on our show. I happened to be watching CBS one day, and the saw that the commercials were also being aired on other shows. I called Monty and told him that this was happening, and that I would find out how often it happened. He was amazed how many times they had aired without his permission. He was finally compensated.

Jerry Shaw and I discovered that outside the back gate at CBS was a famous farmers market where you could buy all sorts of foods. Gilmore Bank was also located there, which was very convenient, so I opened an account there.

Another game show *Your Surprise Package* was taped at Television City. I heard that a representative of the show had gone to a bar in Laguna Beach on a Saturday, and struck up a conversation with a Marine Sergeant that was stationed at Camp Pendleton, near San Diego. He mentioned that they were looking for a Jeep to give away on the show, and was wondering if he knew how he might obtain one. The sergeant said that they had some at the camp, and that he might be able to obtain one. He gave the show representative his phone number, and asked him to call him and let him know. The sergeant indeed called him on Monday, and he said that he would be able to get thirty Jeeps if he was interested, since they were surplus, and probably going to be junked. The representative then asked him how much it would cost for each Jeep. Twenty-five dollars each, he was told.

The representative went to the producer, Alan Sherman, and told him the story. Alan agreed to buy all thirty, and would pay the Marines upon delivery. They'd be treated to lunch also. Alan informed CBS about the pending arrival of the Jeeps, and they thought it would be a good news story.

On the day the Jeeps were to arrive, CBS cleared out the executive packing lot, and had cameras ready to tape the event. At 10:30 a.m., the representative got a call from the sergeant, saying that they ran into a little problem leaving the Camp. The guard at the front gate wouldn't let them leave with the Jeeps because they hadn't gotten authorization from their Commanding Officer. The other interesting fact was that the Alan had made up flyers, and put them up all over CBS, and had sold them all. He wasn't happy, but he did refund the money to everyone, and apologized.

One Tuesday, after taping *Video Village*, I wandered into Studio 33 to watch *The Red Skelton Show* dress rehearsal. Red was doing a skit with Lanie Kazan. Lanie sat in a chair, and Red was on his knees attempting to kiss her breasts. Her comment was "How could such a nice man like you have such a dirty mind?" Everybody started laughing. I found out later that his dress rehearsals were called "The Dirty Hour."

I heard another bit of trivia about Red Skelton. Red started doing his show in 1959 at the old Charlie Chaplin Studios on North La Brea Avenue, and in 1960 he purchased it. One of the first things he did was purchase three mobile trucks, so he could do his show in color. In 1962, I heard that part of his negotiations with CBS was for them to buy the Studio. CBS did, and they filmed the Perry Mason series there.

Another great story I was told about Red was that he went to the Rolls Royce dealership in Beverly Hills dressed like a farmer, in plaid shirt and overalls. He also carried a black satchel with money in it at all times. The next salesman up was an elderly man, and since it was lunch time, he went out for lunch. They had just hired a new young salesman, who approached the farmer, and asked if could help him. Red asked, "Do you happen to have a four-door sedan in gray? They did. Red asked the price. It was $75,000. Red asked what came with the car, and was told that the sheepskin rugs were included. Then Red asks if they had one in Maroon, and was is told one would be arriving on Thursday. The price was also $75,000. Red said he would take them both, and opening his black satchel, he paid for them. When the elderly salesman got back from lunch and heard what had happened he almost had a heart attack.

One afternoon I was in my office, and I heard a major crash coming from Merrill's office. I went to see what had happened. Merrill had been practicing his golf swing, and the club came out of his hand, and broke the floor to ceiling window.

Jerry and I decided to start looking for other restaurants near the office. We discovered El Coyote for Mexican, and Kelbo's for barbecue sandwiches.

We had been doing the shows for a couple of months, and everything was going smoothly, until one Wednesday, after lunch,

Jerry, paged me to the control room. He met me outside, and said that there was a major problem with the technical director. He was drunk!

I talked to one of the cameramen and learned that this had been an ongoing problem. We called Technical Services and have them come down and take care of the problem. When his boss arrived at the control room and asked the technical director to leave, he refused. He wouldn't get out of his chair. Two of technical crew had to physically pick up the chair with him in it, and carried it outside. CBS quickly found another technical director, Bob Stone, who was in the engineers' lounge and, after rehearsing for fifteen minutes, the audience was let in, and Bob Quigley apologized to them, and thanked them for waiting.

The producers also came up with *Video Village Jr.*, which was for kids. Since CBS's Prize Department couldn't supply us with enough kid prizes, they suggested that we buy them. They introduced me to Bernie's Discount Center, which would be able to supply the show. We had categories for prizes, such as Surprises, Toys, Banks and Music. Bob Horner, my contact person at the CBS Prize Department, suggested we go to Bernie's Discount Center to look at some prize possibilities for the show. After visiting Bernie's, he suggested going next door to Boardner's Restaurant for a quick bite. I needed to use the rest room. When I went in there was a crap game going on, with six people. As I was leaving, a police officer walked in, and said everyone was under arrest. One of the gentlemen involved in the crap game asked the officer if he was walking or riding in a patrol car. He was in a patrol car, he said. "How would you feel about walking a beat," the gentleman said, taking a badge out of his pocket. He was a

Lieutenant. The officer left.

One Sunday, Bernie himself invited me to go deep sea fishing off Malibu. After about an hour, a gentleman came up to me who had heard that I worked in television, and was doing a game show with children. He told me he wanted his son on the show. I explained I only

handled the production elements, and had nothing to do with the contestants. To make his point, his two confederates then lifted me up over the railing of the boat. He insisted I get his son on the show, or I could swim the ten miles back to shore. I said I would try, and they brought me back on board the boat. After taking a bathroom break, I asked Bernie who the man was, and he told me that he was Johnny Battaglia, a member of the Mafia. He was also known as Johnny the Bat. "The Bat" operated one of the largest bookmaking operations in southern California.

I recommended Johnny the Bat's son to the contestant people, and he was called in for an interview, I found out that his Mother had brought him, and lucky for me he was selected. On the Saturday that he was scheduled, his Dad was the one that turned the chuck-a-luck, and the boy went on to be the winner of that show. Johnny saw me after the taping, and invited me to a party at Aldo's Restaurant, to thank me. He really didn't believe me when I told him I had nothing to do with it.

Merrill & Bob then created *People Will Talk* with Dennis James in 1963 for NBC. We would go out and film interviews of different people on the street of Los Angeles. Nine contestants would watch the interviews and try to guess what the occupations were.

It was also then that Heatter-Quigley became partners with Four Star Television. Dick Powell, Ida Lupino, David Niven and Charles Boyer were the principal partners of Four Star Television. The only information I was given was that they would financially participate with Heatter-Quigley.

I met with Burt Rosen, their finance person, and went over the production costs with him. After a few weeks, he asked to look at the costs for doing the street interviews, and discovered that the the Heatter-Quigley producers were making a lot of money from that account. They were being paid by NBC to go out every week to film segments, while we were only filming once a month.

Bob and Merrill were angry with me for divulging that information, but I had no idea that this was a secret, so they agreed to split the profits with Four Star. He also suggested that the editing of the interviews should be done at Four Star. They assigned Samuel E. Beetley as my Editor. I went over the details of what need to be done, and in our conversation, he told me that he had been the Film Editor on *The Longest Day*. I felt very small at the moment, because all that Sam had to do was put academy film leader between the segments that we were going to use.

One day when I was at Four Star, Dick Powell came into the area that I was working with Sam and said "hello" to all the employees. I was also introduced to him. Sam told me he did this every week, and they never knew what day.

I got a call from Burt Rosen, and he asked if it would be possible to give away as a prize a recording by Charles Boyer. I was able to include it with a stereo system. It was the only recording he made at that time.

In those days, NBC didn't have a commissary. What they had was a truck where you could get coffee and a sweet roll in the morning's, and sandwiches at lunch time. The truck would leave about 3:00 p.m., and come back the following morning restocked. Your other choice for lunch was going across the street to the Carriage House Restaurant or Genio's Italian Restaurant, and The Smoke House Restaurant.

About this time, we moved our office again this time to Ventura Boulevard, in Studio City. This was an easier commute for Merrill and Bob, since they had homes in Beverly Hills.

I decided it would also be better to be closer to the office, so I found an apartment on Colfax Avenue. I also found out that there were some great restaurants in that area. Art's Delicatessen, Tail O' The Cock, Sportsman's Lodge, Du Pars were a few that I loved.

I also met Ron Ellensohn, who had an apartment in the same building. He was a field secretary for Los Angeles Mayor Sam Yorty. One night he invited me to go to dinner with him at the Oak Room in Encino. Our waitress was a woman named Mary. While sitting at our booth, a gentleman came over and Ron introduced him as Frank Wilcox, who was part owner of the restaurant. I found out that he was an actor, and had a regular role on *The Untouchables* and *The Beverly Hillbillies*.

After going there a few times, I found that Ron always asked to be seated in Mary's section. At one dinner, Frank came over and said he was going to have cataract surgery on his other eye. The operation would be Doctor's Hospital on Beverly Glen Boulevard. He asked if

we would come visit him. This would be Frank's second cataract surgery. The first time the surgeon had made a mistake, and Frank lost his eye, which was why he wore a black patch over it.

The operation was a success. Ron and I went to see him on the second day of his stay, and he was in good spirits. He introduced us to the private duty day nurse he had hired, a beautiful, dark-haired woman named Marie. She was there from 7:00 a.m. to 3:00p.m. Other nurses worked the 3:00 p.m. to 11:00 p.m., and 11:00 p.m. to 7:00 a.m. shifts. Frank also told us that he was allowed to have a bar in his room. So we came by the next evening, stocked his bar for him and stayed for a drink. Frank stayed in the hospital for a week and we visited him every day. On the day before he was going to go home, he asked me to do him a favor. He said his nurse, Marie, had taken such good care of him, he would like me to take her to lunch for him. I agreed, and Marie gave me her phone number.

I called that evening to check her schedule to see when she would be free. Since she did private duty nursing, she had a couple of days off. We made a date and she gave me her address in Westwood.

We went to the Tail O' The Cock Restaurant on Restaurant Row on La Cienega Boulevard. We were there for three hours. When I took her back to her apartment, she introduced me to her roommate, Margie. Marie showed me the terrace of their apartment, and the view was breathtaking. You could see most of Westwood. I mentioned that I would like to see her again. She said that would be all right.

Moving to California had been a great change in my life. I was about to embark on another.

CHAPTER 6
MARIE

Marie impressed me from the beginning. Her smile got me right away, and I could talk to her for hours. We had a lot in common, including enjoying seeing movies. She also seemed alright with me being six feet, three inches tall, even thought she was five feet, four.

I was drawn to Marie from the start, and I loved learning about the life she had led. She was born on May 13, 1936 on a farm in Spiritwood, in Saskatchewan, Canada. She had three sisters, Jeanne, Louise and Anna, and one brother, "Al" for Alphonse. She and her siblings were hearty and strong, and she loved living on a farm. She grew up going hunting with her dad, who would carve up and store whatever they caught in the ice house out back.

Sadly, when she was ten years old, Marie got a lung infection. It never healed, and she eventually had to have an operation to remove the lung. This affected her immune system, and the cold climate of Canada made her weak.

Both her sisters Louise and Jeanne became nurses, and Marie, always a good student, decided to go into nursing as well. After her sister, Louise, graduated from nursing school, she decided to look at nursing positions in the United States. She took a job in 1954 in Porterville, California, as an Operating Room Supervisor.

Marie's health wasn't improving in the cold climate of Canada and wanted to move as well. Fortunately, Louise was able to get Marie a nursing job the following year. Marie stayed there until 1961 when she moved to San Diego, and went to work as a nurse at Mercy Hospital.

During that time, she lived in a rooming house, and she had a space on the third floor that had curtains that separated her from her other roommates. One of her roommates was a woman named Marion Anderson, who had been raised on an avocado ranch in Vista, California. Marion preferred to be known "Mimi". Mimi loved sitting in the sun, and would get very bad sunburns. When Marie would get home, she would apply cold compresses to her sunburn to sooth it. Mimi was dating Pat Delaney at that time, and they got married on June 2, 1962.

Marie left San Diego and moved to Los Angeles, California in 1963, and worked at County Hospital for a while. She became a naturalized citizen of the United States on November 8, 1963. Then she went to work as a floor nurse at UCLA Medical Center, She lived nearby in Westwood, California. While there, she met a woman named Margaret Ann Lee in the kitchen. Margaret, or Margie, as she liked to be called, was also from Canada, and she and Marie became friends. Before Margie went back to Canada for a family wedding, they discussed the idea of finding an apartment, because Margie's roommate had problems that would keep her up at night. Marie found an apartment on Levering, and when Margie returned from Canada, she moved in.

Eventually, someone introduced Marie to Monica Storey, who ran a registry of private nurses, and Marie made the switch to private duty nursing. She had found her niche. There were usually three shifts, 7:00 a.m. to 3:00 p.m., 3:00 p.m. to 11:00 p.m. and 11:00 p.m. to 7:00 a.m. Marie usually got the 7:00 a.m. shift, which was usually the hardest, and included getting the patient up, bathing, and then feeding them. But she most enjoyed really getting to know her patients. She would take the bus to her clients' homes, because she didn't drive yet. After finishing a case, she usually kept the friendships with them.

I was drawn to Marie's open heart and caring nature, and I was determined to continue to see her. On our next date, we went to the Nine Muses Restaurant in Hollywood. I introduced her to eating artichokes, and she enjoyed it.

One patient was Marjorie Flour, whose husband was John Simon of the Flour Corporation that did engineering and construction jobs. He wanted to be called "Si". The Flour's were going on a trip to New York City, and Marjorie needed a nurse to be with her. She called Marie, who was available. The Flour's had a suite at the Sherry Netherland Hotel on Fifth Avenue, across from Central Park, my old stomping grounds. Marie had a room adjacent to theirs. She would call and tell me all about what she did with them. She loved going around Manhattan on the Circle Line boat, but what she liked the best was having lunch at 21 Club, and seeing all the stars there.

I told her that next door to the Club was the building for 21 Brands, which owned the restaurant and the Sherry-Lehmann liquor store. I knew Michael Aaron, the son of one of the owners. When she got back, she couldn't stop talking about her week in New York.

Her next case was Arthur Koehler, who lived in Westwood. I would pick her up sometimes, and drive her home, so she didn't have to take the bus. She didn't drive yet. One day she told me that Mr. Koehler was the wood expert for the Charles Lindbergh's kidnapping case. Koehler's particular research interest in the identification, cellular structure and growth of wood gave him the specific training and abilities necessary for the careful examination of the ladder which had been used by the abductor of the Lindbergh baby, and tracing the ladder to a company in McCormick, South Carolina. Koehler, from there, traced the wood of the ladder to a Bronx lumber yard and was used to build a latter Hauptmann used in the abduction.

Marie's roommate, Margie, frequently went back to Canada, and on one of those trips home she met Tom Evans who was an attorney in Bradford. Tom proposed and Margie accepted. She asked Marie to be her Maid of Honor, and she accepted. Margie was not known for being punctual, and she was happy that Marie was there to help her pack for her six-week honeymoon, and for getting her to the Church on time. They remained the best of friends, but Marie needed a new roommate.

Marie couldn't find another roommate, so she heard that there was a smaller apartment for rent on Glendon Avenue, also in Westwood. It turned out that she knew the Managers, Sally & Tip Oneil. Her apartment was on the first floor, and there was no air conditioning. I contacted a friend, and got her one, which also gave her some protection from someone trying to break in.

Marie's next patient was Julie Murphy, the wife of Senator George Murphy, which started a long-term close relationship for both of us. George Murphy was an American dancer, actor, and politician. Murphy was a song-and-dance leading man in many big-budget Hollywood musicals from 1930 to 1952. He met Julie during this time, when she worked as his dance partner. He was the president of the Screen Actors Guild from 1944 to 1946, and was awarded an honorary Academy Award in 1951. At the time we met him, Murphy was serving as U.S. Senator from California, the first notable U.S. actor to make the successful transition to elected official in California, predating Ronald Reagan and Arnold Schwarzenegger. He is the only United States Senator represented by a star on the Hollywood Walk of Fame. His wife Julie Henkel (known on stage as dancer Julie Johnson) teamed with him in Broadway musicals before she retired to raise a family. They'd had two children, but now she had crippling arthritis and was confined to a wheelchair.

I would pick Marie up in the morning with a fresh-squeezed orange juice, and drive her to Beverly Hills, since her shift started at 7:00 a.m. I was working at NBC in Burbank as the Unit Manager on *Days of our Lives*, and I didn't have to be there until 8:30 a.m. I usually finished at 2:30 p.m., and would pick Marie up and take her to the apartment.

The first time I met Mrs. Murphy she was in her wheelchair, and Marie had to make a phone call. Mrs. Murphy asked me to put a cigarette between her fingers, and then I took the lighter and lit her cigarette. She then asked me about my work, and we chatted until

Marie then came back into the den. The afternoon nurse arrived, and I drove Marie back to her apartment.

The next day when I picked Marie up, she said that Mrs. Murphy had invited me to arrive at 2:30 in the afternoon and use their pool, instead of waiting for Marie out front. Mrs. Murphy had learned that Marie couldn't swim, and hired Mrs. Finney to teach her. Mrs. Finney also noticed that I only swam using the side stroke, and showed me how easy it was to do the crawl.

We continued to date for five years. Marie was my first, and last, girlfriend.

In the meantime, I continue to learn and grow in my job at Heatter-Quigley. I'd been in the television business for several years now, and had begun to develop a sense of what values and skills that were important to being successful at work. Of course, I learned early on to care about my work. There were many different parts to my job, and I took pride in doing with little things with as much care and attention as I took doing the big things. If I agreed to take on a task, I wanted people to believe that it would be done well and on time.

I also wanted to follow the example of Louis G. Cowan, the owner of the first production company I worked for. He, a busy, important man, had always treated me with kindness and respect, even when I was an entry level employee. Both he and his wife regularly showed me by example the importance of treating other people the way you would like to be treated. It was a lesson I never forgot. I enjoyed finding ways that I could surprise people with kindness. As a result, I got along well with both my superiors and my co-workers.

In 1964, CBS bought *Celebrity Game* with Carl Reiner. It was a semi-remake of a show called *People Will Talk*, where contestants had to determine how celebrities would answer moral-type questions. The show had an elegant set and a formally-dressed nine-member celebrity panel. Some of the contestants were Eartha Kitt, Zsa Zsa Gabor, Mel Brooks, and Steve Allen. Three contestants competed. Host Reiner posed a moral-type question (e.g., "Can most women keep a secret?" "Should a man shave in a gas station restroom?"), to which the celebrity panel secretly recorded either "yes" or "no" vote. The three contestants also locked in their votes as to how they believed the majority would answer. Reiner then asked the contestants to pick a celebrity and say how he or she voted, then it was revealed how the celebrity answered, and Carl would ask them why.

Celebrity Game With Jim Backus

The producers hired three comedy writers, Sam Bobrick, Howard Merrill and Stan Dreben, to write material for the celebrities to use. The celebrities' responses usually made for the funniest moments in this show. Carl would come up with great comeback lines. The contestants who were right would split the money. On the last question of the evening, the prize would be worth $300.

Celebrity Game with Ronald Reagan

On one show a question was, "Should bald men wear toupees?" They celebrities responded 5-4 that they should not, and Carl took his own toupee off on camera. Carl was perfect, and the celebrities had respect for him. We would tape two shows in a day. After finishing the first taping, we served a catered dinner, with plates and silverware. I had CBS set-up a living room behind the set, where the celebrities were served first, and then the staff and crew. I would often bring Marie to the studio to watch the tapings, and she reminded that her sister lived in Newport Beach, and might be a good contestant. I recommended her to our contestant coordinator, and she was chosen.

The *Danny Kaye Show* taped across the hall from us in Studio 31 on Fridays. One Friday Danny was late coming in for rehearsal, and everyone wondered where he was. I was in the hall when the elevator opened, and there was Danny in a wheelchair with one leg bandaged and elevated. His producer asked what happened. Danny said that they'd had a dinner party the previous evening. He'd been preparing pasta, and when he went to drain the pasta, the pot slipped, and he burned myself. The producer told Danny to go home, and that he would cancel the taping. Danny refused do that to our cast and crew.

He said if they only taped him from the waist up, he would do the show. That's what they did.

Judy Garland also had a variety show in Studio 43. She wasn't happy with the small dressing room, so CBS got her a trailer that sat outside in the hall. They also painted a yellow brick walkway from it to the Studio. She was happy with her new digs.

For one of our date nights, Marie and I made plans to see a musical at the Music Center in Los Angeles. As we walked into the theatre, she recognized a priest, Father Donavan, from the Newman Center on the UCLA campus. She introduced me and said me that she sometimes went to Mass there instead of going to St. Paul the Apostle Church in Westwood. I found out later that this her first time she ever saw a musical, and she really enjoyed it.

One day I was talking with Art Alissi, a co-worker who screened contestants for the shows. I mentioned that I was going to take Marie to see Nat King Cole at Melodyland Theatre in Anaheim, near Disneyland. He said he had a contact there, and would see if I could get backstage to meet him. He arranged it.

I had never been to Melodyland before, and what made Nat's performance special was that he performed on a turntable, so everyone was able to see him. When the concert was over, I told Marie I had a surprise for her, and we went to the stage door, and we were escorted to Cole's Dressing Room. There were three other people there, along with his wife Maria. They were very cordial, and we stayed about twenty minutes. On the drive home, that was all that Marie could talk about.

Then, in 1964, I was given more responsibility. Heatter-Quigley created a show called *Shenanigans* for ABC with Stubby Kaye as host. *Shenanigans* was a children's game show Saturday mornings. Much like *Video Village*, children advanced on a giant game board. After landing on a space, the children answered a question or performed a stunt, earning "Shenaniganzas" that could be traded for prizes. Most of the spaces on the  game board were references to popular board games by Milton Bradley (such as "Operation"), who served as the show's sponsor.

At the production meeting I learned that I would be in charge of putting the numbers together for the budget.

I went to see Stubby to go over the schedule, and discuss the wardrobe requirements. Stubby was a large, portly man, and he asked if he could have extra jackets and shirts, due to perspiring.

We hired animal costume designer Janos Prohaska to design a Shanaghoul costume that he would wear on the show, and to interact with the children. They loved playing with him.

One particular Saturday, we were going to have a race between two children. There would be two sets of 5 gallon empty cans, set up in a row, and the contestants would be on tricycles, with a pole that had a boxing gloves on both ends. At the finish line, they would hand a banana to a chimpanzee, and win. I had contacted Jungleland in Thousand Oaks, California to see about getting a chimpanzee from them. I explained what it would be doing, and they said there would be no problem.

Unfortunately, at the end of the race, the chimp didn't go for the banana and instead went for the arm of one of the children, and bit it. His parents immediately took the boy to the hospital to be stitched up. When he came back to the studio, we asked his parents how he was doing, and they said he was still in pain and shock, and that they had given him some medication to take. We told his father we were glad that he would be alright, and we gave them an assortment of Milton Bradley games to take home.

On Monday, I called ABC Business Affairs to let them know about the incident, and the people at Jungleland, where we rented the chimp. We all met that afternoon at ABC's Video Tape Department to view what happened, and what our liability could be. I asked if it would be alright for me to feel out the father on what he might want. ABC agreed so I called the father to see how his son was doing. He said that he was feeling a lot better. I asked if there was anything we could do for them. He was appreciative of how the situation was handled, and asked if we would reimburse him for his medical expenses. He would be fine with that. I then called ABC Business Affairs, Milton Bradley, and Jungleland, and told them how the incident was resolved. Everybody was happy.

ABC called and asked me to meet them at the Hollywood Palace theatre, where they wanted to move the *Shenanigans* show. The theater had just been refurbished for *The Jerry Lewis Show*, which would be a weekly show. It was a high-tech arrangement. Jerry had monitors for the cameras on his desk, and if he saw a better picture, he had the ability to put it on the air. His dressing room was two stories. On the main level was his bar and seating area. ABC told me that the bar had been outfitted with Steuben glasses, and up the circular staircase was a shower, decorated with his initials JL, and his dressing area. When ABC cancelled his show, he broke all the Steuben glasses, and even tried to get his initials out of the shower.

I had brought a copy of the stage plans to see if it would fit in the theater. After measuring everything twice, I decided the set would fit on the stage, but the cameras would all have to be in the balcony. There was no room on stage for them. *Shenanigans* stayed where it was.

I'd been having some problems with management at ABC who kept changing key stage crew personnel on a whim and without informing me. I went to see Herb Jellenick at ABC, who told me that ABC could do that. I didn't feel I was getting my point across sufficiently, so I went to the storage locker, where I kept the Milton Bradley toys for the show. I took one that was called "Time Bomb," which was black, and had a fuse on top like a real time bomb. I went back to Herb's office, wound the toy part way, opened Herb's door, and rolled it into his office. I held the door so he couldn't get out. When I heard the ping, I opened his door, and he was hiding behind his chair. He said I had made my point, and that he would make sure no more changes occurred without talking to me. He then asked if he could keep the "Time Bomb" for his children, and I said yes.

I had casually mentioned to ABC that we might want to purchase the set for *Shenanigans* to give us the option to move the show for syndication. The producers decided that there wasn't enough interest in the show to merit the purchase. Two weeks later, I learned they had refurbished the set without my knowledge. I told them that because I did not authorized the work that they did, they could now destroy it. To put it mildly, they weren't happy.

In 1965, ABC did a pilot for a new word game show called PDQ. PDQ stood for "Pretty Darn Quick." The show involved three celebrities and one contestant. Two celebrities were paired as the "Home Team"; the third celebrity and the contestant made up the opposing team, known as "The Challengers."

In the game, a player was in an isolation booth attempted to guess a famous name, title, or phrase. Each team took a turn at the same puzzle, with the team using fewer letters winning the game. A tie was considered a win for the contestant. Prizes were awarded to the contestant for every game won. Dennis James was the host, and Kenny Williams was the announcer.

There were two isolation booths on the set. I had mentioned to ABC that I had some knowledge about isolation booths, from *$64,000 Challenge*, and could offer some suggestions about their construction. ABC decided not to listen to me. They built very heavy booths with cement floors. Very hefty stagehands were required to move them into and out of position. ABC didn't buy the show, so the producers went to the NBC-owned and operated stations in New York City to see if they would be interested.

While in New York, I scheduled minor surgery for a deviated septum. Marie had referred me to an ENT specialist, who suggested I needed the surgery to fix a problem I had with my ears. After the operation, my head and nose were both bandaged. When I was still recovering, I received a call from Merrill, telling me that I needed to be at NBC the following morning to see Dick Welsh, Vice President of Production, and explain the show to him, and leave the film of the pilot for him to view.

When I walked into Dick's office, he saw that my head was bandaged and he apologized for bringing me out in the rain. I said I was alright. NBC made a deal with ABC to buy the set. One of the changes that NBC made was instead of trying to move the isolation booths in and out of position, they pre-set them to save money.

One request that the NBC's 5 Owned & Operated Stations had was to record the show on new video tapes. We could put 2 shows on a 60-minute tape, take a lunch break, and come back and do three shows on a 90-minute tape. Four Star Television syndicated the shows after they aired originally on NBC.

After about a month we started getting complaints from some of the stations, that they couldn't play the tapes. I had some of them returned to Four Star, and we found out that they had been dubbing our videotapes onto old stock that they had, and keeping the new tapes for themselves. It took a while, but they finally got it resolved.

Part of my responsibilities was to secure the prizes for *PDQ*, as I had done on other shows. I had met most of the suppliers when I was in New York working on *Video Village*, So I contacted them and let them know what products I was looking for.

Phil Lane, was one of the suppliers, said he was coming to California anyway to have meetings with the various game shows about using his clients on their shows. He would meet with me there, This was a one-on-one meeting. He was staying at the Beverly Hills Hotel, and suggested meeting him in the Polo Lounge. While we were sitting in our booth, a lady walked by with a drink in her hand, stopped, and threw her drink at us. She then fell down, and passed out. The maître d' came running over to our booth, and asked if we knew the lady, which we didn't. He was finally able to get her to her feet with the help of two waiters, and escorted her out. He then came back and apologized for the incident, and informed us that the Hotel would reimburse us for having our clothes cleaned, as well as for our drinks. The following day I had lunch with Phil, and we concluded our business, without any interruptions.

I mentioned to Jerry Shaw, the director, that I was getting frustrated with the work of the second stage manager NBC was supplying. The position was constantly being filled by different people, and they never understood how everything worked backstage. I ended up training someone every time we taped. He told me to look into what it would take for me to become a stage manager myself. I talked with Harry Meuschke, our Unit Manager on *PDQ* about the problem, and he suggested I set up a meeting with Bob Corwin, who was the Manager of Associate Directors, and Stage Managers. I explained my situation, and asked what about the possibility of hiring me to do the job. He said that he wouldn't be able to hire me because the Directors Guild of America needing a thirteen-week commitment, which he was unable to do, because we only taped three days a week. He said he would at least try to make sure we had the same stage manager for those 3 days. Unfortunately, it never happened.

Heater-Quigley came up with another idea for a show called *Hollywood Squares*. The pilot was done at CBS Television City, and the emcee was Arthur Godfrey. He flew from New York in his own DC-3 airplane. The next day I met him at the Beverly Hills Hotel and asked him to follow me to CBS. When we got there he asked why I took the long way. He had studied the map and thought I should have taken the shorter route. I explained that I didn't want to lose him.

CBS passed on the pilot. Bert Parks also came out to do another pilot, and CBS passed on that.

One night, Marie and I were having dinner at The Oak Room. It was a regular haunt of ours, and we often had our favorite waitress, Mary. This night, however, I couldn't shake off my misgivings about the way my work was going. I shared with Marie that I was getting tired of doing game shows. I was ready for a new challenge, and didn't see that things could happen in my current job. I was burned out. I told her that I was going to see if any opportunities were available.

CHAPTER 7
MOVING ON

In June 1965, I mentioned to Harry Meuschke, our NBC Unit Manager on PDQ, that I was interested in a change. He told me that George Habib, Manager of the Unit Managers, was looking for someone to work summer relief. I got an interview with George, and I was hired. I gave Merrill & Bob notice, and said I would help whoever took over for me, which I did.

I had a small office next to the elevator, and for two weeks I studied the manuals and procedure books to get familiar with the various forms. I was assigned to cover shows while the unit managers were on vacation.

The first one was *Let's Make A Deal*. This was a Hatos-Hall Production. Knowing Monty Hall, the host, made it a little easier. Part of the job was to come in at 3:00 a.m. to insert commercials that weren't available when the daytime shows were taped. I observed how this was done for two days. The video tape operators took pity on me and showed me ways to make the task easier, which I appreciated.

Since I would be covering the daytime shows primarily, I would go in for a few days before the unit managers would leave on their vacations to meet the production personnel. Their secretaries would take care of the paperwork needed and I would sign them. After each taping, you would make out a discrepancy report. If there were any problems, you would check the box that applied, and give a brief description. Most of the time, there weren't any.

I also learned how the shows operated and learned how to do use the folders from show Costs to prepare the budget reports. A week after taping, Show Costs would give you a folder with the costs that had come in so far. The secretaries would give me a log sheet of all the purchase orders for the past week, and I would then do the post budget report, and then return the folder to Show Costs. Three week later, the final budget report would be done, and if any PO's were missing, the vendor would eat those costs. This rarely happened. Then the report with the Show Cost backup would go to George Habib for his approval, and if everything was okay, he would initial it, and it would be distributed to the various NBC departments, and the production company. After that I would take the folder back to Show Costs, and sign off, which meant that nothing else could be charged.

Since I was approaching the end of doing vacation relief, George's secretary, Louise Lillebridge, told me George wanted to talk with me. He told me that I had done a good job, and offered me a permanent position in his department. I accepted.

I called Marie and told her, and we went out to dinner to celebrate at Lawry's Prime Rib Restaurant on La Cienega Boulevard. They start you off with a spinning salad. The waitress brings the salad bowl to your table, and as it's spinning, she pours the Lawry Sherry dressing on it. After the salad course, a rolling cart is brought to your table by one of the chefs, and your prime rib is sliced to your preference. Marie liked hers medium rare, and I asked for the end cut done English style, which is cut thin. This comes with a baked potato with sour cream, bacon and chives, creamed spinach and horseradish. She really enjoyed it.

The first show I did on my own was *Chain Letter*, produced by Hatos-Hall Productions. I had met Stefan Hatos when I covered *Let's Make A Deal* during the summer. I had to prepare the studio schedule, select the associate director, stage managers, technical and stage crews, make-up and hair, and videotape machine paperwork each week. Since the schedule was the same for each week, I made a master, and just made copies, and put in the dates and episode numbers for each week of production.

The budget for the show had been prepared by business affairs, and approved by the producers. I received a copy of the signed-off budget, and proceeded to copy this information onto the NBC forms, and then make copies for future weeks. This meant that all I had to do was put the dates, and episode numbers, and fill in the costs per week, as I had done during the past summer.

Jan Murray was the Emcee, and Wendell Niles was the announcer for *Chain Letter*. There were two teams made up of a celebrity and a studio contestant. Jan would give them a category like "gifts for the boss's birthday." The first player had ten seconds to come up with an answer, then the next player had ten seconds to come up with an answer using the last letter of the previous answer. This went back and forth until the chain was broken. They played for three minutes, and whoever had the most points got $100. For the bonus round, the champions were given a chain word and they alternated forming words. The contestant received $20 for each acceptable answer until the chain was broken.

Another project was *Hollywood Squares*. I was called to go to a meeting with business affairs, regarding the purchase of the *Hollywood Squares* set from CBS. I recommended that they buy it, since their studio doors were bigger than CBS's. At CBS they could only get the first two tiers into the studio and the top tier had to be hung in position and then lowered to be attached. At NBC, the entire set could be rolled into any of their studios. This would save them time and money.

Peter Marshall was the Host, and Ken Williams was the announcer. Jerry Shaw was the director. George Habib asked if I would have any problems working with Heatter-Quigley to get the show started, and I said none. Jerry asked if it would be possible to get some of the technical crew from *PDQ*, and I told him I would make every effort for him. I was able to get most of them. It was interesting to see how Merrill & Bob had creatively used the ideas from *People Will Talk*, to *Celebrity Game* to *Hollywood Squares*. On all three shows, they used a panel of nine. What made this show work so well were the comedy writers that would give the celebrities bluffs and joke answers. Then Peter would ask them for their real answers. The two contestants then had to decide if the answer was true or false to get that square. One was O, and the other X. If they guessed wrong the other contestant would get the square. To win you had to have three in a row. If a contestant was trying to block for the win and missed the question, then the other would be give a question to see if they could.

I also worked on the *Pat Boone Show*. This was a half-hour variety show. I went to meet with Al Lapin, who was the music contractor for NBC. His job was to get the musicians needed for the bands or orchestras used for the various shows. I also found out that Al and his brother Jerry founded the International House of Pancakes, also known as IHOP. Al put together an exceptional band for Pat. One day I asked the executive producer, Army Grant if he realized the talent he had in the band. I informed him that Paul Smith was on piano, Ray Brown on bass, and Frankie Kapp on drums. These were great jazz musicians. They finally featured them on a show, and they had a great time.

My next assignment was *Days of Our Lives*. They would tape Monday through Friday in Studio 2. This was my first experience doing daytime drama. Producers Jack Herzberg, and Wes Kenney and I would have weekly production meetings with the art director and the wardrobe and prop department to discuss the next week's scripts, and anything special that was needed. There were two separate stage crews. One would come in at 12:01 a.m. three days a week and at 3:00 a.m. the other two days. The show crew would arrive at 6:00 a.m. to finish up.

On my first day Wes introduced me to Macdonald Carey and Frances Reid, the two main cast members. When it was time for the dress rehearsal, Executive Producer Betty Corday and Jack would come to watch. Afterwards they would meet with Wes and the director to go over notes, and then meet with the cast. I was surprised to learn that after finishing the dress rehearsal, the director wasn't allowed to wear a headset. The associate director would call the shot numbers to the camerapersons, and the director would let the technical director know when to take it. We taped the show from 12:05 p.m. to 12:35 p.m., and put the commercials in as we taped. If we needed to reshoot a scene, the director went back to the last commercial before that scene, and started from there. We had until 1:00 p.m. to finish. We rarely had to do any re-shoots.

One time, Frank Sinatra did a Special, "A Man and His Music, " in Studio 4, across the hall from *Days of Our Lives*. I remember that Count Basie and his orchestra were there, and Dwight Hemion was the director. I was a huge fan of Frank's, and when we finished taping, I went over to watch his rehearsal, but Frank wasn't there. The following day I went over again, and he still wasn't there. They were scheduled to tape the actual show the following day. The next day I went in, and Frank was there. I went and sat in the audience, and I was able to hear the conversation he was having with Ed McMahon, who was hired to be his announcer for the show. Ed asked him where he had been the last two days, and Frank said that he flew to St. Louis for a meeting with Anheuser-Busch about sponsoring the show. They said yes, and they also gave him the Long Beach distributorship. The special aired on November 24, 1965.

Marie and I were starting to get serious, and she said for us to continue dating, I would have to become a Catholic. I was brought up Jewish, but hadn't been inside a temple or synagogue for a long time. She put me in touch with St. Paul the Apostle Church in Westwood, and they told me that Father Dove would be starting a class soon. I signed up for the class, and Father Dove was a very good instructor. I noticed that he had a very old 16mm projector. I started making phone calls to see if I could locate a newer one for him. Finally I called Burt Rosen at Four Star, and they had just purchased one they didn't need, and he sold it to me at a good price. I got to the class early one night, and presented it to Father Dove. He was very thankful, and the feature he liked best was that it was self-threading.

After finishing the class, I still had some questions in my mind, so I signed up again, and Father Dove taught it. The class finished in November. I told Marie that I wanted to be baptized. Marie had mentioned to her former patient, Dorothy Barnes, that I was going to become a Catholic, and she wanted to meet me. The three of us went to The Brown Derby in Beverly Hills, one of Dorothy's favorite places. Upon arriving, she introduced Marie and me to Max the Maître d, and he showed us to a booth. Marie and I found out that two waiters would fight over who would take our orders. One was Gene the other Phil. I guessed I made a good impression on Dorothy. She asked if I would pick her up on Sundays to take her to St. Paul's for the eleven thirty mass, and then go to the Derby for brunch. I agreed. Since I hadn't been baptized yet, I could not receive communion. Marie told me that Dorothy had converted from being a Presbyterian to being a Catholic back in St. Louis. Dorothy said she would call Monsignor Sullivan to see if he would fly out to perform the baptism. He agreed, and Dorothy got permission from St. Paul the Apostle Church for him to do it along with Father Dove.

On December 19, 1965, I was baptized. Afterwards, Dorothy said we would go to the Beverly Hills Hotel to celebrate. She had invited the priests from St. Paul's to join us. The dining room was busy, and bustling with conversation. When the priests walked in, it became very quiet. When Marie and I took Dorothy home, we couldn't stop thanking her.

I was confirmed on January 23' 1966.

I didn't tell my parents that I had converted, because I thought I would do that after Marie and I reached the next step in our relationship.

On Sunday, October 29, 1966, I received a phone call about 10 p.m. from my dad, telling me that my sister-in-law Judy and her daughters Laura and Pamela had been in an automobile crash in Long Island. My brother Steve had borrowed my Dad's station wagon to take the family to get pumpkins for Halloween. He told me Steve was the only one wearing a seat belt, and that he sustained a broken arm. Judy and the girls died. I told him that I would fly out the next morning, after talking with my boss. I called American Airlines and made my reservations, with the return open, since I didn't know how long I was going to stay.

The next morning, I arrived at NBC at 7:30 a.m., at the same time George Habib arrived. I told him what had happened, and he asked me to keep him informed about when I would be back.

My flight left at 11:00 a.m., I was fortunate that the stewardesses could see that I was under some stress. I told them what had happened, and they kept me supplied with alcohol, and food.

Arriving in New York, I was met by Mom and Sally, who drove in from Honesdale, Pennsylvania to be with Mom. We went to the hospital to see Steve, and I told him I was there for him, and I would take care of him. Mom told me that we would be staying at her brother Dave's house in Rye, New York. It would be neutral territory, and Dad liked them. I stayed there that night.

The next day Steve was released from the hospital, and we went to

Dave's house. His wife Lee was there to greet us, and I showed Steve his room. The funerals were scheduled for Thursday. Dad went to Park Avenue Synagogue, where he was a member, and purchased eight cemetery plots together. That afternoon, Steve called his buddy Arthur and told him what had happened. Arthur showed up that evening with a lot of scotch. At about 11 p.m., Steve said he was tired, so Arthur left and I put Steve to bed, and I put a pillow under his broken arm, to make it easier for him to get some sleep. The next morning, I asked Aunt Lee if she had any Saran Wrap so I could wrap Steve's cast without getting it wet in the shower. It worked.

After breakfast, the doorbell rang. I answered the door to two detectives from New York, who wanted to interview Steve about the accident. I asked if they could come back the next day, and they agreed to come back.

I called George Habib at NBC, and told him what was happening, and he told me to stay as long as I had to. I thanked him.

I then called Marie. She told me that she would be traveling with Dorothy Barnes to St. Louis to see her family. They would be there for another two weeks, and I informed her about the accident.

Thursday morning, I dressed Steve in a suit that Sally and Mom brought up on Wednesday. A car came and took us to the Riverside Memorial Chapel on West 76th Street in Manhattan. Rabbi David Putterman, conducted the service. I went over to offer my condolences to Judy's family. After the service, the rabbi, Mom, Sally, Steve and I were chauffeured to the cemetery. There were three graves prepared, and after the rabbi had finished praying, I noticed that the gravediggers all had tears in their eyes. We went back to Dave and Lee's house for the reception.

Dad told me that he had received a call from Fred Donovan for me and he left his number. He said he didn't recognize the name. I told him that Fred was a priest, and a friend of Marie whom I was dating. I called him, and set up a meeting for the following Tuesday at St. Paul the Apostle Church in New York City.

Steve said the meeting with the detectives went well on Friday.

On Saturday, Dad showed up about 11 a.m. and asked if I would go with him to retrieve the license plates from his car at the impound. At that time in New York, custom license plates were transferable to your next car. Just as we were leaving, Steve asked if we would pick up some liquor, since they had consumed what was there. Dad said yes. I told him to wait a minute. It was time for Steve to start doing things. I asked Steve for a check to cover the cost, and reluctantly he gave it to me. When Dad and I arrived to get the license plates off the car, we couldn't believe what we saw. It was as if someone had put the car in a vise, and you can't imagine what the pumpkins looked like.

I called George Habib, and told him I would be there for another week, and I thanked him again for giving me the time to take care of Steve.

That Tuesday happened to be Election Day. I told my mom that I was coming into New York, and was wondering what I could get to give Lee and Dave for being so gracious. She asked if I could meet her at Steuben's on Fifth Avenue. We met at 10:30, and she picked out a vase. I took it with me, to give to them later.

I then met Fred (the abbreviation for Father is Fr. and his first name was Edward, so he wanted me to call him Fred) at the Rectory and we went to the library, where we both finished off a bottle of gin. I thanked him for being there for me, and asked if he would ever be in Los Angeles, and he thought there was a chance.

That night I waited for Uncle Dave to get home for dinner, and when we were finished, I brought out the box from Steuben, and gave it to both of them. The card was from Steve and me. They thought it was beautiful.

On Wednesday, I called George Habib, and told him I would be back the following week.

When I called Marie in St. Louis to tell her that I was going to be flying back to Los Angeles, she asked if I could fly to St. Louis so we could fly back together. I called American Airlines and booked my flight to St. Louis, and then later that night to Los Angeles. I called Marie, and gave her the information.

On Thursday, I told Steve, that I would be leaving the next day. Mom, Sally and I drove him to his apartment. He made a couple of phone calls to see who would come and help him. After we got Steve home, he thanked me for being there for him.

When I arrived in St. Louis, Marie was there with one of Dorothy's friends to greet me. I left my baggage with American, and went to Dorothy's apartment. She offered her condolences on my loss.

After dinner, Marie and I were driven to the Airport, and we checked her bags, and boarded the flight to Los Angeles. I thanked her for getting in touch with Father Donovan, and I told her about the visit I had with him. On the trip back to Los Angeles she told me that Dorothy and her late husband had owned the St. Louis Browns Baseball team.

We landed in Los Angeles, ready to get back to work. I continued to build my skills and my relationships. I became adept at juggling projects and at solving problems. I felt like I had made a good career transition. I had made some big changes in my life in the previous few years—I had a steady girlfriend, a new religion, and a solid career. I had weathered a family crisis. The 60's were winding down, and I looked forward to what lay in store.

CHAPTER 8
WORLD EVENTS, SPORTS & WEDDINGS

The late 1960's were a tumultuous time in the United States. In April, 1968, Martin Luther King was assassinated. Just two months later, trouble came to the city where I lived when Senator Robert F. Kennedy was assassinated on June 5, 1968. He was shot at the Ambassador Hotel in Los Angeles after winning the California presidential primary. Immediately after he announced to his cheering supporters that the country was ready to end its fractious divisions, Kennedy was shot several times by the 22-year-old Palestinian Sirhan Sirhan. He died a day later.

Meet the Press scheduled a live Broadcast on June 9, 1968, from Burbank. The subject for the broadcast was gun control, in reaction to both the Kennedy and Martin Luther King, Jr. assassinations. This was a fast-paced, challenging program. I was the unit manager assigned to the program. Senator Joseph D. Tydings, a democrat from Maryland, was on the panel along with Alan Barth, Max Frankel, Donn Downing, and Carl Stern. The director was late, and the associate director directed the show until he showed up. On June 12th I received a letter from George A. Heinemann, Director of Public Affairs at NBC News, thanking me for my help.

This was also a time when Elvis Presley was at the peak of his fame. In June 1968, Elvis did his first TV special in Studio 4, which was directly across the hall from ours. The director, Steve Binder, asked if Elvis could come and watch our dress rehearsal in the control room so he would have some idea of what goes on, since he had never worked with TV cameras. Our producer Wes Kenny agreed, and Elvis came in, I introduced him to everyone, and told him what each person's duties were. At the end of the dress rehearsal, he went to each person and thanked them. I mentioned to Steve that he might want to consider taking out the Talley Lights on the Cameras, so Elvis wouldn't look to see what camera he was on. He thanked me for the suggestion.

Wes also directed medical symposiums. They usually taped in New York, and he wanted to move them to the west coast. He asked if I could be assigned to cover them. George Habib contacted Dick Wendelken in Tele-Sales, the contact for any outside business for NBC Burbank, to see if there would be a problem with me being assigned. There was no problem. I found out they usually taped on Saturdays. It would take a couple of hours to bring the set in where the doctors sat, and light it. They wanted to be able to start at 11:00 a.m. The doctors wore lapel mikes, which made it easier for the audio mixer. The first symposium was taped in Studio 6B, which was used by the local NBC station KNBC.

Wes introduced me to Ed Rasp, the producer from New York. During the rehearsal, Wes came out of the Control Room, and noticed the cameramen weren't using their headsets. They told him they could hear him through the glass wall without the headsets. Everything went smoothly. I was asked to do a second one, and this time we used Studio 3, because the local station was doing a show in Studio 6B. There were no problems. On July 8th, Ed Rasp sent a letter to Dick Wendelken thanking him for assigning me.

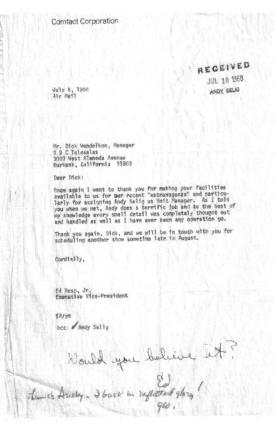

I decided it was time to learn how to play golf. I asked Ron Ellensohn, who lived in my apartment building, if he knew where I could learn. He suggested a pro who taught on Lankershim Boulevard. I contacted him, and he had an indoor driving range to practice on. After a month, he decided to take me to a nine-hole course on Whitsett Avenue in Studio City. It was fun, and I started to enjoy it, and he said that I should start playing with some of my friends at NBC. I asked Paul Pieratt if he would play, and he knew of a nine-hole course in the Burbank, DeBell Golf Course. We played there a few times. Memorial Day was coming up, and Paul mentioned that NBC had a golf tournament, and it only cost $20.00. I signed up and found out that it would be at the Valencia Golf Club in the Valley, and it would be the first time I played eighteen holes. What made it nice was I knew the golfers, and it made me less nervous. My best shot was over the lake. I was one of the lucky ones that got over it on my first try. We took a lunch break after the front nine holes. When we finally finished, my score was 135. The only consolation was that someone that has been playing twenty years had the same score. Because we both had the high scores of the tournament, we each got a dozen golf balls. On the way home, I decided golf was not my sport.

In 1969, NBC decided it needed more Studio space, and they built Studio 9. *Days of Our Lives* would be the first show to use it. Business Affairs wanted to save some money, and asked the show to use three cameras instead of four. This meant that the hour glass used for the Opening & Closing titles would be on film. NBC paid $10,000 to have it filmed. Since most of the commercials were on film, the cost of using the 35MM projector was absorbed by NBC. There would be no cost to the show.

NBC bought another daytime drama, *Bright Promise*, to replace *You Don't Say* with Tom Kennedy. They would share the other half of Studio 9. It was created by Doris & Frank Hursley, who also created *General Hospital*. The stars were Dana Andrews, Susan Brown, Paul Lukather.

MacDonald Carey decided to throw a party for the *Days of Our Lives* cast and crew at his Malibu house on a Saturday afternoon. He supplied the hot dogs and beverages, and invited everyone else to bring the side dishes to accompany them. Wives and girlfriends were invited, and I brought Marie. I stopped at Art's Delicatessen in Studio City to pick up bowls of coleslaw and potato salad before I picked Marie up. He had a volleyball court on the sand, and we split up into teams. Everyone had a great time. The agony came on Sunday, when I found out that I wasn't in the best of shape. My legs ached from jumping in the sand.

I was doing paperwork one afternoon when I got a frantic phone call from NBC in New York. They inadvertently erased their copy of the *Days of Our Lives* being aired the following day. I immediately informed George Habib. He called Business Affairs to make them aware of the problem. I called the producers and let them know. I suggested to Wes that instead of going LIVE to New York, that we tape the dress rehearsal, and if Jack Herzberg and Betty Corday liked it, we would air the taped version in New York and later on the west coast. We got lucky! All we had to do was one minor edit.

That afternoon, I met with the manager of videotape, Craig Curtis, and he came up with a plan that they make a protection copy of all daytime shows done in Burbank. NBC would absorb the cost. After the shows aired, they would re-use the tapes.

Wes Kenny wanted to do something different for the party celebrating the anniversary of *Days of Our Lives*. He wanted to do a parody of the show. Since we had time left after taping the shows, we would tape the spoof segments. We had a model of the Horton house that he wanted to blow it up at the end. The parady was called "Daze of Our Lives." Wes went in to edit the segments together, and then it was transferred to 16mm film. The party was catered, and held in one of the rehearsal halls. Betty Corday, the executive producer, thoroughly enjoyed it. She was really concerned about the Horton house being blown up, and Wes convinced her it wasn't the actual one.

George assigned me to do the inserts for the *Today Show* for the fall prime time shows. Barbara Walters was flying out from New York, and would interview the stars. Her guests included Raymond Burr, who was the star of *Ironside*, a police drama set in San Francisco. The show was about a man called Robert T. Ironside, who was Chief of Detectives for more than 20 years, and was forced to retire when a sniper's bullet paralyzed him from the waist down. In the show, the Police Commissioner hires Ironside as a consultant. Because of his injury, he works out of a wheelchair. For Barbara Walters' special, she interviewed Raymond Burr in the wheelchair. The next show that she did was *I Spy*, starring Robert Culp and Bill Cosby. Robert Culp was there for the interview, but not Bill Cosby. Barbara had started the interview with Robert, when Bill walked into the studio. Barbara saw Cosby, but Robert didn't. Bill walked over to a cameraman, who let Cosby start operating the camera. Barbara asked Robert yes and no questions about Bill. If Robert answered correctly, Bill panned the camera left to right. If he answered incorrectly, Bill panned the camera up and down. After about two minutes, Barbara invited Bill to sit in, and told Robert what had transpired.

Occasionally I would see what was happening in the other studios. On one day, I was in the control room when they were taping *You Don't Say* with Tom Kennedy (who was Jack Narz's brother). They were getting ready to do a live commercial for Peter Pan Peanut Butter. The jar was just about empty, and Tom said, that it was good to the very bottom. He hit the bottom of the jar and it broke off. It took a while to get the audience back to normal, and redo the commercial.

Wes continued to do the Medical Symposiums, and he heard that Ed Rasp wanted to do one in San Francisco. Again, George Habib asked Dick Wendelken from Tele-Sales if I could do it. And thought since I knew Ed it made sense. I contacted KRON in San Francisco to see if the Saturday date would work for them. It did and I told them what we would need in the way of a set and the number of lapel mikes we would need. They informed me that they would charge us overtime for working on a Saturday, and I asked them to call and give me the costs, and follow up with a letter.

They called the next day, and it was still cheaper than doing it in Burbank. I told Wes, and he got in touch with Ed Rasp, who approved it. I asked Wes if I needed to make any air, hotel or restaurant reservations, and he said it would all be handled by Ed's office in New York. Wes and I flew up after taping *Days of Our Lives* and went to KRON, the NBC affiliate, to make sure everything was set up correctly.

We then went to the Fairmont Hotel, where everyone was staying.

That evening the Doctors and their wives, and I were invited to go to Ernie's, a famous restaurant in San Francisco, for dinner. The maître d saw that Wes was wearing a turtleneck under his blazer and informed Wes that he needed a shirt and tie. At which point, Wes showed him that it was a formal turtleneck with cuff links. Our group was already seated, but I wondered what would have happened if our group of twenty had left.

On Saturday, the taping went well, and finished on schedule. Ed had made arrangements for us to have lunch at Alta Mira in Sausalito. Our tables were on the patio with a spectacular view of San Francisco.

On the following Monday, I went into George's office, let him know that everything had gone well. He wanted to see the expenses as soon as possible, so NBC could send the bill. I told him that my airplane ticket, car, hotel and meals were all paid for by Ed Rasp's company. I had zero expenses.

I received the bill from KRON two weeks later, and called Ed, and it was exactly what had been budgeted, and Tele-Sales would be sending it to him for payment, and I explained that there would be an additional bill coming for incidentals.

Two weeks later I received it, and it was for the refreshments, which cost $200. Ed was greatly relieved.

The following year I got a call from Ed telling me that they were going to London for a Symposium. He wanted me to join them and set it up. I asked George Habib about doing it, and a few days later he told me I could go if Ed picked up all my expenses. After two weeks, I had everything arranged.

The week before I was to leave, however, Ed called and told me that the drug manufacturer had reduced their budget, and that I wouldn't be able to go. When Wes Kenny got back, he told me that everything went well. They had finished taping early, and Ed decided he wanted to tape a segment by the River Thames, with Big Ben in the background. Ed got a little confused, or stage fright. He pointed to the Thames, and called it Big Ben, and Big Ben was the Thames. I don't think he ever went on camera again.

One day, George Habib called me into his office and asked if I like sports. I told him I did. He was looking for someone to take over the editing of the commercials for different sporting events. This was a challenging process, weaving pre-taped commercials in to a live broadcast. If the sporting event that happened on a Saturday, the transfer of the commercials would be done on Friday. I would get the information from the sports unit manager's secretary on Fridays, who also gave the rundowns to the film and videotape departments so they would have everything ready to record. I would meet with the videotape operator and go over which commercials were on film and which on video tape. He would transfer the film ones first.

On game days, at 8:30 a.m. the associate director, technical director and audio mixer would view the video tape, and the associate director would write down the last words of the commercial so he could cue the technical director when to cut back to the game. This usually took until 10:30 a.m., and then we took a lunch break until noon. Upon returning we checked-in with the remote truck, and master control to make sure everything was ready to air at 1:00 p.m.

One Saturday, we were getting ready for a baseball game from Dodger Stadium when a major electrical transformer blew up right outside the videotape department. We were told that the manhole cover flew about fifty feet, and when it came back down it shattered. We were fortunate that the explosion didn't affect the telephones.

Master Control called the studio in New York to re-route the game through them. They thought we were joking, and finally realized we had a problem. Within fifteen minutes they were ready to air the game.

Another time we were doing the final round of a Golf Tournament on a Sunday, which went into a sudden death playoff. The NBC producer at the venue was busy finding out who was going to buy the additional time in order to be able to air their commercials. We had about ten seconds to get the tapes cued up and ready to air. When the Tournament finished, NBC Producer Scotty Connal, said that he would be in Burbank the following day, and wanted to see the machines that we used. I introduced Scotty to Craig Curtis, the Manager of the videotape department who showed him our two machines. They were RCA computerized, and all we had to do was tell the Operator the time code, and the machines were ready in ten seconds. Scotty was upset that New York didn't have them. Scotty left NBC in August 1979, to help create ESPN.

I also had the pleasure of doing the Rose Bowl Games. We would come in at 8:30 a.m. to view the commercials and the film inserts of the colleges that were playing. We left those on a separate projector because we never knew when the director at the game would use them. Next door to us was the crew that was doing the Rose Parade, and they had to be in at 4:00 a.m. to get ready. They were envious of us, because we had coffee and Danishes, and they had none. The sports department had a big budget, so the following year I started ordering extra. We would take a break until Noon, and then start our check-in with the remote truck and master control. At 1:30 p.m., we would start the pre-game ceremonies, and then the game started at 2:00 p.m. I had asked George Habib if Marie could come and watch the game. He said it would alright, so I set her up in a viewing room near the videotape Department. After the game, I had a surprise for Marie. George had given me permission to take her out for dinner at Sorrentinos Seafood Restaurant in Burbank. I found out later that George had submitted the receipt to the Sports Department for re-imbursement.

Another year, I was invited to attend the production meeting for the Rose Bowl Game at the Universal Sheraton Hotel. The sports department had a huge suite. As I walked into the room, there were cases upon cases of liquor. At the meeting were the director, producer and Curt Gowdy, one of the play-by-play announcers, who would do a voiceover the following day. When the meeting was over, I asked Bill Palmerston, the unit manager, what all the liquor was for. He told me that they would give some to the spotters from the colleges, who helped identify the players on the field, and other people who helped. The next day I met Curt at the artist entrance, and took him to the control room, and showed him the audio booth where he could view the video, and rehearse his audio. This took about a half hour, and afterwards I walked him back to his car, and he left to go back to Pasadena.

I asked Bill Palmerston about the possibility of giving the film technical director credit at the end of the games, like the rest of the technical crew. I argued that the film technical director is the person responsible for getting the games on the air, and Bill said he would give him an audio credit at the end of the games. I never told the technical director, who we called "CB". CB was really surprised. He had a suspicion that I had something to do with it, and thanked me.

On November 17, 1968, I was doing the football game between the New York Jets and Oakland Raiders. We went on the air at 1:00 p.m. Pacific Time (4:00 p.m. New York time). The game went long, and as we were approaching 4:00 p.m. on the West Coast (7:00 p.m. in New York), New York Broadcast Operations informed us that they would be cutting away to air the movie special *Heidi*. I told New York to contact Scotty Connal, Director of Sports at home, and let him make the decision to stay with the game, or go to "Heidi". New York refused, and with just 65 seconds remaining in the game, made the switch to *Heidi*. Oakland scored twice in the next minute. Viewers were outraged. The next morning, I told George Habib what had happened. An hour later he called me into his office and told me after checking with Broadcast Operations, I had done everything that I could. I felt relieved.

I had my plate full of a wide variety of television products. But I still worked on a game show pilot called *Sale of the Century*. This was a game show pilot, with Jack Kelly as the host. The set was two stories. The game was played on the upper level, to see who would them go down to the stage level to play for prizes. The pilot went well, and it picked up. NBC decided that they had Studio 8H vacant at 30 Rockefeller Plaza in New York, and decided to have the set shipped back there. Willie Stein, the producer called to tell me about the many problems they were having. All I could do was sympathize with him, remembering how the limited space of New York studios made some things difficult. One of the biggest problems they had was getting automobiles as prizes for the show. Since there was no simple way to get them into the freight elevator, they would have the car companies remove the motors and drive trains, so that their cars could be cut in half to get them into the elevator. Once in the studio they would bolt the pieces together. I would've loved to have been in on those conversations.

Another big change happened in the late 1960's for me. Marie and I were getting to be more and more serious, and I was certain that I wanted to marry her. Marie mentioned to Julie Murphy that I was getting serious about marrying her. Julie suggested that we might want to go to Ruser's Jewelry Store in Beverly Hills to look at rings. Marie mentioned it to me, and I said I would also like to go to Donovan & Seamans. We went to both places, and I could tell that Marie like the ring at Ruser's better.

Just before Christmas of 1968, Marie wanted to go and get a Christmas tree. I found out that she only looked at trees that no one else would buy. Well, she found one on a lot, and she got it. We took it back to her apartment on Glendon Avenue. Marie was an amazing woman.

On Christmas Eve, Marie and I were invited to a Christmas Party. I went to her apartment with a bottle of champagne to celebrate with. I noticed how great the tree looked, and told her. She went and got the glasses, and as I was pouring, she went to finish getting ready. When she came back I proposed a toast, and as she went to take a sip, she noticed something in the bottom of her glass. It was the engagement ring!! She was so excited, because it was the one from Ruser's Jewelry Store that she really liked. She couldn't wait to show it off at the party. Marie didn't want to be a June Bride, so she picked May 31, 1969. Marie was a devout Catholic, and wanted to share her faith with me. I agreed to convert to Catholicism before we were married.

I phoned my brother Steve to see if he would be my Best Man, and he accepted.

I phoned my parents, who were divorced, and informed them of my conversion, and that I would be married in the Catholic Church. My mother was happy for me, and my dad was a little surprised. I tried to make light of it by mentioning that it was partly his fault, because he had painted Archbishop Francis Joseph Cardinal Spellman's residence. That didn't go over well.

Dad was still friendly with Rabbi David Putterman of the Park Avenue Synagogue, where he was still a member. I got a phone call from Rabbi Putterman, who asked me a few questions. His final one was, are you happy about being a Catholic, and I said I was. He then wished me and Marie a long life together.

Marie contacted St. Paul the Apostle Church in Westwood, and found that we could be married on May 31st at 1:00 p.m., and Father

Dove would be available to marry us.

Marie called home to Saskatoon, Canada, and told her Mother that she was going to be married. Her parents also were divorced. Her mother was happy about the wedding, but she wasn't well enough to make the trip to California for the wedding. She asked Marie if she wouldn't be upset if her Aunt Laura stood in for her, who lived in Santa Monica. Both Marie and I got along well with Aunt Laura, meeting her for dinner occasionally. Laura spoke French, and Marie enjoyed speaking with her in French so she wouldn't forget the language. She was an excellent stand-in for Marie's mother.

We found an apartment in Santa Monica with an unobstructed view of the Santa Monica Mountains. We ordered furniture for the apartment but arranged to have it delivered by the middle of May. I moved out of my apartment, and stayed in the guest bedroom until our wedding.

Marie and I took care of ordering everything for the flowers needed for the church, the wedding cake, liquor and bartender, and the finger sandwiches for the reception.

My dad called and asked if two of his wife's friends could be invited to the reception, so they would have someone to talk with. Marie and I agreed we would do that.

Sadly, Marie's father passed away in early 1969. Mrs. Murphy asked Senator Murphy if he would give Marie away. He said it would be an honor. Mrs. Murphy suggested that Marie go to Magnum's to look for her wedding dress, where she was able to find one that she liked.

Our wedding day arrived. Marie went to the Murphy's house and got dressed there so Mrs. Murphy could see the dress. Then Marie and

the Senator drove in the limousine to St. Paul the Apostle Church in Westwood. Father Dove officiated. and Marie's Aunt Laura stood in for her Mother. My brother Steve was the Best Man, and Marie's former roommate Margie Evans was her Matron of Honor. Sophie Palmer, another friend of ours,

offered us the use of her back yard for the reception. We accepted her offer, and then she said she would postpone putting the pool in until after our reception. I drove to Sophie's to leave my car, and she drove us to the Church.

Everything went off without any problems.

After the reception was over, Marie and I went to the Murphy's house to drop some champagne and cake. Mrs. Murphy really appreciated it. Mrs. Murphy hadn't attended the wedding. She was wheel-chair bound, and hadn't wanted anyone to see her being lifted out of the limousine and put in her wheelchair. She wanted to hear all about the wedding.

We then spent our wedding night in Bel-Air Hotel to start our honeymoon. We were so busy planning the wedding, that we hadn't planned the honeymoon trip. Marie suggested we just start by driving up the California coast.

On Sunday we started driving up the Pacific Coast Highway, and decided to stay at The Tickle Pink Inn in Carmel Highlands. They gave us a room with a view of the ocean. They didn't have a restaurant, but said they would make reservations for us. That night we drove to Carmel, and had dinner at the Marquis Restaurant, which served French food.

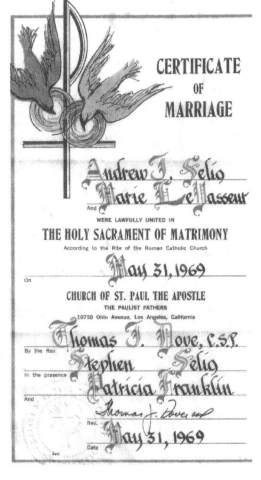

The next day we drove to Carmel, and looked around, and then went on the famous 17-Mile Drive through Pebble Beach. That evening Marie was in the mood for a steak, and Tickle Pink made a reservation for us at the Steak Ranch, which is now Clint Eastwood's Mission Ranch. Marie's steak hung over the edges of the plate.

From Carmel, we drove up to San Francisco, I knew my mother

was going to be there to see some of her relatives. I think she was happy that Marie got to meet them. We had dinner at Trader Vic's, and Marie said she would like to go to the one in Beverly Hills when we got back. We stayed at the Jack Tar, and the next day we left for Lake Tahoe. We found a very nice motel, and they made a reservation for us for dinner, and to watch the *Milton Berle Show*. We had never seen his act before, and he really does give the audience one great show.

The next day we headed back to Santa Monica, and upon arriving at our apartment, Marie was surprised that I had slept in the guest bedroom and not the master bedroom for the two weeks before the Wedding. I told her I was waiting to share it with her.

I could still drive Marie to the Murphy's home on Rodeo Drive in Beverly Hills in the morning, and I was able to pick her up at 3:00 p.m. But I told Marie it was time for her to learn how to drive. I contacted the California Driving School to schedule Marie's lessons. After she got her license, the Murphy's surprised her and bought her a VW Beetle.

Marie told me that the Senator was commuting from Washington to Los Angeles, and was wondering if I wouldn't mind picking him up at the airport. I contacted Ron Ellensohn who worked for the Mayor's office, he had given me one of his business cards, and he told me where I could park at the Airport for free. So, on the Friday's when the Senator flew in, this made it very easy. After doing this for a while, Marie said that he and Mrs. Murphy would like us to have dinner with them on Sunday nights, and then take the Senator to the airport for the trip back to Washington on the red-eye.

One afternoon, I heard that Vice President Spiro Agnew was coming to NBC, and everyone who could went to the parking lot to see him. His traveling companion was Senator George Murphy. The Senator saw me, and waved, and I just stood there, and applauded like everyone else. Marie and I had been invited to dinner that night, and he asked me why didn't I wave, and I told him that there were Secret Service personnel on the roof, with firearms, and I was really scared to do anything.

We settled well into our lives as a married couple. Going to the supermarket with Marie was eye-opening. We were buying things that I had never cooked. I was used to cooking Chef Boyardee out of the can, or Hebrew National hot dogs. Sometimes I added Heinz Vegetarian Baked Beans to my menu, or the occasional frozen dinner. But Marie knew how to cook properly, and I enjoyed a new world of fresh produce and well-cooked meals. The only mistake I remember her making was the first time she cooked artichokes. She put the leaves in the garbage disposal, and we had to call a plumber to fix it.

Early on in our life together, Marie told me that because of her health issues, she couldn't have children. I accepted our childless fate without question. I had Marie, which felt like more than enough. Talking through the situation only make our marriage stronger.

I've had a lot of wonderful experiences in my life, and done many amazing things. But marrying Marie was the best thing I ever did.

CHAPTER 9
EVERY DAY IS DIFFERENT

Then I graduated to nighttime shows. My first show was *Pure Goldie*, a special with Goldie Hawn from *Laugh-In*. The producers were Bill Persky & Sam Denoff. The associate producers were Harry Waterson & Lee Miller. I asked them who would make the decisions if any questions arose. Their answer: whoever was in the studio. This made my life a little hectic, to say the least. The guests were Ruth Buzzi, Bob Dishy and the Muppets. The routine between Goldie and the Muppets in the  rehearsal hall would be a show stopper. The producers brought their children to the rehearsal and they were able to interact with the Muppets. It was charming to watch. Too bad they weren't able to tape it for prosperity.

Marty Pasetta, the director who also did the Academy Awards. decided to tape all musical and dance numbers on the first day, and do the skits on the second day in front of a studio audience. We were supposed to start taping at 10:00 a.m. The stage manager went to get Goldie, and came back and told me she wasn't ready. I went to her dressing room to see if I could help and knocked on the door. Her hairdresser (I got permission from NBC so she could have her own hairdresser take care of her) answered the door. Her hairdresser informed me that this was Goldie's time of the month and couldn't come out. I went to Bill and Sam and explained what was happening. I told them that NBC didn't give rebates for an Act of God. We started taping at 10:30 a.m. and stopped at 1:00 p.m. for lunch. The taping continued after lunch, and as we approached 6:00 p.m., I asked if we were going to break again. Marty said no. I reminded him that meal penalties could be levied for the stage and technical crews if we didn't stop for dinner, and he really didn't care. At 11:00 p.m., I told him that he would have to stop at midnight, so everyone could get a good night's rest. He insisted on getting all the musical numbers done. At 11:30 p.m., I told him he had a half hour left, and he didn't want to stop. At 11:50 p.m., I picked up the phone, and was going to ask the NBC operator to get me Dick Welsch, who was Vice President of Operations at NBC. Marty stopped taping.

The next morning I was in early to inform George what had happened the night before. At 10:00 a.m., as Marty was getting to start rehearsing the skits, Dick Welsch came in, and he and Marty went off to discuss what had happened. Afterward Marty came over and apologized.

Jim Hensen of the Muppets came and asked if he could have a special TV monitor so he and his crew could see what was happening on stage. They wanted to be able to better interact with Goldie. It took about half hour to set-up, it worked well, and Jim appreciated what the technical crew had done. After lunch, Jim Hensen came to me and said that the monitor he was using disappeared. I asked the technical director if someone came in and took it, and he said no. I went to the stage crew, and asked them if they had seen anything. They hadn't. I then called head of security, to come and take a report. While he was doing that, someone said they saw a bundle up in the rafters among the lighting equipment. One of the crew went up and retrieved it, and I asked security to check for fingerprints. One of the stage crew admitted he took it, and put it up there to take home later, thinking it was an actual television. Ironically, the technical director told security that it would not have worked in someone's home. That evening the audience was brought in to see the skits, and we finished on time. The special aired on February 15, 1971.

Once, Harry Waterson and I were talking during rehearsals, and I found out that he also knew Bill Egan, my friend from my early days in television in New York City. Television is a small world. Harry told me he also had been a unit manager, at NBC New York a few years earlier. I mentioned that I also did sports, but that I stayed in Burbank, and just put the games on the air. He told me an interesting story. When he became a Unit Manager, the one thing he told his boss was that he didn't want to cover Sports, because he didn't understand the different venues. As fate would have it, one Friday the sports person got sick, and Harry was the only one to cover the Giants football game. His boss told him everything had been ordered, and all he had to do was sit in the remote truck, and take notes. That Sunday Harry showed up as assigned. everything was going fine until one of the Giants started doing amazing things on the field. Now in those days, you only had 2 people calling the play-by-play. The only person on the field was the Stage Manager to let the referees know when to go to the commercial. The producer turned to Harry, and tells him to go down to field to interview the player. Harry tried to convince the producer that it wasn't a good idea for him to do it, but the producer insisted. Harry went down to the field, the stage manager gives him the ear piece and the microphone, and cued Harry to start. Harry couldn't think of anything to ask this stellar player but: "What's your name? How long have you been playing football?" You can see why Harry was never asked to cover another sporting event.

Marie and I were settling well into married life. Mrs. Murphy suggested to Marie that we might need the services of Bea Halstead, who had a business management company. Senator and Mrs. Murphy were her clients. We set up a meeting with Bea, and we liked what she said. One of the things that she suggested was to buy a house for tax advantages, and to look in the Sherman Oaks area. That evening I called Arlo Hults who I knew as the organist on *Video Village*. I knew his wife Doris was a real estate agent. Doris said she would be glad to show us house. I told her our budget was $45,000, and she said she would start looking for us. The following Saturday, we went looking. We saw houses in Coldwater and the Beverly Glen areas. Marie and I both said we would prefer something not in the Canyons, because of the heavy traffic. Doris had some properties in the flats that we looked at, but were not to our liking. She said could we get together the following weekend.

We got together, and the fourth house she should us was perfect. The location was ideal for us. It was on a quiet cul-du-sac. Marie could take either Coldwater Canyon or Beverly Glen Canyon to get to the Murphy's, and I would take Riverside Drive to get to NBC.

The only problem was that it was priced at $47,500. Doris said she would talk to the owners. She called back and said they would accept our offer of $45,000.

That Saturday, we met Doris at her office to sign the papers, and give her our deposit. That evening she and Arlo took us to dinner at The Odyssey Restaurant in Granada Hills to celebrate. The food was excellent, and the view of the Valley was spectacular.

After moving all our belongings, we found that we needed a few more things to fill up the house. Marie and I went back to Rapport Furniture Store on La Brea, and fortunately for us our saleslady was still there. We asked her to come to see our home that Saturday. After seeing what we needed, she made some very good suggestions, and told us that her husband could do the minor construction that we needed to do, and that he was reasonable. Sunday afternoon he came, and looked over what needed to be done, and he asked us if we wanted to gamble and have the paint on the outside of the house sandblasted for about $300, and then he would seal the wood with two coats of varnish. The whole project would be $500. We agreed, and talk about being lucky, all the grain in the wood matched. The neighbors liked what we did, and I think it helped us become friends. The next project we noticed was that the wood fence around our back yard was falling apart. Marie and I decided to build a cinder block wall instead. We could plant shrubs that would hide most of it. I went to our neighbors Sylvia and Sandy Levine, to see if they would share the expense, and they agreed. It would only be five feet high. It really made a big difference, and they were happy with it.

I did the first season of *Sanford and Son*, with Redd Foxx and Demond Wilson. The show was based on *Steptoe and Son*, which was done in England. The executive producers were Norman Lear and Bud Yorkin of *All in the Family*. Aaron Ruben was the producer, and Edward Stephenson was the production designer. In the cast was LaWanda Page as Aunt Esther, Whitman Mayo as Grady Wilson, Hal Williams as Officer "Smitty" Smith and Noam Pitlik as Officer "Hoppy" Hopkins. He was the only white person in the cast.

In the show, Fred Sanford owned a junk yard, and kept getting into trouble with his "get rich quick" schemes. Lamont also worked for his dad. A running gag was that whenever Fred would feel stress, he would fake a heart attack, and would say, "This is The Big One, Elizabeth! I'm coming to join ya honey." Occasionally, the two police officers would show up at Fred's home, and Hoppy would try to use jive slang, and he would be corrected by Smitty. Hoppy would say "cold" instead of "cool". One day during camera blocking, Bud

Yorkin wanted the cameraman to dolly in to get a tighter shot, and in so doing the microphone picked up the fan noise from the camera. Bud asked to have it turned off, and I told him that turning it off might damage the camera, and that he would have to pay for it. I suggested that the cameraman go back to his original position, and zoom in, and see if he liked it the shot. I was lucky, he did. I found out later, if we had lost the camera, the bill would have been about $40,000. One night when we finished taping, Redd was offered an Old Fashioned to drink, and he said it was too sour, so he poured some Chivas scotch into it. He said that made it taste better.

Another night after taping, Demond was at the water cooler. He saw a lovely lady walk by and, forgetting that he was standing in a little alcove, came up too fast, and cut himself over his eye. I took him to the emergency room at St. Joseph's Hospital. He needed stitches. I called the executive producer, who wanted a plastic surgeon to put in the stitches, because he didn't want him to have a scar. The hospital paged the plastic surgeon. The surgeon had been at a formal dinner, and he really was upset when he arrived and saw the cut. He said any attending physician could have handled it. I explained that Demond was a co-star of an NBC TV sitcom, and this is what the executive producer wanted. The procedure took fifteen minutes, and the surgeon was quickly on his way back to the Party. The good news was that Demond did not have a scar.

Heatter-Quigley also did a pilot for NBC called *Name Droppers*, with Al Lohman and Roger Barkley. I didn't work on it, but I got a call from Business Affairs who asked me to come to their office, since I had knowledge of how Heatter-Quigley worked. They had received an invoice from Heatter-Quigley wanting to be reimbursed for the wardrobe for Al & Roger. It seemed really expensive, and I suggested that they ask for the receipts. Heatter-Quigley submitted a revised invoice, without the wardrobe.

GEORGE MURPHY
CALIFORNIA

United States Senate
WASHINGTON, D. C.

November 30, 1970

Dear Mr. Selig:

I want to take this opportunity to express my heartfelt gratitude to you for your help in my campaign.

The time you gave to Goldie on the Celebrity Committee was extremely generous of you and I am deeply grateful.

My only regret is that our efforts were not successful and, therefore, I will no longer be representing you in the United States Senate.

As I conclude my service, and as I reflect on the many happy days I have spent in office, I shall remember your kindness to me in a special way.

With my thanks and kindest personal regards,

Sincerely,

George Murphy

Mr. Andrew Selig
1321 Centinella Avenue
Los Angeles, California

When I took my two week vacation that summer, I volunteered to work on the re-election campaign for Senator Murphy. One of the celebrities helping on his campaign was Hoagy Carmichael, and I enjoyed our conversations whenever I delivered tickets to him for his speaking engagements. The Senator was running against John Tunney, the son of famed heavyweight boxing champion Gene Tunney. One of the things working against Senator Murphy was that he had had surgery for throat cancer. He had part of larynx removed, which made him unable to speak above a whisper. This was a difficult challenge for a politician. On election night, I drove him to the Miramar Hotel in Santa Monica to watch the results. I was very disappointed when he didn't win. This was the end of his political career. However, Senator Murphy is often credited as being the person who paved the way for entertainers to become politicians. Marie and I remained good friends with the Murphy's for the rest of their lives. When Julie Murphy died in 1973, we were there for the funeral, and to lend a hand to Senator

Murphy. He was very gracious and kind, and gave us his Grandma Moses painting, saying he was sure Julie would have wanted us to have it.

By this time in my career, I was now an old hand, and took an active part in many different programs. I was always working behind the scenes, solving problems and making things worked. Because the shows were different, the problems were all different, and I was never bored. I took pride in being able to find creative solutions to issues that stumped other people. Here are a few of the projects I worked on:

THE FUNNY SIDE

The premise of the show was to look at the humorous side of married life through comedy sketches, music and dance production numbers. Bill Persky & Sam Denoff were the executive producers and Lee Miller was the producer. I had worked with them on the *Goldie Hawn Special*. Lee and I went over the budget, and it was very tight. If there were any problems during the taping, they would go over budget. Whenever I could I would put a discrepancy report, to save them some money.

Gene Kelly was the host, and I thought he would be very demanding to work with. As it turned out, he was the complete opposite....very cooperative. During the introduction to one of the skits in rehearsal, Gene accidently went under a tree branch, and his hairpiece got caught in it. Everyone had a good laugh, including Gene. The cast included John Amos, Teresa Graves, Warren Berlinger, Pat Finley, Dick Clair, Jenna McMahon, Michael Lembeck, Cindy

Williams, Burt Mustin and Queenie Smith. NBC had scheduled it opposite Marcus Welby, M.D., a very popular show on ABC. Since there were no billboards around ABC's office in Century City, the executive producers rented one across the street from CBS Television City to advertise the new show. Their executives had to look at it every day.

We all looked forward to doing the show. On one episode, the theme was about newspapers, and how the only section that you could trust was sports. However, the ratings weren't good enough, and *The Funny* Side wasn't renewed. The NBC crew wanted to let the producers know they enjoyed working on their show, so the day before the producers hosted a Wrap Party, the crew gave the *producers* a party. The idea was to keep it light, and we got them parting gifts. One liked popcorn, so we got him the big bags, and the other tins of peanuts. They were amazed at the gesture, and appreciated it.

LENA HORNE SPECIAL

Lena Horne had a Special, and I was asked to set up a preview party for her. It was going to be held on a Sunday and George Habib gave me permission to bring Marie to the party. They were going to show segments that had been edited from the show. The producers hired Chasen's to cater the food, and they served their world-renowned chili, which everyone enjoyed. The producer asked me to get a piano for the party. The pianist was Lenny Hayden, who entertained the crowd. Few knew that it was Lena's husband. It was revealed just before seeing the segments. When Lena brought her Broadway show to Los Angeles, we were fortunate to go see her. The title was: "Lena Horne: The Lady and Her Music". She really knew how to entertain an audience.

JACK BENNY

It was a highlight of my career to be assigned to do one of his specials. The title was: "Everything You Always Wanted to Know about Jack Benny, But Were Afraid to Ask". The production meeting took place at Irving Fein's office in Beverly Hills. The Friars Club, a private show business club started in 1947 by Milton Berle and other celebrities, was located four doors down on Brighten Way.

The show was set in the early days of movies. The cast was George Burns, Lucille Ball, John Wayne and Dionne Warwick. Jack and George both had the same agent, Irving Fein. Irving's association with Jack went back to 1947, when he was doing radio. Irving then became his manager and producer, and also did public

relations for him. He also got him concert bookings where he would play the violin. Jack was instrumental in getting Irving to represent George Burns after his wife Gracie passed away. On the second day of rehearsals, George went over to Jack, and asked why he had to come

in at 9:00 a.m. when Jack didn't come in until 11:00 a.m. Jack asked, "Do you want to know the truth?" and George said yes. "It takes you longer to learn your lines." Everyone started laughing. Another skit had Lucille Ball playing a dancer, and Jack invited her up to his house. After she entered, a gate came down to prevent her from leaving. Lucy said, "That gate could have hit you!" Jack said that when he did her special, he was almost hit by the scenery. Lucy responded, "When you were on my show, you were insured!"

Another time we went to the commissary for lunch, and Lucy was sitting at a table with a brunette wig, babushka, and sunglasses, and asked Jack to sit with her. His answer was, "I don't sit with strangers."

Another skit was with John Wayne. Jack was playing a big movie star, and he was

telling him that Marion Michael Morrison (John Wayne's real name) was too long to fit on a marque of a movie house. He finally convinced him to change it to John Wayne.

I don't remember the prop man's name, but he invited me to go the Magic Castle in Hollywood. When we got there, he instructed me to go to the library wall and say, "open sesame." The door opened, we walked into a bar, sat down and ordered drinks. After I had a couple of sips, I noticed that my bar stool was going down. I was told that this usually happens to someone who hadn't been there before. We then went to the dining room for lunch. Although the dinner dress code was a tie and jacket, the lunch dress code was casual. On the way back to NBC, the prop man asked if I would be interested in becoming a member. I said yes, and told him about my magic experiences in New York. John Shrum, who was in charge of the art directors at NBC, called me and said that he would get me an application for the Castle. The following week I was accepted as an Associate Member. This meant that I could have use of the Castle, including going to the shows.

I took Marie there for dinner after I got my membership card. I played the same trick on her with the bar stool. After finishing our drinks, I walked Marie over to the piano, and told her to ask Irma to play something. After dinner, we went downstairs where the magicians performed. We both had a great time, and she wanted to go back. That Monday I went to see John Scrum and thanked him. I found out that John also worked with Milt Larsen on designing the Castle. I am now a Life Associate Member.

HALLMARK HALL OF FAME: GIDEON

Gideon, written by Paddy Chayefsky, was a play about the story of Gideon, a judge in the Old Testament. The play had a successful Broadway run in 1961, but was now being taped as a

Hallmark Hall of Fame special. The stars of the television adaptation were Peter Ustinoff and Jose Ferrer. George Schaefer was the director, and he was used to taping the shows in New York, where you asked for a firm bid, any changes resulted additional costs. I convinced him to not use the firm bid, and I got him to trust me. I went to watch the rehearsals at Columbia Studios in Hollywood. It was interesting to see how George worked with the actors. He sat in a wheelchair, with his script on his lap so he could work on his camera blocking. One of the problems we faced was that the show was set in a desert, and the only way we could handle that in the studio was to put the set on five foot platforms. The art director was Warren Clymer, and he did an outstanding job of capturing George's ideas. This also made it easier for George to get some low camera angles, but it made it more difficult for the audio mixer to mike the actors. We had to put the mike booms on platforms also.

George requested that we bring his technical director and one cameraman from New York to work with him. I met with Jack Kennedy, Manager of Technical Services to see how we could make this happen. It got worked out, and O Tambouri, the technical director, and a cameraman came out.

I called George to set the rest of the personnel for the show. He left it up to me, but said that he had his own associate director, Adrienne Luraschi that he wanted. I went to see Bob Corwin to see if that would be a problem, and he said it was alright, but that she had to be paid by NBC. George didn't have a problem with that.

On the first day of camera rehearsal, Peter Ustinov arrived carrying a Snoopy lunchbox. Try to picture this big man walking through the lobby of the Beverly Hills Hotel with that in his hand. He brought it every day and had a picnic in his dressing room.

Peter mentioned to George that he would like to get out a little earlier on one of the taping days, due to a dinner commitment. George

said he would try. Toward the end of the day, during a scene which was rather lengthy, Peter went completely off script. George said that since Peter wanted to get out early, he would use that take. Peter insisted on doing it again. Another time we were in the middle of a scene, and all of a sudden we heard the sound of a jet plane coming in for

a landing at Burbank Airport. They really didn't have jets in Biblical times.

When we finished taping the show, George invited everyone to go the Carriage House Restaurant, across the street from NBC, to celebrate and thank everyone.

George had made several changes to the set, and when I gave him my post estimate a week later, there were savings. I called him and gave him the good news, which he appreciated.

BOB HOPE

I was excited to be able to attend the rehearsals of Bob Hope. On one show, one of his guests was Arnold Palmer. They had become friends at the Bob Hope Desert Classic in Palm Springs. There was a lull in the rehearsals, and Bob asked Arnie if he could ask him a question. Arnie said sure. Bob wanted to know what he should do to improve his game, and Arnie asked, "How honest do you want me to be?" Bob told him to go ahead. Arnie said, "Give it up." Everyone started laughing.

Another time Don Rickles was a guest, and he sat on a stool right inside the door to enter the studio. Whenever a guest entered he hit them with a one liner, and they were in hysterics.

JOHNNY CARSON

Johnny Carson loved to play practical jokes from time to time. One evening after taping the *Tonight Show*, Ed McMahon was leaving the Midway parking area where the VIPs parked, when he was stopped by the guard who wanted to look inside his trunk. To Ed's amazement, the guard found a typewriter and other equipment. Ed couldn't explain it, and finally the guard told him that Johnny had set it up.

Michael Landon went to dinner with Johnny and their wives at Beaurivage Restaurant in Malibu. Michael accidently hit a cat as they were leaving. About three weeks later they went back to the same Restaurant, and after being seated they were handed menus. Everything on Michael's menu had to do with cat, which Johnny had set up. Michael finally caught on, and they all had a good laugh. The following week Michael was a guest on his show, and shared the experience.

ANDY WILLIAMS SHOW

One day, while preparing to rehearse for the *Andy William's Show*, I was up in the Control Room of Studio 3, which happens to have a large window overlooking the stage. Liberace was a guest, and he was sitting at the grand piano, with a candelabra on it. There was also a live lion lying on it. I think Andy was going to sing "Born Free." During the rehearsal, the lion leaped to the stage, and went over to where Andy was standing, and started licking his hand. The trainer told Andy not to move, and about two minutes later, had the lion under control. Andy needed a lot of time to recover from the experience. Another time Andy drove up to the artist entrance in a Mercedes-Benz, and there was a new guard on duty. Andy told the guard that he parked in the Midway with the other stars. The guard asked Andy what he did, and Andy said he was a singer. The guard told him he couldn't park there. Five minutes later Andy was admitted, and the guard apologized.

PERRY COMO SPECIAL

Perry was doing one of his specials, and was standing on one of two platforms elevated fifteen feet in the air. After he finished his song, the stage went dark, and the platforms split in half. He was supposed to be on the right platform. Unfortunately, he was on the left one when it split. He took a walk in space, and broke his leg. Two days later he was able to finish the special in a wheelchair. The cameras only showed him from the waist up. When he did his next special at CBS, he insisted everything would be done without any platforms.

DEAN MARTIN SHOW

Greg Garrison was the producer and director. I was covering for Dean Reid, the unit manager, who was on vacation. Dean had warned me that Greg liked to play tricks on Dean Martin once in a while, and to just go with it. One time, they come to the segment where Dean is supposed to jump up on the piano, and sing a song while Ken Lane is playing. Well, he jumped up on the piano, and it broke away. Another time they had a new prop man on the show, and he was told to put black shoe polish on a brass pole, which Dean was supposed to slide down. Well, the prop man forgot to rub it off, and NBC had to buy Dean a new tuxedo.

Dean never knew what Greg had planned for him. After finishing his opening number, Dean usually told the audience a few jokes. Once, as he was talking, four of the Golddigger dancers came out with two on either side of the camera, and they start unzipping their costumes, and showing their bosoms. The audience couldn't see what was happening, and Dean's comment was "Oh my."

BILL COSBY SPECIAL

This was a fun show to do. The opening of the show was Bill driving a Mercedes onto the NBC Lot. The welding shop made a seat that attached to the front of the car where the cameraman would sit. The car was white, which didn't show up very well on camera, so we had the paint shop paint it a light blue color with a water-based paint. After the opening was filmed, I told prop man to drive the car to the

car wash, and I would meet him there, and pay for it. Well......we forgot to tell the guys at the car wash that the Mercedes had been painted. They couldn't believe that the paint came off. It had never happened before. The manager came out, and started apologizing. I told him that I was from NBC, and explained what we had done, and that they didn't do anything wrong. He was relieved.

One of the skits was with Bill and Herb Edelman. In the scene, Herb was a taxi driver stopped at a red light. Bill rode by on a bicycle and accidentally hit Herb's bumper. Herb got out, and kicked Bill's bicycle tire. Bill then pulled Herb's side-view mirror off. Herb retaliated by taking a sledge hammer out of trunk, and smashing the bike's wheels. Bill took the sledge hammer and tried to break the rear window of the cab. Unfortunately, the hammer bounced off. Bill tried several times and got really frustrated, because the windshield just wouldn't break. We finally got it so he break it and finish the scene.

BING CROSBY SPECIAL

I was assigned to schedule the taping of several commercials Bing would do for RCA, and that would air on his Christmas special. His special had been shot on film, and George asked me to do the transfer to Videotape, putting the commercials in during the transfer. I kept calling the producer to find out when I could schedule the transfer as I was worried we were running out of time. I think the special was going to air on December 14, 1971, and I finally got a call that I could schedule it on December 13. Everything was arranged, and the producer walks in at 10 p.m. on the 13th with the print. We were ready to start the transfer, when we saw that the print was very dark. The producer starts complaining the film video operator wasn't shading the film properly. I suggested that we take it across the hall to the film department and use their 35mm projector. It was still dark. The producer made a phone call and left to go get the new print. He finally came back, and this time the film is perfect. We made the transfer, putting the commercials in, and finished at about 5 a.m. I warned the producer that it might not get to New York in time to air that night, and I offer him the option of paying for transmission by telephone line from Burbank to NBC New York. It would cost about $3,000. He decided that it was too expensive. I suggested using a courier to fly it, bit he didn't want to spend the money. The final resort is to pay for me to take it, and that's another no. So he gambled on shipping the tape, hoping that it arrived at NBC in New York on time. He really got lucky, and the tape arrived an hour before it aired.

1972 WINTER OLYMPICS: SAPPORO, JAPAN

During these Olympics, NBC Burbank received the events from Japan to play in the United States. We had a production meeting with the Olympics sports producers, and learned that the schedule would be grueling. One of the problems we would facing was the audio lag from Japan. We would have to sync the audio to the video for broadcast because of the time delays. We used the Lexicon machine to fix the problem. I would be the unit manager scheduling the associate directors, technical personnel and the videotape machines to assemble the packages to play on the *Today* show, and during prime time each day. It took two weeks to do the schedule, and then we had a meeting with all the managers who would be affected. About fifteen technicians would be going to Sapporo from Burbank. I gave them a form to fill out for their sizes, so the clothing that NBC was going to supply, would fit. A week before they were to leave, they came to my office to pick-up their NBC Sports outfits. There were no serious problems during the Olympics.

COMMERCIAL

I was fortunate to get assigned to do commercials for the Tele-Sales Department at NBC. Dick Wendelken and John Spence oversaw getting outside businesses to come and use the NBC facilities. The first ones I was assigned to do was for Hallmark Cards. Hallmark hired Foote, Coyne & Belding, based in Chicago, was the advertising agency. It would take a week to videotape the commercials. Hallmark taped its Valentines and Easter commercials at the same time, and everything went well. When they came back in December to produce commercials for their Christmas cards, they requested me to help them. The following year Hallmark came out with a new line of party goods. They hired a food designer to make sure the color of the food would photograph realistically on their plates. There were four scenes that had to be edited with dissolves. I asked the associate director, Clay Daniels, to go to the videotape department with me and supervise the editing. The director had figured it would take him a full day to do it. Hallmark was pleased with the outcome, and it also saved them money. The director wasn't pleased, however, because Clay and I delivered what they wanted in less time, and the director lost out on some income. He didn't want to work with me again. I was fortunate that the next time I did the Hallmark Commercials, they hired a different director.

I also did the introduction of the Camaro automobile for Chevrolet. It was a three-minute commercial, and was going to be seen on *Bonanza* in prime time. On the day we shot the commercial, the truck arrived at 2:00 a.m. We unloaded the cars and brought them to the stage. Lon Stucky was the lighting director, and the crew the Union sent didn't have a clue of what they had to do. It was cost effective to bring in outside crews to save on overtime. NBC provided the head electrician, and the lighting board operator. Lon asked me to get pads and pens so the new crew could take notes, while learning about the equipment. Lon, the head electrician and the board operator hung all the lights that they needed.

At 8:00 a.m., the NBC crew arrived, and Lon was happy to see them. When the agency people came back at 9:00 a.m., I mentioned that I had found a small problem with the Camaro. I am six-foot three inches tall, and couldn't sit in the driver's seat and turn the steering wheel. The wheel dug into my thighs because the track for the seat wasn't long enough to move the seat back any farther. The representative from Chevrolet asked me to sit in the car again, and he said that all they had to do was lengthen the track for the seat. He said that it would be a quick fix at the factory, and thanked me for bringing it to their attention.

After the 3 minutes was edited, we made a black and white kinescope for them to take to New York to score the music to it. A few weeks later, they brought the track back to us, and we found out that they had recorded 30 seconds to much. I asked them to give us a couple of hours to try and fix it. I went to Craig Curtis, manager of the Videotape Department, and told him about the problem. He said that they had just gotten a new Lexicon machine that would be able to speed up the track. He could make it fit the three minutes. When they came back and saw the finished commercial they were really surprised with the finished product.

The most amusing commercial was for the banking industry. Jack Benny was the spokesperson. We had a production meeting, and the producers decided they wanted Jack to be in front of a blue screen for the commercial. However, when we started rehearsals, the producers had forgotten that Jack's eyes are blue. The background image showed in his eyes. It took a half-hour to change it to a Yellow Screen. That solved the problem.

I loved having a job where every day was different, facing problems that required common sense and creativity. I wasn't unhappy where I was, but soon enough I was given a new opportunity.

FOOTE, CONE & BELDING

401 NORTH MICHIGAN AVENUE   CHICAGO   60611

September 2, 1969

Mr. Andy Selig
C/O John Spence
Telesales Department
NBC, Burbank
3000 W. Alameda
Burbank, California

Dear Andy:

Thank you for all you help and consideration in shepherding
the Hallmark commercials to say nothing of the agency people
and the clients. I appreciate your patience and understanding.

Cordially,

Mimi

Dayton Rommel
Copy Supervisor

DR:pab

FOOTE, CONE & BELDING

andy

2727 WEST SIXTH STREET   LOS ANGELES 90057

NEW YORK CHICAGO SAN FRANCISCO HOUSTON LONDON MEXICO CITY TORONTO FRANKFURT PARIS MILAN COPENHAGEN
MELBOURNE SYDNEY STOCKHOLM MALMÖ AMSTERDAM THE HAGUE ROTTERDAM BRUSSELS

August 29, 1969

RECEIVED
SEP 4 1969
GEORGE HABIB

Mr. John Spence
NBC
3000 W. Alameda
Burbank, California

Dear John:

The Christmas commercials are great. The time spent in
producing them was a pleasant experience.

Please convey my appreciation and regards to all who helped
in their production. A special thanks to Andy, Terry, Stu,
Bob, Joe, Chuck, Art and Art, and above all to Ed Flesh and
Dick Darley. I know there were many others behind the walls
and behind the scenes who made contributions that I am not
aware of, you know who they are and I would be grateful if
you relayed my sentiments to them.

Hope we work together soon on another exciting project.

Sincerely,

Tom Rook

TR:pc

*George —
Please pass along
thanks! Andy*

157

CHAPTER 10
A NEW JOB

I had kept up my friendship with Bill Egan in New York, and he informed me that Goodson-Todman Productions, where he was the production supervisor for their game shows, that they were going to expand their offices in Los Angeles. He asked if I would be interested in interviewing for the job of Production Supervisor. I said yes, and two weeks later, I met with Mark Goodson and Howard Felsher, who was the executive producer of *Password*. I told them about my game show experience in New York, and Los Angeles.

Three weeks later, I received a call from Bill, telling me that I was hired.

The first show I did was *I've Got a Secret*. The executive producer was Ira Skutch, who came out from the New York office, and the show would be produced at KTTV Studios. I set-up a meeting with Lou Steinberg, who was like the Tele-Sales Department for Metromedia, and we went over the budget and the studio schedule. Included in the budget was office space for the staff and parking. I met with Ira and Ted Cooper, who came out from the New York office, regarding the set he designed, and was being built at KTTV. The set went over-budget, but when Bill Egan negotiated the deal at KTTV, he had put in some padding in case of any emergencies that might arise. Those extras took care of the overages. Ted was relieved when I told him the overages would be amortized, and it was our "secret." Ted and I became good friends after that. Ira put together the staff, and I took care of scheduling the stage and technical Crew with Willie Geiger, unit manager at KTTV.

Steve Allen was the emcee, and Marc Breslow was the director. Johnny Olsen also came out from New York to be the announcer.

Bill sent out the masks that the celebrities had used on the show in New York, which also saved money.

On one episode, we were going to have a U.S. Army tank. I notified KTTV three weeks in advance, to see if there were any problems. The day before rehearsal, I was notified that the stage floor wouldn't be able to hold all that weight. The alternative was to park it outside the studio and put a camera out there, at their cost, I suggested trying to put down some planks on the floor to re-distribute the weight of the tank. They went for that, and it worked!

Another time, the panel had to guess what the occupation of a gentleman guest. In rehearsal, he told us that he didn't do rehearsals. It became clear later what he meant. When we taped the show, the panel couldn't come up with his occupation. So, as the curtains parted, you saw a platform 30-feet in the air, and a wading pool with two feet of water in it. He did a belly dive from the platform, and hit the water, and then came out of the pool. We then understood why he didn't rehearse. The finished segment showed him doing it in slow-motion.

Marc Breslow left as the director to do *The Price Is Right*, and Stu Phelps came in and finished the run.

A week after we taped the show I would have a meeting with Lou Steinberg and Willie Geiger to go over the costs. There were never any surprises.

I had told Willie that Bob Barker was going to be the host of *The New Price Is Right* on CBS. Willie mentioned that Bob was taping *Truth or Consequences* right then, so we went into the control room. Bob was saying words, but they were breaking up. He was also mouthing words silently. He asked the audio mixer, Bud Linquist, to come down to the Stage and fix his microphone. Bud went to the stage, very concerned. Bob told Bud that he'd been with the show a long time, and that maybe he needed a rest. At this point, Bud started to sweat. and didn't know what was happening. Bob told him that maybe a vacation would help, and he gave Bud tickets for a two-week, all-expenses paid vacation. Bud was really surprised, and relieved at the same time.

Ira Skutch and Howard Felsher had been assigned by Mark Goodson to find enough office space for *Password*, and *The Price is Right*. After looking at what was available, they decided on 6430 Sunset Boulevard. It was convenient to ABC, CBS and KTTV Studios.

The Price Is Right was produced at CBS Television City. I had a meeting with Charles "Cappy" Cappleman, the Director of Design and Production Services, to go over the studio schedule. The budget had been done in New York with Jerry Chester and Bill Egan. This was the half-hour version. We would tape in Studio 33, sharing the studio with

Carol Burnett. Cappy [also introduced me to Rita Burton, who would be our production supervisor. She had just transferred from CBS Studio Center in Studio City, where they did film shows. The first thing I did was take her to the Videotape Department to show her that videotape didn't have sprocket holes like film does. I could tell by her reaction that we would get along. I then took her around to meet all the department heads. Frank Wayne was the executive producer, who also transferred from the New York office.

We found out that Bob learned the various games very quickly. Part of my job was to go to the CBS warehouse on Fridays to make sure

that the CBS Prize Department had all the prizes there for the tapings. I usually arrived at the studio at 7:30 a.m. on Sunday to make sure that prize pictures for the trips were there for Marc Breslow to select for the tapings that day. We would camera block with the models, Janice Pennington and Anitra Ford, and the announcer, Johnny Olsen, from 9:00 a.m. to 10:00 a.m. One of the games was the *Grocery Game*, where the contestants were shown five grocery items. They had to specify the quantity of each item, trying to get a total between $20 and $21, without going over. Then the prices were shown, to show who had guessed well.

Part of my job was to find the cash register for the game. Luckily on the fifth call, I talked with National Cash Register (NCR), and I explained what the machine had to do, and they had one that could do the multiplying. I convinced them that it would be on national television, and they would get free advertising. They delivered it, and showed Janice how to operate it. I said that we would paint the NCR logo black, so it would stand out. They asked if they would be able to exchange it when the new models were introduced, and I agreed. The sound effects man, Gus Bayz, set up his equipment in the orchestra area on the stage. He was able to put a microphone on the cash register in order to hear it doing the calculations. We let him know about any new games that we were going to use, so he had time to get the effects. Gus asked me if it would be alright for him to paint sometimes when

he wasn't needed for rehearsals, and I said yes. At Christmas, he gave me a print of a street in San Francisco. One day Marie and I were in Geary's in Beverly Hills, and we saw some of Gus's work there. We appreciated his gift even more.

After watching the rehearsals, Jay Wolpert, the producer, would go outside where the audience was waiting and would talk to them, using a different code word for selecting who would be selected as contestants for that show. CBS Program Practices assigned Nancy Wiard to go with Jay on the line so that she could check to see if the selected contestants had been on the show before using a micro fiche to check their name and social security numbers. A few tried, but were caught.

On one show we taped, a lady called down by Johnny Olsen was wearing a tube top, and it fell down. We stopped taping, she fixed it, and we continued taping. Afterwards Nancy went down to the Video Tape Department to see how it was edited out.

We were fortunate to have Nancy assigned to other shows that Goodson-Todman did.

We always displayed automobiles on the show, but one day after rehearsal, the head prop man asked one of his assistants to take the car outside and park it. He forgot to ask the assistant if he had a driver's license. He didn't, and he ended up crashing the car into the fence. When we taped the *Money Game* that show, Marc was unable to show the front of the car.

Bob Barker asked me if it would be possible for him to park his car by the loading dock instead of parking near the artists' entrance because it was closer to the Studio, and he would only be there for about an hour. I went to Rita, our production supervisor, and she was able to arrange it. Later, I asked Bob's wife, Dorothy Jo, if there was something special we could do for Bob. She suggested a sign with WGMC (World's Greatest MC). When he arrived and saw it, he was pleased. After a couple of months, we put a light on it with a rotating color wheel around it.

That November, I called Bill Egan, to find out what the procedures were for Christmas presents for the crews. He said that they preferred to give gifts, and not liquor. I told him how hard the crews worked on *The Price Is Right*, and that I thought that adding liquor would also be appreciated. I also asked him what the budget would be, and he said about $5,000. Two weeks later I called him, and gave him a list of possibilities. He called me back and gave the okay on the gifts, and the liquor. In January, I sent Bill the list of everyone that had received the gifts, along with the invoices from the vendors that I used. He said the following year just send the invoices, without the back-up.

Since the daytime *The Price Is Right* show was doing so well, Mark Goodson offered CBS a half hour night-time version. They passed, and NBC picked it up and Dennis James was the host.

The prizes were a lot bigger and more expensive. Walter Kresel was hired to handle the procurement of them. On one particular show, we had a pontoon boat. I gave CBS in advance all the information of size and weight. The day we were going to display it, it couldn't make it up the ramp to the studio. I went to Mark and suggested that we get a backdrop, put the boat in front of it, and pre-tape it with the models and Johnny Olsen's description. I asked Rita to keep track of the costs. Because of CBS's mistake, they would be paying for the taping, and playback of boat for the show.

Because of the size of some of the prizes for the night-time version, CBS put a fence around an area with surveillance cameras. The only problem was that they never hooked them up. One Friday when I went to look for the outboard motor, that we were going to give away that Sunday, it had been stolen. Walter Kresel was able to get a replacement, and CBS paid for it, and decided to post a guard out there. Nothing was stolen after that.

Once in a while, CBS would have some specials, and they would ask to use some of our cameramen. I asked Marc if he would let them, and he refused the request. They appreciated me trying, but were disappointed. A few weeks later, two of the cameramen called in sick, knowing that the only cameramen available in the lounge had never observed the show. Marc said he wouldn't do the shows. I went to Frank Wayne, and informed him what had happened. He had a long conversation with Marc, and Marc ended up giving permission for the cameramen to do the shows. It turned out to be a really hard day for Marc.

When the engineers went on strike and CBS Management had to do the show, I showed them where to set up all the audio and monitors that were needed. They really appreciated my assistance, and in return I was invited to dine with them. It took them longer to learn the camera blocking. After the first show they did, they sat down on the camera pedestals, they were so exhausted. Management then realized how difficult our show was and were anxious to get the strike settled. During that time, I called Bill In New York to get his permission to have coffee and Danish delivered to the technicians walking the picket line. He approved it. The strike lasted a week, and everyone was happy to get back to normal.

A few years earlier, I met Jack Shea when he directed an episode of *Sanford and Son* at NBC. We would talk during breaks in rehearsals, and one day he asked if I would be interested in working on a show called *Insight*. He told me it was a religious show produced by the Paulist Fathers, and they usually taped on Saturdays. I was committed to doing sports at that time, so I told him I couldn't help. Now we jump forward a couple of years, after I have converted to Catholicism. One day I saw Jack in the halls of CBS, when he was doing *The Jeffersons*. He asked me again if I would be interested in doing *Insight*. This time I said yes. He set up a meeting with the producer, Father Ellwood Keiser, and it went well, and I agreed to do a season of shows. I donated my time. The show taped at CBS Television City, which made it very easy for me. CBS donated everything but costumes. Father Keiser set up a deal with Western Costume, who supplied costumes for free. I picked up the costumes on Friday, and return them on Monday. They did these shows very frugally. I volunteered to supply coffee and pastries for all to enjoy. The cast members and directors all signed over their checks, and gave them back to Father Keiser as a donation. When we finished the season, Father Keiser invited the actors, directors, and supporters to a party at the home of Jerry Lewis. I brought Marie. I found out that everyone who knew Father Keiser very well called him "Bud". Jerry stayed away, but Patti was a very gracious Hostess.

When Mark Goodson visited the company, he stayed at the Beverly Hills Hotel. Since he was spending so much time there, he decided to purchase the suite. He called me and said his television reception was very bad, and that the hotel didn't want to fix it. He wondered if I could do something. I spoke with the hotel manager, and asked if it would be alright to install an antenna on the roof, and run the cable down to Mark's room. He approved it, as long as the cable wouldn't be too obvious. I contacted my antenna installer, and he was able to do it that afternoon. He called me when it finished, and said that Mark was pleased. Mark called me to thank me for doing it so swiftly.

About a month later Mark called to have his Rolls Royce Corniche convertible brought up to the front of the hotel. The valet told him that someone had taken the keys when he wasn't looking, and took the car. The following day it was found at Manhattan Beach. There must have been a major wind storm because the car was pitted from the sand. The hotel paid to have the car painted.

In 1976, *The Price Is Right* went to an hour, they added an additional model, Dian Parkinson. Bob Barker asked if he could have a stage manager assigned to let him know which game was going to be played. I was able to get Willie Dahl assigned. After playing three games, the contestants spun the Big Wheel, with amounts from $5 to $100. Whoever came closest to $100 without going over was the first contestant to go on to the showcases. The same thing happened after playing the next three games. After seeing both showcases, whoever had accumulated the most money would have the option to bid on it or pass it to the other contestant. Whoever was closest without going over the retail price was the winner.

I found out that Bob liked martinis, so after one of the shows, I asked Willie Dahl if he would mind serving Bob one after the last show of the day. He agreed to do it. The next week, I met Willie, put a white napkin on his arm, gave him the martini on a silver tray, and he served it to Bob as he exited the stage.

To show my appreciation for the hard work the crews did, I had a refrigerator installed backstage with cold drinks, and beer. In one of the Prop Boxes, I had a shelf and door installed, for liquor for the producers only, and put a padlock on it. The only exception was the technical director, "Pappy" Cunningham. On the last night of taping he would have a getaway drink for his drive to Palm Springs, where he grew fruits on his farm Ludie Acres. At Christmas I was one of the lucky few that got an assortment.

The following year, I got a call from Charles Cappleman, telling me that there would be an increase in the below-the line costs for the services that CBS provided. I reminded him that we had rate card protection from New York. This was a complete bluff on my part, but we never saw an increase while I did the show.

On April 9, 1998, CBS changed the name of Studio 33 to Bob Barker Studio, to coincide with his 5,000th show.

Bob's last show aired on June 15, 2007, after 35 years of emceeing *The Price Is Right*, and to coincide with his 50th year as a TV Host. Marie and I sent him a retirement card, and he sent us a note telling us that he took the "WGMC" sign home.

BOB BARKER

DEAR MARIE & ANDY —
THANK YOU FOR MY LOVELY
RETIREMENT CARD.
ANDY, AS THE CREATOR OF
IT, YOU SHOULD KNOW I AM
TAKING MY WGMC SIGN WITH
ME. MY VERY BEST TO BOTH OF
YOU ALWAYS.

CBS ran re-runs until October 15th, and then started airing new shows with Drew Carey as emcee. That was the start of the 36th year.

I was doing well as Production Supervisor, and felt that my skills were a good match for the job. The hours were long, though and I worked six days a week. Marie noticed that I was getting grouchy and suggested that I see our physician. He recommended that I find some kind of outlet. I asked if tennis would work, and he thought that would be a good release for me. Marie said that she would also like to play. We found a small club in Sherman Oaks that had four courts. The pro's first name was Pat, and he made it easy to learn. After three months, he thought we ready to start playing. Marie wanted me to see our doctor again, to see how I was doing. He said I was doing better, and suggested that if anyone was giving me a bat time at work, to visualize his face on the tennis ball.

Marie told her friends that we were playing tennis, and learned that the friends play at Notre Dame High School on Saturdays. For $100 a year contribution, we could both play. We joined, and it was a lot of fun. I also joined the Racquet Center in North Hollywood, which had about sixteen courts.

Looking back, one of the funniest things that happened was when Marie decided to babysit Carolyn Waterson's cat, Muffin, one weekend. Muffin was dropped off on Friday evening, and she was amusing. I do not like cats, and Muffin picked up on that. Marie and I were watching TV in the bedroom, and I had made some popcorn. To keep Muffin out of it, I hid it under the blanket. It drove her wild. That Saturday, as I was leaving to play tennis at the racquet center, Muffin was nowhere to be found. Marie said that I should go, and she would call me when she found the cat. At 10:00 a.m., the front desk called our court, and said that Muffin was found. It took my mind off her, and I started winning after that. When I got home, I told Marie that I won two out of the three sets, and she told me that Muffin had gotten out climbing up the inside of the chimney, and gotten into the tree in our front yard. She got our six-foot ladder out of the garage, and was able to coax Muffin down. When Carolyn came on Sunday, Marie told her the story, and said she wouldn't babysit again. We all had a good laugh.

Match Game with Gene Rayburn was the next show CBS bought. Ira Skutch was the executive producer, and Marc Breslow directed. There were six celebrities on the Panel. The three regulars were Brett Sommers, Charles Nelson Reilly, and Richard Dawson.

After the first three months doing the show, Gene approached Ira about doing something different at the opening of the show. Ira asked me if we could afford to do something. We were under budget, and I suggested that instead of having the doors slide open when Gene made his entrance, that we make the doors out of balsa wood, and have Gene crash through them. Ira asked Gene what he thought, and he liked it. Well, the day comes when we are going to do this, and Mark Goodson had flown in from New York and was in the control room for the taping. We forgot to tell him about the plan. Gene played it great. He burst through the doors at the opening, saying he couldn't wait any longer for the doors to open. Ira had a red phone connected to the control room, and Mark Goodson called him on it during the commercial break, and asked what we were going to do for next show. Ira explained that they were fake doors.

Another time Charles Nelson Reilly informed us he was going to be late for rehearsal, so we just left his seat vacant. Before we started taping, we got Charles into a harness suspended above the set. When he was introduced, the audience saw feathers floating down, and then Charles was flown in to his seat. He said, "You wouldn't believe the turbulence over Denver!"

We were taping one Saturday, and next door they were taping *The Dinah Shore* show. We were about ten minutes into our show, when we heard this band coming through the walls of our studio. I went over to find out that they had part of the USC Marching Band performing. They apologized, and compensated us for their mistake.

Mark Goodson overheard Johnny Olsen talking about how he went to Lawry's for dinner about three times a week. Mark hadn't eaten there. He asked Johnny to make a reservation for six people for the following Saturday after we finished taping. Ira and his wife Libby, Marie and I, and Mark and Johnny made up our party. When we all arrived, there were a lot of people waiting for tables. The maître d recognized Johnny, and sat us right away. Mark was really impressed. Everyone enjoyed their dinners, and thanked Mark.

Ira asked me if I could help with obtaining studio space for the *Variety Club Telethon*, with Monty Hall. In the past, they had taped it at NBC Burbank, which cost them a lot of money. I set up a meeting with KCET, the Public Broadcasting Station in Los Angeles. I gave them the dates and times that the telethon producers were looking for, and the possibility of using their phone banks, since they did pledges for their station. I told Ira that by doing it at KCET they would save a lot of money, they could use their phone banks, which would also save them, but they would have to secure a phone number. Ira agreed, and told me to lock the date. I wasn't able to attend the event because of a prior conflict, but the day after the telethon was done, Ira called and told me that it went off perfectly, and that the Executives from Variety Clubs were pleased.

Since I was working six days a week, Mark Goodson decided that Ted Cooper, from the New York office, and whom he relied on, and I both needed to have beepers so he could get a hold of us. I would get beeped at 7:30 a.m., which was 10:30 a.m. in New York. I also decided that since we were not taping any shows on Wednesdays, that would be my day off. However, I was still expected to be available by beeper. Marie and I decided to see how far the away the beeper would work. We went to Port Hueneme, and found a Mexican restaurant where I was out of beeper range. Every Wednesday we knew how far we had to travel. When we got back within range it would go off, and I would call the office to see what the problem was as soon as we got home. It usually wasn't anything important, and I would take care of it on Thursdays.

I worked on many different shows as part of my job. Here are a few of them:

TATTLETALES

In this show, husbands were pitted against wives. Bert Convey was the emcee, Paul Alter was the director, and Jack Clark was the announcer. I hadn't seen Jack since *The Big Surprise* in New York, and it was good to catch up with him. Jack would later go on to do the announcing on *Wheel of Fortune* with Pat Sajak.

Three couples competed. One set of partners would be on stage and give answers about what their mates would say. The mates couldn't hear, because they had headphones on with music playing. To make it a little more exciting, the audience was split into three sections and assigned to each couple. They would win money if their couple won. We tape fived shows, and after the first two, we would take a dinner break. during that time the audience members would receive their checks as they left. The same thing happened after we finished the next three shows.

Bert Convey was usually at the studio by 3:00 p.m., but one day, he was late. Paul Alter, the director, asked one of male celebrities to substitute for him until he arrived. Bert finally arrived, and was really surprised they started without him. He was never late again.

SHOWOFFS

This show was based on the popular game of Charades with two teams competing to act out words. The pilot was taped in May, 1975 at ABC with Larry Blyden as the emcee. There were two teams, Reds and Blues. Each team consisted of two celebrities and one contestant. While one team was playing the pantomime game, the other was in a soundproof isolation booth backstage so they couldn't hear. They were given the same words, and whoever got the most words in two rounds would win $1,000, and then play the End Game. Unfortunately, Larry was in a car accident while on vacation in Morocco, and passed away on June 5. It was devastating to everyone who worked with him.

Bobby Van was brought in to replace Larry, and he did a great job.

The End Game was changed to allow the celebrities a given amount of time for the first, second, and final word. If the contestant elected to go forward, and missed, they would lose half of the accumulated money.

FAMILY FEUD

This was another show for ABC. The emcee was Richard Dawson. There were two teams of five family members who competed to give answers that matched popular surveys (i.e., What time do you get up in the morning?). The surveys used on the show came from the audiences. When the audience members arrived for the tapings, the ushers would hand them questionnaires, and before they started taping, they would collect them and give them to one of the production assistants to take back to the office for future shows. Gameplay started with one person from each team would being asked a face off question. Whoever buzzed in had the option of playing or passing it to the other side. If they decided to play, each member had to give an answer. If the answer was wrong, they would get a strike. Three strikes and the other side had the opportunity to win the points. The family was allowed to collaborate to decide on one answer, and if they were correct they would steal the points. I believe the first one to 500 points won the game.

For the End Game, one family member went into an isolation booth so they couldn't hear the answers that the other member was giving. They had 20 seconds to give their answers to five questions, and then the person in the isolation booth would come out, and have twenty-five seconds to give answers. If there was a duplicate answer there would be a buzzer, and they had to come up with a different one. If they won, they received $5,000.

Richard was using a hand microphone, and always getting tangled up in the cable. I suggested to ABC that they use a lapel microphone and run a cable up Richard's leg. An engineer off stage could take care of feeding and retracting the cable. Richard was extremely happy. Eventually he used a wireless mike.

CONCENTRATION

Mark Goodson decided to bring back *Concentration* for syndication.

The show had originally been created by Jack Barry, Dan Enright, Robert Noah and Buddy Piper. Since we had had a good working relationship with KTTV, I called Lou Steinberg to see if he could accommodate the show. Stage 1 was available, along with the office space, and parking. Ted Cooper designed the Set, and KTTV built it. Howard Felsher was the producer, and Ira Skutch directed. Jack Narz was emcee, and Johnny Olson was the announcer.

One week Jack learned that when we finished taping the shows, he needed to do 60 promos for the various stations that had bought the show. He was amazing, he did them all in one take!

The only problem that occurred on a regular basis was with the game board. When a puzzle part had to be revealed, the board would malfunction, and we would have to stop to do repairs. For Christmas gifts that year, the show gave carving boards that were made by Prison Preventers. Both Howard and Ira were involved with this organization, which sent ex-convicts to various schools, and let the students know what life was like behind bars.

NOW YOU SEE IT

This was another show for CBS. It was created by Frank Wayne. Jack Narz was the emcee, who also worked at the same time on *Concentration*. Johnny Olson was the announcer. The object of *Now You See It* was to answer general knowledge trivia questions by finding the answers which were hidden on a grid, similar to a word search puzzle. The special effects department had to conceive and build a 56-grid game board (4 lines with 14 column positions) that was connected to a special computer in order to play the game.

There were four new contestants split into two teams, each with one "outside" and one "inside" contestant, and was played on an electronic game board on the opposite side of the stage from the contestant desks. The letters were referred to as "positions" for scoring purposes. The board was shown to the contestants momentarily, then quickly turned off before any of them could fully memorize it.

To start the round, the "outside" contestants turned their backs to the board as Narz read a question. The first "inside" contestant to buzz-in would say which line the correct answer appeared on. If the correct line was given, it remained lit and the "outside" contestant for that team turned around to give the position of the first letter of the word, then give the answer that Narz was looking for; the entire response would therefore be in the form of "line x, position x, word". If the wrong line was guessed, the other team got a free guess.

For instance, if the answer was in line 3, and the answer was in position 7, they would receive 10 points. Halfway through, they would switch positions during a commercial break. Then the other contestant would see the board, and write a secret answer. If someone did have the secret answer, and showed it, they would receive 10 extra points. Whichever team was ahead at the end of the second round, they would split up, and now compete against each other.

For this game, they would be using only 1 line of the board, and Jack would give them a clue, and reveal one letter at a time, until one had gotten four words correctly. The winner then went on to play against the Champion. Now they would have to buzz in with the line and position. The contestant that was in the lead after that would play the Solo Game. At Jack's podium, they would see the entire Game Board. They had 60 seconds to circle and call out the answers. The only problem was that the stylus didn't erase after each answer, usually took about ten minutes to fix. Each correct answer they would get $100. When the Jackpot isn't won, it would increase by $1,000, until someone won. There was a limit of $25,000 that CBS imposed.

I met once a month with Cappy (Charles Cappleman, CBS Director of Design and Production Services) to go over the Studio schedules for *The Price Is Right, Match Game, Tattletales* and *Now You See It* so that there weren't any conflicts. Luckily, we never had one.

DOUBLE DARE

Double Dare was created by Jay Wolpert for CBS. Alex Trebek was the host, and Johnny Olson was the original announcer, later replaced by Gene Wood. Two contestants, each in separate isolation booths, attempted to correctly identify a person, place or thing based on one-sentence clues that Alex gave them, one at a time, on an electronic game board. The correct response was shown to the home audience before the first clue was given. A maximum of 10 clues were played per subject, typically starting with obscure pieces of trivia and progressing toward more widely-known facts.

Either contestant could buzz in at any time to guess the subject, and doing so closed off the opponent's booth so that he/she could not see or hear anything. A correct guess won $50 for the contestant, while a miss closed his/her own booth and gave the opponent a chance to see the next clue (referred to as a "penalty clue") and offer a guess unopposed. If the opponent also missed, both booths were opened and play resumed with the next clue after the penalty.

When a contestant correctly identified a subject on a buzz-in, he/she was shown the next clue in sequence and could dare the opponent to answer. When a contestant gave the answer on a penalty clue, it was used for the dare since the opponent had not yet seen it. If the contestant chose to dare, the opponent's booth was opened and he/she had five seconds to study the clue before guessing. A correct answer awarded $50 to the opponent; a miss awarded $100 to the daring contestant, closed the opponent's booth again, and gave the contestant a chance to offer a double dare based on the next clue. A correct answer on a double dare awarded $100 to the opponent, and a miss awarded $200 to the double-daring contestant.

The winner of the main game competed in a bonus round against the spoilers, a panel of three Ph.Ds. placed in separate isolation booths so that they could not see or hear each other. The booths were turned off to begin the round.

The contestant would be shown eight clues, and then decide which four to use to try stop the spoilers. If the spoiler missed an answer, the contestant got $100, but if the spoiler guessed correctly the spoiler would get $100, and would be out for the remainder of the round. If the spoiler still didn't know the answer after the fourth clue, the contestant won $5,000.

In May, 1977, I received a call from Harry Waterson, with whom I had worked at NBC on *The Goldie Hawn Special*. He had done the pilot for a new comedy series called *SOAP* for Witt-Thomas-Harris that would air on ABC. I had no idea at that time what I was expected to do as the associate producer, but I was looking forward to finding out, and looking for a new challenge I said I would.

When I got home, I told Marie about the phone call, and she thought I should at least go to the meeting and see how it felt.

Harry set up a meeting with one of the executive producers, Tony Thomas. I went to his home in Beverly Hills for the meeting, and found out that he was Danny Thomas' son. I thought the meeting went well. A couple of days later, he asked me to meet with Harry, and go over the budget with him. He told me I would be responsible for hiring the secretaries, associate director, script supervisor, stage managers, wardrobe supervisor, and staff for makeup and hair. Harry gave me a list of personnel that had worked on the pilot, and probably would be available for the series. I continued to go to more meetings, getting information about the duties of the job. After a few more meetings with Tony, I finally asked him when they were going to make the decision about hiring me. He apologized, and said I was their new Associate Producer. He then gave me the phone number of their agent, Leonard Hanzer, to go and finalize my deal.

I was excited to have a new challenge in my career, and ready to get started. I called Bill Egan at Goodson-Todman in New York, and informed him I would be leaving. I would be available to give any information to my replacement. It was time to move on.

MARK GOODSON

GOODSON-
TODMAN
PRODUCTIONS

NEW YORK   375 PARK AVENUE · NEW YORK, NEW YORK 10022

June 7th, 1977

Dear Andy:

I did not have a chance to speak to you before
your departure, so this is in the nature of a
goodbye note.

I regret any misunderstandings which arose between us, and I am sure that time will heal
all wounds.

I want to thank you for the many contributions
you made over the years to our success in California. I know how dedicated you were to us
and I, by no means, underestimated the hours
you put in, or the attention you gave to details. So once again, thank you for that.

I hope that your new position gives you the
greater financial reward and responsibility
that you were looking for.

Best,

Mark Goodson

Mark Goodson

4818 Mary Ellen Avenue
Sherman Oaks 91423

MG/peg

181

CHAPTER 11
SOAP

I started my new job in June, 1977. The show was scheduled to start airing in September. We had a lot to do.

I was given an office at ABC Prospect, and started to put together the staff for *Soap*, most of whom had worked on the pilot. The director, Jay Sandrich, had done the pilot. He had also been the director for the *Mary Tyler Moore Show*. We met, and he asked me to set up meetings with associate directors, stage managers, script supervisors and wardrobe designers. I had met the set designer, Ed Stephenson, when I was a unit manager at NBC on *Sanford & Son*. The lighting director, Larry Boelens, had done the Pilot and was also available. ABC didn't have room at the Prospect lot, so they rented space at Ren-Mar Studios in Hollywood. As I was starting to interview people for office staff, and starting to put together the technical and stage crews from ABC, the ABC technicians went on strike, and I was put in the position of hiring everyone.

It was really baptism by fire. I had never been in that situation before and I was fortunate enough to be put in touch with Cliff and

Susan Renfro of Acey-Decy Lighting. They would supply the lighting equipment and stage crews. This was the first time I ever had to put everything together for a show. I was very fortunate that NOTHING went wrong.

ABC had already contracted with Pacific Video to use their remote truck. Unfortunately, it only had two videotape machines, and I needed five. Four would record the four cameras, and the fifth would record the line feed that the audience saw. Pacific Video had only two VHS ¾-inch tape recorders. Ren-Mar told me that Vidtronics, which was across the street from them, had underground wiring to their facility I went over and talked with Burt Lippman about the possibility of using three of his videotape machines and three of his VHS ¾-inch tape recorders, and editing the show at his facility. I was able to negotiate a good deal for everything.

Everything was going smoothly until the set was delivered. The stage we were going to use had been used as an indoor tennis court, with very soft floors. The sets sunk into the floor, and we had to put ¾-inch tempered Masonite fiberboard down, and then put the sets on top of them.

The crews were taking shape, but I was still looking for a head property master. Tony Thomas suggested Tommy Fairbanks, who had worked for his father, Danny. Tommy was available, to my relief.

Harry Waterson asked if it would be possible to hire Carl Lauten as the second stage manager, as he had worked with him on the *America's Junior Miss* Specials. I called Jay Sandrich and told him of Harry's request of using Carl as the second stage manager, and he agreed to use him. Since we had a thirteen-week commitment from ABC, I went to the Directors Guild and they said he could submit an application for membership. He was voted in, and received his Guild card.

I called Jay to let him know that I had people ready for him to interview for his key positions. He selected J.D. Lobue as the associate director, Phil Ramuno as the first stage manager, Linda Day as script supervisor, and Judy Evans as wardrobe designer. I had worked with Judy when we worked at NBC. I contacted Ken Ziffren, who was the attorney for Witt-Thomas-Harris, to see what paperwork he needed. I sent him the preliminary deal memos, and he sent me the formal contracts for these people to sign.

Linda Otto and Judith Weiner were already in place to do the casting for the show. They really did an outstanding job, and they were very conscientious about not going over budget on the additional guest cast members.

George Allison Tipton was the music composer, already in place from the pilot. I informed him how much money he had for the twelve episodes. He said he would schedule four scoring sessions, doing 3 shows at a time.

I contacted Albert G. Ruben, who provides insurance for movies and television shows, and informed him that we would start rehearsals in July. They gave me the phone number for the doctor to schedule the physicals for the director and cast. This was so we would have an insurance bond in the event we were forced to shut down, due to any illness. This had to be done for every show every year, and this was a line item covered in the budget.

Rehearsals started in July. On that Monday, the cast, producers, Jay, and the rest of the staff gathered for the reading of the script. I gave Linda Day the format information that I had received from ABC, telling us how much time to allow for the show content, and she would time the reading, so that everyone had an idea where we were. It also gave the producers an idea of where to make changes before the final run-through on Wednesday. After the reading the doctor started doing the physical exams. Judy Evans, the wardrobe designer would find out what the producers wanted the Actors to wear, and she would keep them informed. The only actor that had a problem with wardrobe was Katherine Helmond, because she had a small waist and big bosoms. Judy asked the producers if she could design Katherine's outfits if she stayed within the budget. They agreed.

Jimmy Baio, who played Billy, was only permitted to rehearse four hours a day, because he was a minor. We hired a teacher who schooled him the other four hours. Because we taped on Fridays, he could work until 10:00 p.m.

Jay would then start staging, and that would last until Wednesday afternoon. During that time, he would block camera shots with his associate director, J.D. Labue. Then there would be a producers' run-through with wardrobe, and Linda would let them know how they were on time. Jay and the producers would then meet to discuss any changes. Thursday morning, J.D. would meet with technical director and the cameramen to give them their camera shots. Before starting camera blocking, Jay introduced the technical crew to the cast, so they knew who they were.

At 5:00 p.m., there would be a rehearsal with wardrobe and ABC programming executives, and afterwards a meeting to go over any needed changes.

Fridays started at noon with make-up and hair, and Jay started rehearsing with cameras from 1:00 p.m. until 4 p.m. The audience would be seated, and Marc Summers was hired to do the warm-up and introduce the cast which usually started at 4:30 p.m. The taping of the early show at 5:00 p.m. Usually Jay didn't stop to correct anything during the taping.

We would break then for dinner, which was catered. The cast, Jay and the producers ate in a separate area, so they could give notes to the cast, and the crew and staff in another.

Taping started again at 7:30 p.m., and if there were any mistakes, Jay would stop and redo those scenes. We usually finished at 9:00 p.m., and would let the audience leave. If there were still scenes that needed to be fixed, they would start at 9:30 p.m., and be finished by 10:30p.m. at the latest, because the stage and technical crews had to be off the stage by 11 p.m. or it would cost overtime..

After the taping of the first show, Columbia Pictures Syndication Division ("CPT") had a party for the cast and staff because they had bought the syndication rights for *SOAP*. The only problem was that the party started after the taping, and I kept telling CPT that we were still doing pick-ups. To make a long story short, when all the pick-ups were finished, there wasn't anything left for the cast to eat or drink.

The following Monday at 3:00 a.m., the crew would take down the sets from the previous week and put up the new ones.

There was an available office near the studio that I converted into the producers' room. It was equipped with 5 television monitors, one for each camera, plus the line feed. I had a phone installed from the producers' room to the remote truck so they could talk with Jay. We also had five ¾-inch VCR's that could be used on Monday mornings to select the best takes with Jay. Then J.D. would go across the street to Vidtronics to start the editing process with Gary Anderson, the editor. They would use these cassettes for editing. J.D would bring an edited cassette back to the office so the producers and Jay would look at it, and make changes. When the final decision was made, the script for the opening of the show was written, and Rod Roddy was hired to be the announcer, would go in and record it at Vidtronics. Gary then created an electronic editing list, which controlled the 1-inch tape machines, which created the master which included the show's Opening, show content, three one-minute commercial inserts, and closing credits. This would take a day to complete. Gary always made a protection copy.

The following week, the master was delivered to Compact Video sound department in Burbank, where they would transfer it to a ¾-inch VCR with time code in the picture, and a 2-inch videotape with the audio on it. Music was the first track to be added by George Tipton, who composed all the music, then sound effects, and last was the additional laughter and applause. The time code in the picture made it easier to go back and redo any scenes if necessary. After that process, the new composite audio was recorded to the master videotape.

Back at Vidtronics, they made two copies from the master to be delivered to ABC for broadcast. When the show aired, ABC added the commercials. The master always stayed at Vidtronics.

After taping three episodes, the cast and technical crew took a week off.

During the first hiatus, ABC settled the strike with the engineers, and decided to move the soap opera *General Hospital* to Ren-Mar Studios. I told them about the problems with the stage floor, and ABC had Ren-Mar install a concrete floor. I suggested that, after pouring the cement, they leave the big stage door open so it could cure. I had learned this lesson when I worked at NBC. They hadn't left the stage door open then, and it created waves in the concrete. Ren-Mar didn't listen, and the next day when they opened the door, the floor had waves in it. They had to jack hammer out the cement at odd hours so it wouldn't disturb our rehearsals.

SOAP debuted on a Tuesday night, and the producer's decided to have a gala party. We were fortunate enough to have Bob Seagren, who played Dennis Phillips on the show, volunteer the use of his home. ABC Programming Executives were also invited, and everyone was excited to see the show on the air.

As we were nearing the end of our 13-week commitment from ABC, we received a pick-up for the remaining 9 episodes. ABC had just built two new Studios, 57 & 59, on the Prospect Lot, and wanted us to move there to save money. The only problem was that the control room for Studio 59 wasn't completed yet. They wanted us to use a remote truck for a control room. Chris Cookson, from ABC technical services, and I flew up to Oakland to see the truck in operation at an

Oakland Raiders game to decide if could work for us. I told him it was a bit noisy because of the air conditioner compressor noise, but we would try to use it.

On the first day of camera blocking, I received a frantic call from Jay Sandrich, telling me he couldn't hear the actors. I met Chris at the Truck, and realized there was a problem. The air conditioning compressor was too loud. There was a dressing room available near the stage, which they converted into the control room. We were amazed at how fast they got it done. We used that dressing room for three episodes, and then moved across the hall to Studio 57's new control room for the last six episodes.

After taping two episodes at ABC, I received a call from Bob Trachinger, who oversaw technical operations, saying that he wanted to have a meeting regarding the scrim that we used behind the camera lens to soften the look. The meeting was held at ABC's Century City office, and Tony Thomas, Jay, Larry Boelens, Director of Photography, and I attended. Julie Barnathan, President of Technical Operations, flew out from New York. Bob Trachinger, and Chris Cookson also attended the meeting. For over an hour, Julie complained that we had "bastardized" his cameras. Larry said that we might get the look by adjusting the lighting. When it was time for us to leave the conference room, we realized how short Julie was. He asked Bob and Chris to please help him out of the chair, since his feet didn't reach the floor. As soon as we got out of the room, we all had a good laugh.

After we had finished the last episode, the producers threw a Wrap

Party with the cast, crew and the ABC executives. I brought Marie. The highlight of the party was showing out-takes from the episodes, and everyone enjoyed them. They continued doing this every year.

At the end of the season, the executive producers asked for a meeting with their business managers to go over the profits. According to my calculations there was a profit, but I couldn't prove it, because the accounting firm's books said there wasn't any. The firm's books didn't make any sense. They wanted to fire me, but I convinced them to let me take the books to three different entertainment accounting firms for them to peruse. All three said they couldn't make heads or tails out of them. I also asked the ABC auditors to look at them, and they couldn't make any sense of them either. Of all the three accounting firms that we had look over the books, I suggested we hire Cappell, Coyne & Company from then on. Tony Thomas agreed. I found out later that Danny Thomas Productions also used the same firm.

I also implemented a system that each check would have two signatures, One from Cappell, and one executive producer. Tony was the one that would sign. I made sure the checks were correct before Tony signed them.

ABC picked up the show for a second season, with a guarantee of twenty-two episodes.

ABC decided to move us again. Columbia Pictures had recently sold their Hollywood Studios to Saul Pick and Nick Vanoff, who changed the name to Sunset-Gower Studios. Nick told me that he was also involved with Complete Post, a post-production facility, located across the street from the studios. I toured the facility, and was impressed. I told ABC that I thought SOAP could be edited there, but the post audio would still be done at Compact Video in Burbank.

I was also looking for a new secretary. Robert Spina, who was a production assistant on *SOAP*, recommended a woman named Adria Horton. I interviewed others, and Adria understood what I needed, and that made my job easier.

I asked Tony Thomas about the possibility of doing some of the post-production audio work myself, as I had done much of this work many times in my career. I told him that I would have to have a thirteen-week commitment to get into the Directors Guild of America. He talked it over with Paul and Susan, and they agreed. I became an Associate Director in the Guild. After attending three monthly meetings, I was recommended to be on the Membership Committee for incoming members, and was asked if I would have any problems since I was also an Associate Producer for a production company. I told them I wouldn't.

Susan Harris requested having a car and driver so she could have more time to be creative. I contacted Barry Gordon, ABC Business Affairs, to see if this could be included in the budget, and he said he would let me know. A week later it was approved.

I called Leonard Hanzer, Witt-Thomas-Harris's agent, to go over the budget for the second season before having my meeting with Barry Gordon, to finalize it. After getting Leonard's input, I met with Barry, and he approved it. We were very fortunate in those days that we didn't have to worry about deficit financing, as most shows now face.

ABC decided that they would air a 90-minute retrospective before the start of Seasons Two, Three and Four. This was a reminder of what had happened, and what was in store for the coming season. I called Barry Gordon at ABC Business Affairs, and told him that this would require additional compensation for the actors and the director. I contacted Anita Cooper our AFTRA representative (American

Federation of Television and Radio Artists) to work out a compensation package based on the clips from each episode they appeared in. We agreed at $225.00 per episode, and I said that the agent's commission would be on top of that so their client would get the full amount. Jay Sandrich's deal was handled by Tom Hoberman, who worked for Ken Ziffren..

ABC also decided to move the show *Barney Miller* from the Vine Street Studios to Sunset-Gower, and would be next door in Studio 15.

Since there were no control rooms or producers' room for *SOAP* or the *Barney Miller* show, ABC brought in trailers, which we situated outside the stage. The Producers Room was set up with the five monitors, and I supplied the 5 VCR's that we had used at Ren-Mar Studios. Plus they installed phone lines, so they could talk with the Control Room. ABC also installed videotape machines and ¾-inch VHS machines in another building.

Two weeks after completing the first show for *SOAP*, I went to see Vic Rose at Cappell, Coyne, who was the accountant assigned to us. I wanted to see if changing accounting firms made a difference in reporting a profit. He shared with me the report from ADP (Automated Data Processing), and it showed a profit. I took our copy of the report, and the checks back for Tony to sign, and he in turn told Paul and Susan. We never had a problem again, and the producers started making profits. I felt vindicated.

One day, the lighting crew called me down to the stage, and said they weren't happy coming in at 3:00 a.m. three days a week. They never really had time with their families. I talked with Larry Boelens, the lighting director, about the problem with his crew, and suggested coming in on Saturdays to do the lighting. He refused the idea. I went back up to our offices, and told Tony about the problem and my solution. Tony asked Larry to come up to his office and discuss it. As a result, Larry quit.

I quickly called our ABC Unit Manager, Barry Haworth, and asked how fast a new lighting director could be assigned. Half an hour later, Richard Hissong showed up. After meeting Richard, I explained what was troubling his crew. I asked him how he felt about working on Saturdays, so the 3:00 a.m. calls could be eliminated. He had no problem with it. Barry, Richard and I then met with the crew, and I explained that there would now be a staggered call. The carpenters would come in at 8:00 a.m., to start putting up the sets, then the lighting and prop crews. No more 3:00 a.m. The only condition that was, that no-one would work more than an 8-hour day. They agreed, and thanked me.

Cathryn Damon, the actress who played Mary Campbell on SOAP, gave birth to a baby girl, which was written into the script. I learned that we would need a nurse on the set when we taped the early show. I hired Marie, who was a registered nurse, to take care of the baby. It was fun to have her at work with me for once. I also needed a social worker, so I used the teacher I hired for Jimmy Baio.

Barney Miller, also taped on Friday's. They had a great cast, including Hal Linden, Abe Vigoda, Jack Soo, James Gregory, and Steve Landesberg. They taped without an audience, which they would add in post-production. They started taping around 2:00 p.m. I also found out that they rarely got a complete script before taping. They were also upset that we were finished by 11:00 p.m., while they were there much later.

Paul Witt decided to play a practical joke on Tony for his birthday. He asked Tommy Fairbanks to get some donkeys to put in Tony's office by 9:00 a.m. Tony walked into his office that morning and saw the four donkeys. Three were on the floor. One donkey stood on Tony's desk, and decided it was time to go to the bathroom, right on cue. We were all laughing so hard, including Tony.

ABC decided to re-run "SOAP" from 11:35 p.m. to 12:05 a.m., Mondays through Fridays. As we had only allowed three minutes for commercials in the original taping, the show would have to be edited for an additional three minutes. The cost would be $10,000 per episode. I did a little investigating, and found out that there were no time limits for broadcasting after 11:00 p.m. I called Barry Gordon at ABC Business Affairs and told him what I had learned. Barry called me back that afternoon, and said New York wasn't aware of this ruling, and thanked me for saving them money.

Marie and I were approaching our tenth wedding anniversary. I thought I'd surprise her with a weekend in San Francisco. I made reservations at the Stanford Court Hotel, and dinner reservations on Saturday at The Shadows Restaurant. We flew up on Saturday, and as we got to the baggage area, Marie saw a man in a black suit and sunglasses holding a sign with the name "Selig." She thought he was from the Mafia. I had arranged with the Hotel to have a limousine pick us up. She gave a sigh of relief when I told her.

That evening, we took a cab to the restaurant, but our driver had never been there. Don't ask me how, but I remembered where it was, and directed him. We had a delicious meal, and took a cab back to the Hotel. The Shadows closed in the early 1990s.

In May of 1979, I saw an advertisement in the *Los Angeles Times*. The Buckley School was having a fundraiser at the Universal Amphitheater. Nancy Sinatra's children attended Buckley, and had asked Frank Sinatra to star. I was able to get two tickets. As the June 19th date was approaching, I told Marie that I had purchased the tickets as another surprise. At the entrance to the amphitheater, we were greeted by a person giving Frank's records as a souvenir. We each got three different ones, then we were handed a book of matches and a candle. We would be told later what they were for. We went to our seats, which were excellent. As the show was about to begin, Nancy Sinatra came out and explained that she would give us the signal when to light the candles. This was Frank's 40th anniversary in show business, and we were going to help celebrate.

Don Rickles was there to get us ready for Frank. One of the stories he told was about George Shearing flying from Los Angeles to New York, with a stop-over in Chicago. George, who is blind, was flying first class, with his seeing-eye dog. When they arrived in Chicago, all the passengers got off for the lay-over. The captain came out of the cockpit, and seeing George was still sitting there, asked if there was anything that he could do for him. George asked the captain to take his dog off, so he could relieve himself.

After about half an hour, the passengers were informed that they could re-board the plane, and started lining up at the gate. At the same time, the Captain went up the gangplank holding onto the harness of George's seeing-eye dog. Many of the passengers started asking for another flight to New York. After Don finished, Nancy came out and asked everyone to light the candles, and then she introduced her dad. When Frank walked out, the lights were turned off, and all you could see was the light from the candles. Everyone sang "Happy Anniversary" to him. It was an amazing sight to see, and I expect an anniversary that he would remember.

Towards the end of the second season of *SOAP*, the producers decided to do a spin-off for Robert Guillaume, who played the butler Benson DuBois. It would be called *Benson*, and Robert Guillaume would be the governor's director of household affairs. James Noble played the governor, Inga Swenson played the maid, Missy Gold was the governor's daughter. Because Missy was a minor, we needed a teacher, and a stand-in for  her. We hired her mother, who would be able to go over any changes. Jay Sandrich directed the pilot. When Missy wasn't in a scene or at school, she stood next to Jay, and if another actor missed a cue, Missy would give them the line. She had memorized the entire script.

For the exterior of the Governor's Mansion, we found a house at 1365 South Oakland Avenue in Pasadena, California. It had been used before, and I explained that we were only interested in the exterior of the house, and would need to tape it at night also. We agreed on a price, and the owner's signed the release. When ABC tested the pilot, I decided to go to the screening to see how this was done. They had someone explain what the premise of the show was, and how to use the dial to indicate their reactions during the screening. It tested very well, and in July, production started at ABC Prospect Studios. John Rich was hired as the director. I had heard rumors that John usually liked to pick on someone on the staff during a season. I didn't want to be this person. I mentioned to him that Bob Guillaume usually didn't hit the same mark in the early or the later taping. After he did his first complete show, he grabbed me by the arm, and escorted out of the control room. I was really scared, and then he told me that I was right.

To make sure that the executive producers, Paul, Tony and Susan, would be able to attend the tapings, *Benson* taped on Tuesdays and *SOAP* taped on Fridays.

I'm not sure when the following incident happened. We were taping the early show of *SOAP*, and the audience was about twenty seconds late on the laughs. I went to investigate and found that part of the audience was deaf, and they were waiting for the dialogue to be translated into sign language. We weren't able to use much of the material that was taped. ABC apologized, and would really be more careful in securing the audiences in the future.

While we taping the early show of SOAP, Paul and Tony mentioned to Susan that they were having a problem coming up with a script for the upcoming episode of Benson. She asked what the concept was, and they told her. She said that she could probably do it over the weekend, and they asked her to write it, and they were relieved.

Before the start of the third season, I was called into the producers' offices, and they informed that I was being promoted. My new title would be Executive in Charge of Production. I was surprised! Jerry Bucci our technical director, started calling me EICOP, whenever he needed to see me.

Tony and Paul asked me to see what the possibility was of getting them a car and driver like Susan had. After many long conversations with Barry Gordon, it was approved.

One day, Tony saw Danny Arnold, executive producer of *Barney Miller*, whose offices were below ours, driving a golf cart to get from his offices to the stage. He was wondering if we could get ABC to get one for them. I contacted Al Simon at ABC and asked about the possibility of getting one. He said he would have to talk it over with Business Affairs, and then get back to me. ABC agreed, and it was put into our prop budget, so it wouldn't stand out.

During the third season, Jay had to direct a scene with Cathryn Damon falling down the staircase. I hired a stunt double, because we didn't want Cathryn to hurt herself. Jay wanted to rehearse the fall, and I suggested that we tape the rehearsal, since we could use all four cameras to cover it. We got lucky on the first rehearsal! It was perfect. The next week the stunt person came to pick-up her check, I told her how much I appreciated what she had done, she was surprised that I had paid her extra. I told her that she had saved us money, and I wanted to show my appreciation. She said that never happened to her before.

The executive producers pitched two pilots to ABC for the next

season. Witt-Thomas-Harris did *I'm A Big Girl Now*, starring Danny Thomas, Sheree North, Diana Canova, Rori King, and Martin Short. It dealt with Diana and her younger daughter moving back home to live with her father.

The other pilot was *It's A Living*, by Paul Witt & Tony Thomas. The cast included Ann Jillian, Gail Edwards, Wendy Schael, and Susan Sullivan as waitresses in a hotel restaurant. Their boss was Marian Mercer, and Paul Kreppel was the piano player. When we started rehearsals, Paul said he could play piano. We quickly learned that he couldn't. So we had to deaden the piano keys and put a small camera above the piano, with a monitor backstage, so the real piano player could see what Paul was attempting to play. This show was also picked up by ABC.

During the time we were rehearsing the pilots, Marie and I decided we were going to go on a "real vacation." We booked a cruise from Florida to Southampton, England, with plans to then go on to the British Isles and the Norwegian fjords on the Royal Viking Line. We had arranged everything through American Express. After the pilots were delivered to ABC, we packed our bags and flew from Los Angeles to Hollywood, Florida. Senator Murphy was living close by, and we arranged with him to pick us up at the hotel we were staying and visit

with him until it was time to board the ship. It was good to see the Senator again. The hotel shuttled us to the dock where we boarded the ship.

After being welcomed and given our table assignment, we were shown to our stateroom, and found our luggage had been delivered. Later that afternoon, after leaving the dock, we had our first fire drill, and then relaxed until dinner. The next morning there was a note under our door, telling us that our table assignment had been changed to Table #1, which I knew was the Captain's table. I guess American Express must have told them I was a television producer. At breakfast, we met three other couples. The rest of the morning we explored the ship, and at 11:00 a.m., bouillon was served. For lunch, we had the option of going to the buffet at noon, or waiting to sit in the dining room at 1:00 p.m. At 3:00 p.m., it was time for Bingo, or to see a movie.

At dinner, we met the captain, and we were lucky enough to sit next to him. He was very charming and entertaining. There was wonderful

after dinner entertainment as well. And if you were still hungry, there was the midnight buffet. The following morning at breakfast, we found out from the other tablemates, that the captain didn't like one of the other couples, so we made sure that they never sat next to the Captain for the rest of the crossing. The captain learned that Marie was found of chocolate truffles. Well, one night before dinner we were invited to the Captain's Stateroom for cocktails, and in the breakfront was a plate with a doily and chocolate truffles for Marie. One of the other couples picked up on it, and when we got back to our stateroom, they had some more truffles delivered to her. She had a good laugh.

Another night after dinner, the entertainment was a Polish band, and if you shut your eyes, you could imagine being serenaded by the old Glenn Miller Band. It was pure joy.

The night before reaching Southampton, they transformed the dining room into a casino. This was the only time there was any real gambling on the ship. We were able to enjoy the ten-day crossing, and a day of sightseeing in England off the ship.

That evening I got a transatlantic phone call to get back to Los Angeles as soon as possible. Both shows had sold. We had planned to spend a few days in London after our cruise, meeting with Columbia's Syndication Division. We had set everything up before we left. I called the person in London at Columbia, and told him that our plans had changed. We would be in London the next day. I also called Tom Hoberman, the attorney for Witt-Thomas-Harris, to inform him I would be coming home early. He said I made his day. He had never received a ship-to-shore phone call before. I went to the ship's purser and told him that we needed to make flight arrangements for the next day from Amsterdam to London. Marie and I left the ship in Amsterdam, and flew to London. When we arrived at our hotel there was a message from Columbia, asking us to join them for dinner. I called and accepted their invitation. When he picked us up, I gave him a box, and asked him to put in the trunk. I would explain later.

We went to a restaurant called Parks and had a delicious dinner, and afterward when we getting into the car, I asked him to look inside the box. It was full of *SOAP* souvenirs that he could use to promote the show.

On the way back to our hotel, he asked if we had made arrangements to get to the airport. We had planned to take a cab, but he insisted that he send a car and driver for us. The next morning the doorman called, and said our car was there. It was a Rolls Royce limousine! It made us feel a little better about leaving.

We flew back to Los Angeles. On Monday, I started on the schedules, and started hiring personnel for both shows. Since I knew that there was no way for me to supervise all four shows, the executive producers hired Harry Waterson to supervise *Benson* and *It's A Living*. These shows taped at ABC Prospect.

There were some changes made for the fourth season of *SOAP*. Jay Sandrich left, and J.D. Lobue moved up to director. Phil Ramuno moved to Associate Director, and Carl Lauten moved up to first stage manager. We now needed a second stage manager. I asked Anita Cooper, who was the AFTRA (American Federation of Television and Radio Artists) representative to our show for the three seasons. Anita would come about twice a month to talk with the actors to make sure everything was alright. I asked her if she be interested in becoming a stage manager. She said she would have to think about it. Two weeks later she said yes. I was very happy to be asked to be one of her sponsors on her DGA application. Anita would go on to be the Chairperson of the Associate Directors/Stage Managers/Production Associates Council-West. She would also receive the Franklin J. Schaffner Achievement Award from the Guild in 2002, in recognition of service to the industry and to the Directors Guild of America.

While we taped *I'm A Big Girl Now*, Tony Thomas kept asking me where Danny Thomas, his father, hid his vodka. I told him I didn't know. Tony looked high and low, but couldn't find it. The only place he didn't look was in the freezer in the prop room, which was where it was.

The other scary thing about Danny was that he carried a Derringer pistol in his waistband. He said that he liked to be prepared for any emergencies.

Tony asked if I would be interested in helping with the St. Jude Telethon that Danny hosted. That year they arranged to use Merv Griffin's studio on Vine Street in Hollywood to tape the Telethon. Before Merv started using the studio, it was where they did *The Hollywood Place*. I had a meeting with Murray Schwartz, and he put the schedule and crews together. Jeff Margolis was the director, and there were no problems with the taping.

The following year, I was asked again, and this time I made the arrangements at CBS Television City. I sent them a letter in March, letting them know the dates, and which personnel we wanted. A week before, I was notified that CBS had made major changes to some of the key personnel, and at that time it was too late to change venue. After we finished taping, I went and retrieved the videotapes, and delivered them to Tony Thomas. They would make copies for syndication purposes, and when they aired in the various cities, they would superimpose the telephone numbers at the bottom of the screen, so people could make their donations.

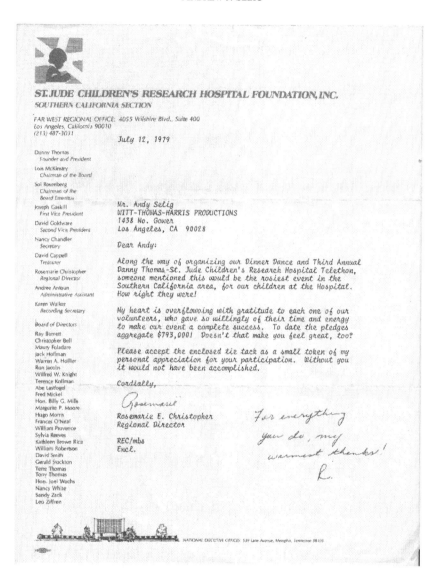

July 12, 1979

Mr. Andy Selig
WITT-THOMAS-HARRIS PRODUCTIONS
1438 No. Gower
Los Angeles, CA 90028

Dear Andy:

Along the way of organizing our Dinner Dance and Third Annual Danny Thomas-St. Jude Children's Research Hospital Telethon, someone mentioned this would be the rosiest event in the Southern California area, for our children at the Hospital. How right they were!

My heart is overflowing with gratitude to each one of our volunteers, who gave so willingly of their time and energy to make our event a complete success. To date the pledges aggregate $793,000! Doesn't that make you feel great, too?

Please accept the enclosed tie tack as a small token of my personal appreciation for your participation. Without you it would not have been accomplished.

Cordially,

Rosemarie

Rosemarie E. Christopher
Regional Director

REC/mbs
Encl.

For everything you do, my warmest thanks!

R.

NATIONAL EXECUTIVE OFFICES: 539 Lane Avenue, Memphis, Tennessee 38105

Two weeks later, I received a call from CBS to go over the costs for the Telethon. I showed them a copy of the letter from March, and the bill went away.

During our fourth season of *SOAP*, ABC wanted to change it from a half hour to a full hour show. We started taping the episodes in July so there would be sufficient time for editing. After the shows aired, ABC had agreed to pay to have them edited back to a half hour for syndication.

As it was getting close for ABC to pick-up the show for another season, which would have been the fifth, we were notified that *SOAP* had been canceled. It had been an exciting show to work on, and we felt we had done good work.

SOAP had been nominated for seventeen Emmy Awards:

- Outstanding Comedy Series: 1978, 1980 & 1981
- Outstand Lead Actor in a Comedy Series: Richard Mulligan won in 1980 and was nominated in 1981
- Outstanding Lead Actress in a Comedy Series: Cathryn Damon won in 1980 and was nominated 1978 and 1981
- Outstanding Lead Actress in a Comedy Series: Katherine Helmond was nominated in 1978, 1979, 1980 and 1981
- Outstanding Supporting Actor in a Comedy Series: Robert Guillaume won in 1979
- Outstanding Directing in a Comedy Series: Jay Sandrich was nominated in 1978 and 1979.

Jay had invited the producers, Marie and me to the DGA Awards banquet in 1978 and 1979. On our table, there were miniature director chairs with our names and the date. If my memory recollects, the entertainers was Robert Goulet in 1978 and Bette Midler in 1979. They both did exceptional shows.

Soon after, *I'm A Big Girl Now* was also cancelled. Since those were the shows that I was responsible for, I was also let go. It was the summer of 1981, and I needed to find a new job.

CHAPTER 12
THE EIGHTIES

In March of 1981, I got a call from Al Simon at ABC telling me that Peter Palmer was looking for an associate producer for a sitcom. Peter and I had worked together on *Match Game*. I met with him at Carson Productions, (Johnny's Production Company) and he said the new show was *Lewis & Clark*, starring Gabe Kaplan. The show would tape at ABC, but air on NBC. He told me the executive producers were George Shapiro and Howard West, whom I had met when he was agent with the William Morris Agency in Beverly Hills. I thought that getting my foot in the door at Carson Productions might lead to other projects I might be offered.

The show was about a New Yorker named Lewis who moves to Texas and buys a country and western bar managed by a man named Clark, played by Guich Koock. The big event every week was the armadillo races on the bar. Also in the cast were Ilene Graff as Gabe's wife, Michael McManus, Wendy Holcombe, Clifton James, and Amy Linker and David Hollander as Gabe's children.

Although all of this was planned in 1980, the show was delayed due to the 1981 strike of the Writers Guild of America, which had to do with original programming for pay television, video cassettes, and video disks. Peter asked me to wait until the writers' strike was over to start working on putting together the office staff, which I did. The strike wasn't settled until July 11, 1981.

Lewis & Clark

Guich Koock (left) and Gabe Kaplan (right) as Lewis and Clark

One night while taping the late show, one of the female extras wandered away from the holding area that was set up for them and went by the fly system (pipes that are used for lighting the shows), and tripped. The only thing she could grab was one of the lines of the fly system. Some object fell, and hit her on her head. We took her to see the nurse on the lot, and she said she was alright. A couple of days later, she said she wanted to sue ABC and Carson Productions. I informed Al Simon at ABC about the problem, and he put me in touch with an ABC lawyer. After telling him what happened, I suggested we call AFTRA (the extras union), and I would explain to their representative what happened. We held the meeting on his speakerphone, so we both could hear. They agreed that ABC and Carson did nothing wrong. They would get in touch with her, and let her know the result.

We had fun doing the shows, but it only lasted one season.

NBC had received the rights to televise the Summer Olympics from Moscow. The first Games ever held in Eastern Europe. Then the Soviets invaded Afghanistan, and on March 21st, President Jimmy Carter announced that the United States would boycott the Games. NBC was very lucky that they were able to get all their equipment back.

I don't know who put me in touch with Bill Fisher at Columbia Pictures Television. I went in for an interview to be the associate producer on *Filthy Rich*. The show was about a very dysfunctional family, and a satire on the nighttime soap opera shows, like *Dallas* and *Dynasty*. In *Filthy Rich*, a wealthy man dies and leaves a videotaped will. In it, the heirs learn that they won't collect a dime of their inheritance until they accept the man's illegitimate son and his wife into their family.

Bill and I hit it off, and this was the beginning of a very good working relationship. Bill asked me to meet with Executive Producer Larry White, whom I knew when he was a vice president at CBS. The director was Wes Kenny, with who I had worked on *Days of Our Lives*. The other executive producer was Linda Bloodworth, who also created it. I got the job.

We did the second pilot for CBS at Television City, and the show was picked up. CBS didn't have any stages available, so Bill contacted Al Simon at ABC to see if they had any space. They did. Bill and Al did the budget, and then Bill showed it to me. I said I thought I could get a better deal for facilities from Al. Bill was really surprised when I came back with a better deal.

I also asked Bill if I could do the post-production audio, so I would be able to keep my medical benefits with the DGA. He checked with Business Affairs, and they agreed.

One of the props for the show was a huge bathtub, and we didn't want to have any problems with it leaking. The drain was soldered shut, which took care of the problem. The prop crew would siphon the water out after each taping. The show was set in Memphis at a fictional mansion called Toad Hall. When Big Guy Beck (Forrest Tucker) passed away, instead of leaving a will, he left video tape cassettes, which were played to them by his attorney every episode.

Big Guy's snobbish oldest son, Marshall Beck was played by Michael Lombard, his snobbish wife was played by Dixie Carter. Also adding complications was Big Guy's younger wife, played by Delta Burke. His illegitimate son was played by Jerry Hardin, and his wife Bootsie was played by Ann Wedgeworth.

Nedra Volz played Big Guy's senile first wife, Winona Beck, also called Mother B. Rounding out the cast was Charles Frank, who played the younger son Stanley. Stanley was the only member of the family that wasn't depending on getting any of the inheritance, because he had invested his money wisely.

Don Roberts, who was on staff at CBS, had designed the sets for *Filthy Rich*, but since the show was going to tape at ABC, we needed another art director. Don recommended David Sackeroff, a freelance art director, take over those duties. David and I hit it off, and this would lead to a lot of shows that we would do together.

In one episode, Nedra Voltz's character dreamt that they had a money tree in the back yard. We needed to find a real tree for the filming. David and I agreed on a location, and I explained to the owner of the property what we wanted to do. He signed a location agreement and I paid him a small fee. We taped fake money to about ten trees to get the effect, put up a stepladder for Nedra, and then videotaped it.

Linda and Larry started getting complaints from the actors that the director was being abusive in the way he talked to them. They asked me to look into it. I went into the audio booth off stage and heard him berating some of the cast. I reported back to Larry and Linda what I heard, and the director was fired. They got Wes Kenney to come and direct that episode, and do the rest of the shows. The cast was very happy again. At Christmas, the producers handed out silver pigs, with Filthy Rich engraved on them.

Bill invited me to Columbia for their Christmas Party. Columbia's new president, Frank Price, was there, and welcomed everyone. Mr. Price told a story that his predecessor told him after he was hired. The predecessor gave him three letters that he had prepared.

"After being here six months," he said, "you will be summoned to the board room. Remember to take the first envelope with you. They are going to ask you about the movies that are already in production, and why are they over budget. You will open the envelope and read your answer, which is: 'They were already in production when I was hired, and I had nothing to do with giving them the okay.' About nine months later they will summon you again, and they are going to ask about the movies that are in post-production, and also over-budget. You will open the second envelope, and read your answer: 'These were given the green light before I was hired, and I am not responsible for the overages.' Two years later, you will receive another notice to come to the board room, and while you are in the elevator, open the third envelope: 'It's time to make out three new envelopes.'"

If nothing else, we all got a good laugh from it.

I also worked on a show called *Reggie,* which was a remake of the popular BBC show *The Rise & Fall Of Reginald Perrin,* starring Richard Mulligan. There was never a normal day in Reggie's life. He was a little crazy, and would have dreams of doing different jobs in every episode. We would go out and tape these fantasies, and edit them in to the episodes.

Barbara Corday was the executive producer. She and her husband, Barney Rosenzweig, invited the cast and some of the staff to an afternoon social at their home so we could all meet prior to starting rehearsals. I asked if I could bring Marie, and she said yes.

Richard was happy to see me, and to know that we would be working together again. He asked for a favor. Could he could possibly have the same costumer that he had worked with on SOAP? I called Don Rehg to see if he would be available, and he was.

213

Barbara mentioned to me that the cast was having problems with the director. After she informed me what was going on, I called Bill Fisher about the problems, and he asked me to come to his office at Columbia, and discuss it. I told him I had a good working relationship with the DGA, and we could probably negotiate a way to let the director go. I set up a meeting, which lasted about an hour. The DGA offered a settlement amount that was better than what Business Affairs had estimated, but it would only be on the table until 2:00 p.m.. When I got back to Bill's office and gave him the figures, he called Business Affairs, and they said to make the deal. I called the DGA to finalize it. When I got off the phone, I asked Bill if I would get any of the money they saved. You can guess what the answer was.

In one episode of the show, Reggie dreamed he was running an ice cream company, and David Sackeroff, our art director had an ice cream cone made out of Plexiglas that would light up. Barbara had mentioned that she liked it, and after the show was cancelled, David had it modified, and we hung it in her office at Columbia before she came in. She was really surprised and delighted.

Marie was having problems with the smog in the valley, and was wondering if we could move to the Westwood area. We looked in the real estate section of the *Los Angeles Times*, and finally found an ad for new townhomes in the Brentwood area. They had built four buildings with two townhomes in each. Five were still available, and we found one that we liked. The best part was that we shared only one common wall, which was in the living room. Each patio had its own Jacuzzi in it. The original builder had defaulted and Carpeteria, a carpeting and hardwood flooring business, had come in and finished the project. We told them that we were interested in Unit # 2, but we needed to speak to our financial advisor, before making a commitment.

We met with our advisor, John Larkin, and showed him what they were asking for the Unit, he called Carpeteria, and asked if they would be interested in our Mary Ellen house in Sherman Oaks. After seeing the house, they were interested in buying it. We had another meeting with John, and we called Carpeteria with our offer, and they accepted it. When Marie and I went to sign the papers, I noticed that they had the wrong figures in the contract, and called John right away to have it corrected, which they did.

When I saw David Sackeroff on the set of Reggie, I told him about the condo, and asked if he would be able to help us get some furniture. He said yes, and the following Saturday we met him at Charles & Charles showroom. Marie liked what David had chosen, and we ordered the pieces. David arranged to have them delivered afterwards. Whenever we needed additional furniture that's where we went.

Marie was getting tired of doing private duty nursing. One day while we were at the dentist for teeth cleaning, she overheard a conversation that the dentist was looking for someone to answer the phones and make appointments. When she saw Dr. Rifkin coming in to see me, she came in and asked him if she could be considered for the receptionist job. A week later she received the phone call, and started working there.

Columbia was going to do the television adaptation of *Ain't Misbehavin'*. It was to be part of the NBC Live presentations. Bill Fisher was interviewing for associate producers. I told him I would as interested. He set up a meeting for me with Alvin Cooperman, the executive producer, which I thought went well. Two days later I was hired. The cast would be from the Broadway show: Nell Carter, Andre De Shields, Amelia McQueen, Ken Page, Charlene Woodard, and Luther Henderson, the piano player. They were also able to get Arthur

Faria, who did the choreography on Broadway. Don Mischer directed. I got a rehearsal hall at NBC so Don could see the musical numbers with Luther playing the piano. Don told Luther that the piano that he would be playing would move across the stage. The set was designed as a night club, with small tables and chairs. The guests would be in the audience were told to be in evening attire for the occasion.

I asked Marie if she would like to come to the taping, and she said yes.

Don Mischer told the cast that when we taped the show, we would do Act 1, take a half hour break, and do Act 2. If any pick-ups were needed they would be done the following day.

Marie told Dr. Rifkin that I was doing *Ain't Misbehavin'*, and he asked if he and his wife could come. I put them on the guest list, and Dr. Rifkin said he would pick Marie up and bring her.

When we started rehearsing on set, our audio mixer, Bill Cole, realized he had a problem. Nell, Andre, Amelia, Ken & Charlene were all on wireless microphones, and trying to mix them with the band was impossible. We met with Don Mischer, and decided to bring in another mixer just for the Band. I asked Bill who he would like to have, and he asked if Joe Ralston was available. I went to technical operations, and pleaded my case, and they came to the control room to see the problem for themselves. They agreed that Bill needed help, and they got Joe for him. We put an auxiliary mixing board in a room near the stage with a headset, so Joe would be able to talk with Bill. NBC also approved giving Joe Ralston credit.

The final problem happened on the day of taping. I called over to Columbia's casting department to see if all the contracts had been signed. I found out Nell's was the only one signed. I asked them to get the contracts to me as soon as possible. I only had an hour to get them signed, or there would be no show. I went to each dressing room. The only question anyone had was if anyone was getting anything extra. I said that only Nell was. They trusted me, and signed.

When Marie showed up with Dr. and Mrs. Rifkin, I had already told the usher where I wanted them seated. They had an unobstructed view of the stage. When we finished Act 1, I went down and told them that there were refreshments in the lobby, and that I wouldn't be able to see them again because Don wanted to schedule the pick-ups for the following day.

Don had asked that the post-production be done at Compact, and asked to have Ed Brennan as his videotape editor, and Allen Patapoff for post-production sound. I was able to get both of them because of my good working relationship with Compact.

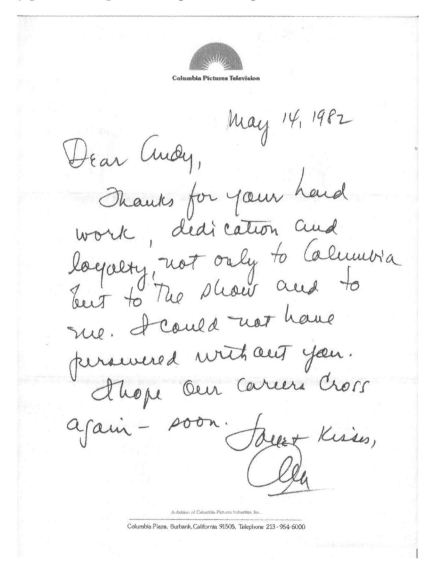

Ain't Misbehavin' aired on NBC June 12, 1982. It was nominated for 8 Emmy Awards, and Nell and Andre won.

Cable television was starting to grow, and the Networks were afraid of losing revenue. On November 23, 1982, the broadcasting industry and the Justice Department agreed to eliminate the duration of television commercials. What this meant was they could put as many commercials as they wanted in a television show.

The old standard was that during the daytime, which ran until 8:00 p.m., the networks aired six minutes of commercials in a half hour. After 8:00 p.m. to 11:00 p.m. they aired three minutes of commercials per half hour.

In 1983, I did the Pilot for *Mama Malone* for CBS. It was about a very unusual family, with Italians, Irish, and Greeks. Lila Kaye was cast as the mother, who did a cooking show out of her apartment. To make it more interesting, Lila was an English actress, trying to play an Italian. There was a lot of ethnic humor that wasn't offensive. What really made it interesting was that it was a show within a show. CBS only aired thirteen episodes in 1984.

Bill Fisher had been working on budgets for some upcoming pilots, and he sent them to Michael Grossman from Business Affairs for approval. One day Michael stopped by Bill's office, and he gave him one of the budgets. He kiddingly said to him, "If you find anything you don't like, shoot holes in it." The next day, Michael comes in, and gave Bill the budget back with holes in it. He had taken the Budget to the shooting range, and used his 45-caliber gun.

Ken Corday, the producer of *Days of Our Lives*, asked Bill Fisher if he knew of someone who could help him with a pilot called *Rituals*, which was being done for syndication. Telepictures Productions would produce it. Bill mentioned that I was available. I met with Ken, and he told me what he wanted me to do. I agreed to do the pilot, but told him that if it went to series, I would not be available. Ken agreed. He asked me to attend a meeting with Frank Konigsberg, President of Telepictures Productions. The meeting took place at Frank's office on South La Cienega Boulevard. The offices were not in the best part of town. I think Frank was trying to tell us they didn't have a lot of money for the project. A few days later, Ken said there would be another meeting, and asked if I could have a budget ready. This time the meeting was in Sherman Oaks at the corporate offices, which was completely different than La Cienega. We gave them the budget, and explained that I had talked with ABC about using their studios, and the possibility of using some sets for the pilot. Frank said that would be okay. Ken hired Herb Stein, who was one of the directors on *Days of Our Lives*, Jill Farren Phelps as producer, Charlene Keel as writer, Lynne Osborne as casting director. I was the supervising producer.

I contacted David Sackeroff, and asked if he would be available for the pilot, and told him he would have access to ABC's scenery used on General Hospital. There would also be a restaurant location. He agreed. Al Simon assigned Ray Savoy as our production administrator. We had worked together before, and this would make my job easier. Steve Auer was our unit manager, and Karen Wolpin would be the remote one. Dick Robertson, Senior V.P. Sales & Marketing at Telepictures Productions, was looking for a room to use for prospective buyers to view the show. I found a large dressing room, and equipped it with coffee, sweet rolls, and soft drinks.

David, Jill, Karen and I went out looking for the restaurant to use, and we found one. I negotiated a fee with them, and told them that the cast and crew would have lunch there. They went out of their way to accommodate us. The best part was that we finished on time.

The pilot was edited at Vidtronics. Telepictures signed up enough stations to syndicate it.

I received a phone call in December, 1983 from Art Fisher, who had directed Donny and Marie Osmond, about doing a pilot for a show with Bobby Vinton. I told him that I was interested, but that I needed to ask Bill Fisher if it would be alright with him. Bill said yes, and Art set up a meeting with Bobby and his agent at his home to go over the idea for the show. It was to be a variety show and one or two of the company would be featured each week. There would be about six co-stars.

Bobby was going to be appearing at Knott's Berry Farm for a concert, and he invited Art and me to go see it. He wanted Art to see how he interacted with his audience, and give him some insight for the kind of set needed for the show. I brought Marie. We drove to the venue, and Art flew his helicopter there.

I had contacted John Spence at NBC Tele-Sales about the possibility of doing it there, and Art had contacted KTLA. I explained to Art that due to the confines of the budget, I could get a better deal at NBC. Art finally agreed. The scenery would come out of NBC stock, and I suggested going with a staff art director to save money. He was already familiar with the Crew that I would get since he had directed various shows at NBC. We met with Worldvision Enterprises, a television program distributor who would finance and syndicate the show, and finalized the budget. Art would be the producer and director of the project.

Dennis Roof was assigned as the art director, and we had another

BOBBY VINTON

meeting with Bobby to go over his thoughts on the sets. Dennis presented his ideas, and both Bobby and Art agreed to his drawings. I told Art that when the show went to series, the scenery would have to be built, and the costs amortized. I also called Worldvision and informed them, and they were alright with it.

I set up a meeting with the AFTRA (American Federation of Television & Radio Artists) representative, to discuss that this was an ensemble cast, and that each one would be featured in different shows. It took a while, but they finally agreed to our concept, which would save the producers money.

Everything was going smoothly until a week before we were going to tape the show. I got a call from Worldvision, telling us that the budget would include a second run. This would add costs to the budget that I had not included. I walked into Art's office and told him about it, and he called Worldvision and told them he couldn't worry about that.

Finally, it was the day to tape the show. We had allotted an hour and a half to do the first show. Well, we didn't have enough time to do everything. After giving notes to the Ensemble, and before doing the second show, Art was told by Worldvision that he had to stop at 10:00 p.m., whether he had all the segments taped or not. As we approached the time, I went and locked the doors to the control room, and told Art not to stop until he had everything he needed. Art finished at 11:00 p.m., and you can imagine how mad Worldvision was.

The next day Art started editing at Compact Video, and everything went together very well. I started doing the post estimate, and found that we had saved some money. I called Art and suggested that we give gifts to the key crew people at NBC, and that the enclosure cards would be from us. He agreed. When Worldvision saw the edited version, they wanted to make changes, and Art explained that there would be some jump cuts due to Bobby's wardrobe not matching. I delivered the master videotapes to Worldvision. Art called and thanked me, and said he hoped that we could work again. The night it aired I was dining with friends, and we didn't believe the butcher job that had been done with the editing.

About two weeks later, I got a call from John Spence at NBC, and he told me that Art had died while piloting his helicopter. He was blinded by the sun, and didn't see the power lines. I went to his funeral, and it was a fitting tribute to this wonderful man.

ART FISHER

Andy:

Just wanted to let you know that you are doing one helluva good job.

I know that we have not worked together before, for whatever reason, but I am damn glad that you are on our team putting together the myriad of details that go into the making of a GOOD television program.

Thanks for your presence.

New World is indeed fortunate to have Andy Selig on their aide...and I don't write these letters often.

VERY RARELY INDEED.

CHAPTER 13
WHAT'S HAPPENING NOW

My working relationship with Bill Fisher continued to be a good one, and one that kept me working. We met both professionally and personally. He asked me if I would like to go to the American Music Awards telecast on January 28, 1985. Without asking Marie, I said yes. When I told her, she was very excited, and I told her that we had to wear evening wear. Luckily for me she had a dress that I had given her for Christmas, and this would be the perfect occasion for it. I rented a tuxedo. Bill said to meet him at his house, and we would ride in his limo along with his date, Susan Abramson, who was the talent coordinator for the show.

The American Music Awards were held at the Shrine Auditorium, and we had seats in the sixth row with a great view of the stage. Lionel Richie was the host. Prince performed "Purple Rain." It was a fabulous show, and when it finished, we all went backstage to the party and saw most of the performers. Marie was in her glory.

To reciprocate, we took Bill and Susan to an English pub called The Cock and Bull on the Sunset Strip. We started our meal with their famous Welsh Rarebit, then the salad. For the main course, it was buffet. They usually had roast beef with Yorkshire pudding, turkey with stuffing, and vegetables, plus a fish dish. The carver gave you a fairly good size portion that covered the plate. Bill went back for thirds, that's how much he loved the food.

Bill worked as Vice President of Live and Tape Productions for Columbia, and was also involved in syndicated programming. After finishing my work on the Bobby Vinton show, Bill asked me if I would be interested in working on a budget for an upcoming project. I found out that they were going to bring back *What's Happening*, which had

The cast of "WHAT'S HAPPENING NOW!!" (from left to right) HAYWOOD NELSON, ANNE-MARIE JOHNSON, DANIELLE SPENCER, ERNEST THOMAS and SHIRLEY HEMPHILL say "thank you very much for watching our show!!"

been a hit on ABC from 1976 to 1979. They changed the name to *What's Happening Now* for syndication.

Syndicated shows were created to be seen in local markets. The syndicator would finance these shows. First they produced a pilot and tested the market before making a commitment for thirteen or twenty-two episodes. In the case of *What's Happening Now*, the show already had a proven track record as *What's Happening*, and the major leads would continue to do the new show. It was already likely to be popular, but we could produce the syndicated show on a lower budget than when it was produced for network television. I told Bill it seemed like an interesting project.

Bill had found a warehouse in Glendale, California owned by Sam and Al Makhanian. They were in the auto parts business, and wanted to convert their warehouse into television studios. Bill asked me to go and see if it would work for *What's Happing Now.* There was a lot of work that needed to be done. I was told that it had to be up and running in forty days, which would be a real challenge. I went over all the things that needed to be done for the conversion. Sam and Al met with the Mayor, whom they knew, to see if this was feasible. They were able to convince the city that it would increase its revenue. Al took the information from us, and had the plans drawn up and approved. It would be called Glendale Studios.

The first thing that had to done was to fix the floor in the warehouse. Al Makhanian wanted to jackhammer it, but I told him about a special cement product you could just pour over the top and it would level out the floor. This is what we did, and Al was surprised when he put a level on it. It worked!

The space would also need a steel center beam installed on the roof to hold all the lighting equipment. While waiting for the fabrication of the beam, construction started on the control room, lighting board room, wardrobe, make-up, and dressing Rooms. Al also put in an elevator to the second floor, where the dressing rooms were, just in case an actor needed it. I was there seven days a week to make decisions. I informed Bill when the beam was to be installed. Al, Sam, and Bill all signed it before it was lifted into position.

The next project was to get the contracts for the crews. Bill got in touch with Howard Fabrick, a labor relations attorney, who suggested setting up two separate entities, so Glendale Studios could do both union & non-union shows. I told Howard the biggest stumbling block would be with stage crew, and I suggested that we sign with I.A.T.S.E. Local 33, if at all possible. For the engineers, we would have to go with Local 659. I found out that I had met George Dibie, the Local 659 president, while he was the lighting director on *Barney Miller*. Howard set-up meetings with the unions, and asked me to sit in. The negotiations went very well, and Howard informed Al Makhanian, that the contracts had to be signed by him, as he was the owner of Glendale Studios.

Bill knew John Poliak, who owned a television remote truck. We asked him if he would be interested in renting his truck Wednesday through Fridays. We would need four cameras and three 1-inch videotape machines, and the same number of VHS machines. He was agreeable, and Bill asked him to submit a bid. The numbers were good, and Bill put him in touch with Al Makhanian to sign the deal.

Everything was completed in forty days, and the only stumbling block we faced was with the City of Glendale. They came in for an inspection and told us that we had to install a sprinkler system under the bleachers. I explained that the bleachers were not a permanent installation, because they would have to be collapsed and rolled into the other studio. Then they insisted that we hire a Glendale fireman to be there when the audiences were present. Al finally got the city to sign off on the bleachers, and we didn't need a fireman.

In the meantime, I asked David Sackeroff to be art director, and Toni Vitale to be wardrobe supervisor. They were both available.

David would have the sets built by Scenic Express, who would also deliver them.

I then started putting together the office staff, associate director, stage managers, script supervisor, and the stage and technical crews. I would be competing with other shows that videotaped on Fridays.

Barbara Corday asked me to interview Mark Cendrowski as a possible second stage manager. The meeting went well, and I hired Mark, and helped him get his DGA Card. (In later years, Mark went on to become a successful director, best known for

Al and Sam showing their appreciation

his work on the highly popular CBS sitcom *The Big Bang Theory*.)

Now it was time to bring in the sets, and do the lighting. The City of Glendale wouldn't sign-off on the electric for the stages. I went out and rented a generator so we would have sufficient power for the studio. The inspector came by, and refused to let us use the generator because it would make

too much noise for the neighbors. I informed him that it was up and running, and to prove my point, we opened the doors of the generator, and he was amazed how well the insulation worked. He then signed off on it.

Al also built a room for the producers with monitors and phone access to the control room. David Sackeroff hired Kate Murphy to be his assistant, and I was able to find a room where she would be able to have a drafting table that she could work from.

Al Simon called and asked if I would interview his daughter, Leslie, for a position on the show. I met with her and I offered her the job as my assistant. It was good timing. We would be using a computer for the first time. I had gone to Columbia to learn how to use them, and I had a really bad experience. Leslie felt comfortable with the computer and also tried to teach me, but every time I tried to input something the same five letters came up on the screen.....ERROR! Al forgot to tell me that Leslie was a member of Mensa, an organization for people with high IQ's.

About two weeks before production started, Columbia had a luncheon at which the producers, Michael Baser and Kim Weiskopf, and the writers, Larry Balmagia, Bob Peete, and Jay Moriarty, would meet the cast. The original cast included Ernest Thomas, Haywood Nelson, Fred Barry, Danielle Spencer, Shirley Hemphill. Anne-Marie Johnson was later added as Ernest Thomas' wife.

Bill and I sat down to review the budget, and I found out that I had only $100,000 per episode to work with. There was very little room for any mistakes. Two weeks after we taped the first show, I did a final cost report and went to the financial department at Columbia to discuss the costs. They informed me that because of the large number of shows they were working with, they wouldn't be able to input my information to the computer for at least four weeks. They asked me how close was I with my numbers. I told them I put in an extra $1,000 for contingencies I didn't know about. After taping four episodes, and coming in under budget, I learned that they had left out the royalty for the creator of the show. We were able to cover it with the extra $1,000 that I had added.

One of the rooms we built doubled as a rehearsal hall, where we would read the scripts on Monday. Then on Friday, it became the dining room. Al wanted to put a soda machine in the room, and told me he had contacted Pepsi. I called Bill Fisher to tell him, and he said there would be a problem, because of a conflict with Coca-Cola, who had just purchased Columbia Pictures. Bill made a phone call, and a Coke machine was delivered to the Studio. As long as we were there, Coca-Cola would supply Coke products for the machine. I arranged for a catering company to provide the dinner on Fridays, and if there was any food leftover, I asked them to donate it to a local food bank, which they were happy to do.

After finishing our 22 episodes, we had a wrap party, where we passed out *What's Happening Now* sweaters that Toni designed, and showed out-takes from the shows. We also learned that we would be back for another season.

During the hiatus, CBS agreed to do a show with Melba Moore, called *Melba*. Saul Ilson was the executive producer, and the other producers were from *What's Happening Now.* Along with Melba, the cast included Gracie Harrison, Barbara Meek, Jamilla Perry, Lou Jacobi, and Evan Mirand. In the show, Melba is divorced and raising her pre-teen daughter Tracy (Jamilla Perry), with the help of her mother Rose (Barbara Meek). She hangs out with her long time best friend Susan (Gracie Harrison), and works at a New York City visitor center with Jack (Lou Jacobi), and Gil (Evan Mirand).

Bill Fisher allowed me to do the post-production audio on *Melba.* After completing the first episode, I had Vidtronics make a ¾-video cassette so I could show it Saul Ilson. After he viewed it, he called me into his office and said I did a good job.

Melba premiered on January 28, 1986, the same day as the space shuttle Challenger disaster. CBS pulled the show and aired the remaining episodes during that summer.

Also during the hiatus, Al Makhanian of Glendale Studios decided to buy his own cameras. I advised him that it would not be a good idea,

because new CCD (Charged Coupled Device) cameras were being developed, and he was better off using a remote truck instead of keeping someone doing maintenance on a full time basis. He didn't heed my

"What's Happening Now   Cast & Crew   December 1985"

suggestion, and bought them. Al found out the hard way that it was costing him a lot more than he expected.

When *What's Happening Now,* came back for the second season, there was a dispute with Fred Berry, and he left the show.

The Technical crew approached me, and asked if there was any way to include medical coverage for the two days they worked. I called George Dibie, the president of their union, to find out what the cost would be. It was reasonable, and it wouldn't put us over budget. I informed the crew that they would be covered, and they were grateful.

The producers decided to do something special for our Christmas episode. We invited underprivileged children to see the taping, and afterwards they went next door and had their pictures taken with Santa. We also found out what gifts they wanted for Christmas and we were able to get them.

We were very fortunate that the show was doing well in syndication, because we were able to do another two years of shows.

During the hiatus, Bill Fisher called me to

"Season 3"

come to his office to discuss finding facilities for doing a syndicated version of *Let's Make A Deal.* He had made the arrangements for me to fly to look at studios in San Francisco and San Diego. In San Francisco, I only went to one station, and their studios were too small. My flight to San Diego was on a small 10-seat airplane, and I had a woman sitting next to me by the window. She asked why we were flying over the ocean, and I said it was easier for the pilot to land in the water than the mountains if the engines failed. She dug her nails into the backrest of the person sitting in front of her. We arrived in San Diego without any problems. Unfortunately, the studio there was also too small. After going over all the information I brought back, Bill agreed.

The following week he asked me to go to Las Vegas to the Caesars Palace Hotel to discuss another show, *Up Pompeii*. From there I would go to Orem, Utah so see the Osmond Studios. Marie was also invited to go to Orem.

I went to Caesars Palace and met with their person in charge of entertainment, explained that *Up Pompeii* would star Buddy Hackett. He told me they loved Buddy, and asked if they could have *From Caesars Palace Hotel presents Buddy Hackett* at the top of the show. I told him that I would discuss that with Bill Fisher, but that I wanted to explain the show to him. It was called *Up Pompeii*, based on the British comedy with double entendres, and risqué gags, and that it would be done in the nude. He said we could do the show there, but without *from Caesars Palace*. I left the hotel and took a cab to the airport. I told the driver that I was meeting a private jet there, and that he would take me to the special area where they landed.

Marie would be coming from Van Nuys on a Clay-Lacey private jet with our luggage, and I asked her to pick me up in Las Vegas at McCarran Airport. I waited about fifteen minutes until she landed. The pilot said it would be about a half hour before we could leave because our lunch wasn't ready yet. Marie said that this was the best, and that she could get used to flying private jets. After taking off, the co-pilot served us our sandwiches and cold drinks. About an hour later we landed at Provo, Utah, and were met by Paul Jensen, the owner of the Osmund Studios. Paul offered us a ride in either a Rolls Royce convertible or a limousine. We opted for the limo. He took us to his office at Osmond Studios, and I explained that we wanted to do a syndication version of *Let's Make a Deal*. We would need to put up the producers, director and staff. Paul said that they had a couple of condos they could offer, and the rest of the staff could stay in town at a hotel at 50% of the regular price.

I agreed that the set could be built there. I told him that they would tape four shows a day for a week, and then take a week off. I also informed him that he would be supplying the technical crew and stage crew. He said that he had enough information to come up with a budget, and told us that we would be staying at Sundance, at one of Robert Redford's condos. He provided us with a car and directions to the condo, and asked us to be back at his office at 6:00 p.m. to go to dinner. The directions were easy, and I was glad that Marie remembered what the code word was to open the gate.

We relaxed for an hour, got dressed for dinner, and then drove back to his office at Osmond Studios. Paul was there his wife and another couple, and we got in the limo for the drive to Salt Lake City. As we started driving, we came to a street that had iron gates. Paul said that was Osmond Lane, and that was where all the Osmonds lived.

We arrived at the restaurant La Caille, which was just outside of Salt Lake City in Sandy, Utah. At the entrance was a pond with wild turkeys around it. After being seated, Paul asks if we would like something to drink, and we both said wine. After looking at the menu, we decided on red. Marie and I both forgot that Utah is a dry State. Paul said not to worry, and went and got us each a glass. After dinner, we drove back to the studios. Paul asked if we wanted someone to come the next morning and cook breakfast for us, and we said no. We would see him at 10:00 a.m. the next morning and go over the numbers. Marie and I really didn't want to leave, but we made the trip back to the studios, and while I was in with Paul, Marie had another cup of coffee. The budget was good, and I told him I had to go over it with Bill Fisher, and that he would be in touch with him.

Paul then drove us back to the airport, and we boarded the jet. When we arrived in Van Nuys, we thanked the pilot and co-pilot for an experience we would never forget. Since Marie's car was there, she drove me to the Burbank Airport so I could retrieve mine. I drove to Columbia Pictures Television, and told Bill about what Caesars Palace said about *Up Pompeii*, and about the Osmond Studio bid for *Let's Make a Deal*. I said that the savings would be about $200, and that was without any hiccups. Bill waited a day before calling Paul and letting him know that it wouldn't work, and thanked him for taking good care of Andy and Marie.

I don't know the circumstances, but in 1987, Bill Fisher was let go, and Al Simon from ABC was brought in to replace him.

Towards the end of Season 4 of *What's Happening Now*, I read in *Variety*, that Jay Sandrich was going to join Grant Tinker in a new venture called Grant Tinker Garnett Entertainment. Jay had worked

236

with Grant at MTM Productions as director of *The Mary Tyler Moore Show*, and I had worked with him on *SOAP*. They were going to be at The Culver Studios, where *Gone with The Wind* was filmed. I got in touch with Jay to see when they might be getting into production. He said to call him the following week. That night I told Marie about phone conversation with Jay, and she said this would be a new challenge for me, and go for it. He put me in contact with Jack Clements, who was Vice President of Production. My meeting with Jack went well, and then I met with the executive producer Sam Bobrick, whom I had met when he was a writer on *Celebrity Game*, and Producer Louie Anderson. I was hired as the associate producer for *The Johnsons Are Home*, a pilot for CBS based on Louie's life.

On my first day I went down to see Stage 15, where we would tape the show, and found that the Stage floor was uneven. I notified Jack Clements that they would have to cover the existing floor with tempered Masonite, and he put me in touch with the carpenter. I asked if he knew how to do it, and he said yes. That was done on a Friday. On Monday, when I went down to the Stage to look at the floor, it had buckled. I called the person who had supervised the work, and he met me on the Stage. He couldn't believe what had happened. I explained that the Masonite needed room to expand and contract. That all he needed to do was use a matchbook between each piece of Masonite. The second time, there were no problems.

Since GTG was a new entity, they needed to have contracts with the engineers, stage crew, make-up & hair, and wardrobe. I suggested using Howard Fabric, with whom I had worked before, to do the negotiations. I informed Howard that I would like the engineers to be with Local 659, and the stage crew with Local 33. My main concern was I didn't want to use Teamsters to do all the trucking of sets and props. He was able to negotiate that out of our contract.

Jay, Sam and Louie were busy casting the show, and Edward Stephenson was the production designer. Edward and I had worked on various shows before.

Geoffrey Lewis was cast as Andy Johnson Sr., Lynn Milgrim as Ora Johnson, John Zarchen as their son, Andrew Johnson, Audrey Meadows as Aunt Lunar, and Billie Bird as Mrs. Simms. The rehearsals were going well, until one day we heard music coming from the studio next door. We shared a common wall. I called Jack Clements and told him about the problem. He set up a meeting that afternoon. I found out that Michael Jackson needed to re-shoot part of his Music Video, and he really needed to hear the music. I suggested that they turn the speakers into the Studio to help alleviate the problem, which it did. The following day, I was able to go into the Studio where Michael was filming, and they had to recreate the subway station in New York. This was built on platforms in order to get the proper angels.

Jay asked if he could see how our set looked on camera, I got a camera on a tripod, and put a dolly under it so it could move around the stage. He was pleased with what I did for him. I also set up a 21-inch color monitor. I contacted Video One to see if we could use their mobile truck, and it was available on the dates I needed. Post-production was going to be done at Complete Post in Hollywood, and Jay wanted Rick McKenzie to be the editor. On the night we taped the pilot, Rick was in the control room to take Jay's notes. The post production audio was be done at Compact Video's Audio Department in Burbank.

After all the post production was completed, GTG had a party for the producers and cast to see the finished product.

We were waiting for CBS to let us know if was going to be on to the fall schedule, but they passed on it.

Jack Clements asked me to meet with Deborah Aal, executive producer for *Raising Miranda*. It was about a father who has to raise his fifteen-year-old daughter alone. We had a good meeting, and I was hired as the producer. The show would take place in either Racine or Sheboygan, Wisconsin.

Deborah asked to find out the availability of set designer David Sackeroff. He was available, and after having a meeting with Deborah, he started designing the sets. Once they were approved, and being built, I found out that we would go to Racine to videotape exteriors. I contacted the Racine Visitors Bureau, to see if this could be done. They had just filmed a feature with Goldie Hawn and Mel Gibson, called *Bird on a Wire*, for Universal Pictures, and they had a good experience working with the production company. I then contacted the local television station to see if I could use one of their crews for the shoot, and also to provide the videotape stock. After agreeing on the fee, they could accommodate us. I then contacted a lighting rental company in Chicago to provide the equipment that we would need, and put our lighting director Andy in touch with them. I agreed to put their driver up at our hotel, to make it easier for us to get to the locations at the same time.

Before leaving, I got the GTG's location agreements, for the owners to sign.

I should mention that we doing this in the middle of August.

My contact with the Visitors Bureau, arranged for us to stay at the Marriott, and she agreed to accompany us to the various sites, which would make it easier for us to deal with the property owners.

Deborah, David and I went looking for exteriors of houses that would match his interiors. We found three that would be perfect, and narrowed it down to one. I went to talk with the owner and explained that we would tape only the exterior of her home in daylight and at night. She agreed.

The next stop was the high school, and the principal couldn't have been nicer. His only problem was accepting the money. I explained that he could use it to do upgrades to the school, and he finally agreed to take the money.

The last stop was the shopping mall, and the owners were agreeable, as long as we showed the name, which Deborah agreed to do. While we were at the mall, I mentioned to Deborah that I only brought a summer weight jacket, and it was colder than I expected. I went and bought a warm windbreaker, and she told me to submit the bill to GTG. She was pleased how everything was going, that she decided to go back to Los Angeles a day early.

I called Marie that evening to tell her everything was going smoothly, and that I missed her. I mentioned that in the lobby of the Marriott, they had a wall hanging that would look great on our living room wall, and that I would be home in two days.

The next morning, I mentioned the wall hanging to David, and he agreed that it would work on our living room wall. I asked the receptionist if they could give me any information on the artist. I found out that she lived in Los Angeles.

The next morning as we were leaving the hotel, we saw the local newspaper with a banner headline saying: SORRY SHEBOYGAN!!!!!!!! Meaning Racine had been picked for the location.

Since we were able to complete all our daytime exteriors early, we decided to tape Lake Michigan for an additional transition, and the nighttime exteriors went well also. I took everyone out to dinner as a thank you for an excellent job.

The next day we drove back to Milwaukee for the plane trip back to Los Angeles.

The following Monday, I had all the exteriors transferred from the 1-inch videotapes to ¾-inch VHS cassettes, so they could be inserted during the editing process. I brought the cassettes back to the office so Deborah could see the how everything turned out, and she was pleased with the taping.

I contacted the artist who had done the wall hanging I saw at the Marriott, and she was willing to do one for Marie and me. We scheduled a meeting with her, and asked David Sackeroff if he could come also. At the meeting, she said that she would do a three-dimensional design of pine trees, and would send us a drawing for approval. We showed it to David, and he liked it. I called the artist and gave her the go ahead. Two weeks later she called and delivered it, and

David came to hang it for us. It really turned out better than the one we saw in Racine.

After long audition sessions, Deborah and the show's creator, Jane Anderson and writer, Martha Williamson, selected the Cast. James Naughton would be Miranda's father, Royana Black would be Miranda, Miriam Flynn and Steve Vinovich were the next door neighbors, the Hoodenpyles, Bryan Cranston was Uncle Russell, and Amy Lynne was Marcine Lundquist, Miranda's schoolmate.

Instead of using a remote truck, GTG went out and purchased CCD cameras, and I arranged to rent the audio booms from Mole-Richardson. A room near the stage was converted into the control room and producers' room. On Mondays following the taping on Fridays, the director and Deborah would view the cassettes, and select the best takes. Then the associate director would start the editing process.

It was decided to tape the show without a studio audience. This sometimes made the acting more challenging for the actors to gauge reactions. We were able to get about twenty people from the studio to come every week, so the actors had an idea where the laughs were.

Since there was a commissary on the lot, we used them for our catered meals, and we would use it after they closed. we were able to have two separate areas, one for the producers, director and cast, and the other for the crew.

The directors for these nine episodes were John Pasquin, John Whitesell and James Widdoes.

When we got close to finishing the episodes, Deborah Aal, suggested that I should look into getting an agent to find jobs and also negotiate for me. She put in touch with Beth Uffner with The Broder Agency. Our meeting went well, and she would let me know when she heard of a project.

Beth had heard that Steve Papazian at Warner Brothers was looking for a producer for the show *Molloy*. After meeting with Steve, he had me meet Grant Rosenberg, one of the executive producers. Our meeting went well, and he hired me.

Molloy was about an 11-year old living with her single mother in New York, and her father was on the West Coast, whom she would see on weekends. After her mother dies, she moves to the West Coast to live with her father and his new family. Here she is confronted with a self-absorbed teenaged step-sister, and a younger step-brother. Her Dad gets a new job as program director, at a local television station, and Molloy is lucky enough to get a regular part on a children's variety show.

Steve told me that there wasn't enough office space for the staff, and that we would have to split up. The executive producers and the writing staff would be in one trailer, and the production personnel in another.

Ken Johnson was hired as the set designer, and Dwight Jackson as the set decorator. I then started putting together the rest of the crew. At that time, we only had a six-episode commitment from Fox.

Mayim Bialik played Molloy, before her big break in *Blossom*. Kevin Scannel played her Dad, Pamela Brull was her stepmother, Jennifer Anniston was her stepsister, Luke Edwards as her stepbrother, and I.M. Hobson was Simon on the children's show. This was Jennifer's debut before *Friends*. The directors were Andy Weyman & Jack Shea.

As we were nearing the start of production, I contacted Steve, to find out where they purchased the videotape stock for the shows. I thought that their prices were a little steep. I then called my contact at 3M and asked him for his prices. He informed me that he couldn't sell at Warner Brothers. I asked him to come anyway for a meeting and go over his pricing sheets. I did a comparison of the costs and I called Steve for a meeting. He was surprised that 3M was a lot cheaper, and he was going to make a change on his other videotaped shows.

Just before the first hiatus, I received a call from Bob Jeffords. Bob was the unit production manager for *Murphy Brown*, overseeing the cost on film shows. He informed me that Mayim was going to do a guest appearance on their show. I told him that Mayim would have the script memorized after the first day, and that he might want to warn Candice

Bergen. I also mentioned to Bob that if he needed to borrow any wardrobe for her, it was available, because we didn't have any idea when our show would air on Fox.

When we completed our six episodes, I asked Bob Jeffords if I could come over to see how a film situation-comedy was done. I was amazed at how long it took, and I learned that they have only one video camera so the audience could watch. I then realized that my world of videotape was a lot faster, and more cost effective also.

Marie and I received a phone call from my cousin Burt, telling us that he was going to be in San Francisco for a meeting, and asking if we would drive up and have dinner. Marie was able to get off work early, and we drove up to San Francisco, and found the French restaurant where we were meeting. Burt was already there with his wife Janice, and two other couples. After everyone had looked at the menu and ordered, Burt asked me to pick the wine. The sommelier came over and I pointed to the wine that I selected. I asked him to put a napkin around it, so no one could see the label. I said our host would taste it. Burt said that it was the best French wine he tasted in a long time. I then asked the sommelier to remove the napkin, and it was BV (Beaulieu Vineyards) from Napa, California. After having a great evening, Marie and I thanked Burt and Janice for inviting us, and we drove back to Los Angeles.

My agent Beth phoned to tell me that KTMB (Kathy, Terry, Mort and Barry) Productions were looking for an Executive in Charge of Production for a show called *The Fanelli Boys*. Ken Stump had been hired for the job, but he passed away on January 1, 1990. Their offices were located at Disney Studios in Burbank. I had worked with Kathy Speer and Terry Grossman when they produced *Benson*.

After my interview with the four, they put me in touch then with Mitch Ackerman, Vice President of Television Production at Walt Disney Studios. I was hired, and my temporary office was in a trailer. Mitch told me that the pilot for *The Fanelli Boys*, would not be taped at Disney, because they didn't have a stage available.

Rita Burton, with whom I had worked at CBS Television City, had been transferred to run CBS Studios on Radford in Studio City to see if she could accommodate us. They would have studio space, but I would have to bring in a remote truck for cameras and videotape. I contacted Video One, whom I had used in the past, and they were able to accommodate us.

I moved over to CBS and started putting together our Crews. I received a call from Rita inviting me to come to a production meeting where they discussed upcoming studio activities. I let them know when we would start using Stage 20, and I passed out the calendar that showed what would be happening from April 2nd to April 27th. They were impressed, because no one had ever given them that much information before.

Jane Fletcher was the production designer, Richard Decinces was the set decorator, and Richard Brown was director of photography. Jim Burrows would direct. He was the son of Abe Burrows, and he had also directed *Cheers*. Deborah Barylski was the casting director and, along with the producers and Jim Burrows, they came up with an outstanding cast.

Ann Morgan Guilbert played the mother, while Joe Pantoliano, Christopher Meloni, Ned Eisenberg, and Andy Hirsch played her sons. Richard Libertini played Father Angelo Lombardi.

The pilot was for NBC, and the premise was about a woman who, after her husband passes away, plans to sell her home, and move to Florida. However, her sons decide to come home after making messes out of their lives, hoping Mom would be there to comfort them.

During a break one day, I mentioned to Jim that I had the pleasure of meeting his dad, Abe Burrows, when he was one of the Celebrity Panelists on the game show *What's It For*. He said his dad rarely spoke about those times, and enjoyed hearing the stories.

While *The Fanelli Boys* was in post-production, NBC gave KTMB the green light to do another pilot called *Anna*. Noam Pitlik would be the director. I had worked with him on *Sanford and Son*, when he was an actor. Jane Fletcher would be the production designer.

The show was about Anna, who was in a wheelchair, and her male roommate. Anna was played by Maria Charles, and the roommate by

Keith Diamond. Also in the Cast were Tom La Grua, Bill Macy, Dennis Lipscomb, and Herb Edelman.

Maria was an English actress, and the producers tried very hard to for her to get a Brooklyn accent, but it didn't happen. She struggled through.

There were a couple of scenes that took place inside a subway car. I made arrangements with the New York Subway Authority, to tape the subway segments that we needed. Since I couldn't get away, Noam and I met with the Disney Production Executive, and explained what we needed, and he did an excellent job for us.

The Disney Studios were approached by Sony to try out their high definition cameras. I informed Noam, and we had a lengthy meeting with the Sony representative, and Mitch Ackerman, Vice President of TV Production. We were informed that Sony would also provide the remote truck, and the special monitors for the playback of those scenes. Since we would be using blue screen for the background areas, they would also supply the special paint to use. I was so grateful the Noam was there for the meeting with Sony.

When it came time to rehearse these scenes, Sony left out a very important detail at our meeting, that these cameras would not be on the normal studio camera pedestals we were used to, but instead would be on tri-pod dollies. This meant that the cameraman wouldn't be able to raise or lower the cameras. After trying various heights, Noam made it work.

After the taping of the scenes, Noam edited them in the Sony high-definition remote truck, so they could be played back during the taping.

On the day the Pilot would tape, Sony brought in their special high-definition monitors, which took 30 minutes to set up.

Lots of Disney executives were in the audience, including Michael Eisner, Randy Reiss, Garth Ancier, and Warren Littlefield, who was V.P of Primetime Programming at NBC. There were many NBC Executives there, as well. Everything was going smoothly until it was time to see the scenes taped in high definition. The Disney production executive, wanted to help get the monitors in position for viewing, and in doing so, he unplugged the monitors. I informed Noam, and he was not comfortable waiting thirty minutes to have the monitors recalibrated, and neither were the Executives. They had to watch them on the regular monitors.

After we finished taping, I noticed that the producers, Disney executives, and NBC executives went off for a meeting. About a half hour later, Mitch Ackerman, approached me and asked how much it would cost to re-shoot the pilot. NBC wanted to re-cast the part of Anna with an actress with a more convincing Brooklyn accent. I told him it would be about $500,000. He then asked the Disney accountant and I to come up with a more realistic number, which we did. The difference was $2,000 more.

NBC decided not to redo it.

NBC did pick-up *The Fanelli Boys*. Disney still didn't have any room at their studios, so I started hunting for space. Since I had a good relationship at Sunset-Gower Studios, I approached Ed Lammi, to see if he had any stages. He told me that Stage 16 would be available, and I put a hold on it until Jane Fletcher could approve. She did, and I was also able to get the office space that *SOAP* had used. Jim Drake and Jack Shea were the directors.

Unfortunately, I started having problems with Disney, and not being able to work them out. I called Beth, and informed her about the problems, and I left after completing six episodes.

I explained to the crews that I was leaving, and that I hoped we would work together again.

CHAPTER 14

END OF AN ERA

Marie was getting burned out at Dr. Rifkin's office, and a friend of hers told her about a job opening at UCLA. They needed a patient coordinator for the head of the Cardiothoracic Surgery department, Dr. Hillel Laks. Marie applied for the job, and a week later she was hired. On her first day, she met Bambi Wojciechowski, Dr.

Laks' secretary, who explained what he wanted her to do. She would schedule future patients for surgery, and make sure they brought their x-rays and other medical history for Dr. Laks to look at. She said goodbye to Dr. Rifkin.

In reading about Dr. Laks, I found out that Dr. Laks was a professor

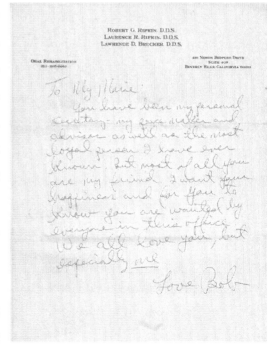

at the David Geffen School of Medicine at UCLA, In addition, in 1984 he established the UCLA Heart, Lung and Heart-Lung transplant program. With his team, they implanted one of the world's first total artificial hearts. He performed open heart surgery on Tiger Woods' father, and while he was recovering Tiger would visit the pediatric heart surgery ward. Another patient was Andre Agassi's dad. Andre was so appreciative that the surgery was successful, he brought warm-up suits for Dr. Laks' staff. Marie asked if she could have a large to give to me, which I still have.

One day when dropping something off for Marie that Dr. Laks had ordered, I met Bambi, Dr. Laks, and Tess Sood, who scheduled the operating rooms for Dr. Laks. That June Marie and I were invited to attend the graduation for the cardiothoracic doctors. This was not your usual graduation. Some of the other doctors in the department told amusing stories, and one even wrote a poem about the new doctors.

Another year Dr. Laks was having a convention at Disneyland, and I was invited. Bambi told Marie that the printer forgot to deliver two boxes that they needed, and asked if I would drive back to Los Angeles to get them, which I did. That evening, while having cocktails before dinner, Dr. Laks thanked me for getting the material, and I thanked him for inviting me. The next morning nothing was planned. We were given passes for Disneyland, so we took the monorail from the hotel to Disneyland.

Marie and I were happily living in Brentwood, and enjoying our townhouse. One day, I went out to retrieve the *Los Angeles Times*, and noticed as I passed by Unit #4 that the windows in the kitchen were all fogged up. I told Marie, and she also went and looked. When I got to my office at Warner Brothers, I called Carpeteria and told them what I had seen. That afternoon they called and said that they were letting one of the sons of the owner used the unit, and that he had brought his pet snake with him. He had put the snake in the bathtub. Somehow the snake turned on the hot water and flooded the Unit. He thanked me for informing them.

I was by then entering my fourth decade working in television. I had moved up from office boy to producer. I knew a lot of people in the industry, and I had learned how to solve a lot of different sorts of problems.

In early 1990, I received a call from Erwin Stoff, (Deborah Aal's husband) to see if I would be available to produce a show for HBO, called *Down the Shore*. The show took place at the Jersey Shore, where three buddies got a beach house for the summer, and to help defray expenses, they had three female co-workers move in.

Erwin set up a meeting with Alan Kirschenbaum, the creator and executive producer. HBO had bought his idea. I met Alan at his office at the Directors Guild of America building on Sunset Boulevard. It was a good meeting, and I was hired. I was given a small office at the DGA building, where I started putting together the staff and crew. Erwin told me that this would be in association with HBO Independent Productions, and put me in touch with Carmi Zlotnik, Vice President of Production. Carmi wanted to set up a separate production company that would handle paying all bills, and asked me to be that entity. The name I came up with was for that company was

Giles (Selig spelled backwards) Productions. HBO took care of all the necessary paperwork to make it work.

Carmi also asked me to see if I could find an available stage at Warner Brothers Hollywood Studios. They had Stage 1 available, along with office space nearby. I had Erwin and Alan look at the office space to make sure it would accommodate them. Erwin asked if there would be an office for him, and I told him that there was one on the second floor, that was quiet. He liked that it was separate.

I called David Sackeroff to see if he was available to be the art director, and he was. Beth Hymson was the casting director, and John Sgueglia was the director. He gave me a list of who he would like me to hire. I was able to get them.

I got a call from Roxie Evans, with whom I had worked at CBS. She told me that Adria Horton, who worked with me on *SOAP*, was looking for work, and she gave me her phone number. I called Adria to come interview as the associate producer. It went well, and I hired her.

In order to make Giles Productions work efficiently, HBO hired a production auditor, Fay Moss, who would be on site, and a payroll company to prepare all checks. Fay & I were the signatories.

The *Down the Shore* cast included Louis Mandylor as Aldo, Tom McGowan as Eddie, Lew Schneider as Zack, Anna Gunn as Arden, Cathryn de Prume as Donna, and Nancy Sorel as Sammy.

Alan had wanted some stock footage to use for the transitions. Stock footage transitions are used for going from one scene to another. They could be used for daytime or nighttime to set up what was being taped at the studio. I asked Alan to explain exactly what he wanted. I found a crew in New York to shoot additional images. When the tapes arrived, I had ¾-inch cassettes made so Alan could view and approve the footage. It was exactly what he wanted, and I called the crew in New York, and thanked them for doing such a great job.

Warner Brothers had a store on the lot where you could purchase their logo merchandise and other items. I have always been a collector of Broadway show music, and the store sold these compact discs at really good prices.

One day I got a call from the store manager, asking if I could possibly help him out with some videotape stock for another show, because his delivery was late. I was able to accommodate him, and he thanked me by giving me some CDs of Broadway shows.

Down the Shore was going to air on Fox. Carmi gave me a copy of HBO's budget, and I could see that we would be deficit financing over $100,000 per episode. After taping three episodes, I received a phone call from Warner Brothers Syndication, asking when we would deliver the shows. Since we didn't have an air date yet, we were taking our time. He informed me that the show had already been sold for foreign syndication, and Warner Brothers needed them delivered as soon as possible. I asked if he was at liberty to tell me how much each they were selling each episode sold. He said they were charging $150,000 per.

I went in to Alan, the executive producer, and told him about my phone call. He was livid. HBO had never informed Alan that the show had been sold for foreign distribution. He was going to call HBO and give them hell, since they had told him that's how much over budget we were for each episode. I told him that if he did that, I would be fired, because I knew too much. He called HBO anyway, and I was terminated. HBO was upset because I got information that I shouldn't have, and they felt they couldn't trust me any longer.

When they finished the six episodes, I heard that they moved the show over to KTLA to tape there. I received a call from one of the staff they told me all the problems they were running into by HBO's constraints, and I was really missed.

A few weeks later, I got a call from Warner Brothers They asked if I would interview for the producer position for a new situation comedy. When I met the executive producer, he said that he wasn't about to hire anyone to spy on him. He then called the Warner executive who had recommended me, and told him that he was going to spend as much as he wanted, and there was nothing he could do about it, and hung up the phone. That afternoon I received a call from Warner's apologizing for the incident.

After that incident, I realized that I had enjoyed a very good career in television. I had learned a lot, contributed to the industry, and met a lot of interesting people. But now the time had come to say goodbye. I retired in the summer of 1992. I called some of the people I had worked with to say goodbye. These were long-term relationships, and we would continue to get together occasionally for lunch. But after 36 years in television, it was time to leave.

CHAPTER 15
AFTER TELEVISION

Marie wasn't ready to leave her job at UCLA, and I agreed with her. She received wonderful letters from patients (see below). But since I wasn't working, I asked her how she would feel about me driving her to UCLA each day, which would allow me to turn in my leased vehicle. She agreed.

I kept up some of the friendships I had cultivated over the years, and we would get together. They were surprised that I didn't want to pursue anything in the television industry. I told them I didn't really want to work in television given the way the industry had changed. Now, with the cable networks, and the three mainstream networks (ABC, CBS & NBC), I wouldn't be able to get the salary I was used to. The producers were all doing deficit financing, and the only way they could make some of that money back was letting the networks syndicate their shows if they had a hit. If it wasn't a hit, the show would probably be cancelled. After years spent making sure we met our budgets or coming in under-budget, I couldn't see making the switch comfortably.

To Marie, With thanks for being so wonderful to all our patients. Hillel ①

Herbert R. Mayer
Lock Box 5426 · Sherman Oaks, California 91413

TEL #: 818/789-5461
FAX #: 818/789-7751

✗ *Please file in Marie Selig's Personnel File*

August 30, 1993

Ms Marie Selig
c/o Hillel Laks, M.D.
UCLA School of Medicine
10833 Le Conte Avenue
Los Angeles, CA 90024

Good morning Marie:

So often in life when something is amiss you always seem
to hear about it.

In like manner when something nice is done we just do not
seem to take the time to do anything about it.

I just want to take a moment to express my thanks and
heartfelt appreciation for the help that you have been to
me and my family.

Your thinking of all of us is way beyond "The Call of
Duty".

My wife is a very special person to me and after 50 years
a special bonding has come about that I do not think that
I would be a whole person without her.

Your easing us through this critical period is very much
appreciated. Marie, you are really terrific and both
myself and my family will never forget how helpful you
have been.

Warmly,

Herbert R. Mayer

nc

JOHN DAVID PORTER

April 6, 1998

Dr. Gerald Levey, M.D.
Provost Medical School and
 Medical Sciences
10833 LeConte Avenue
Room Number 12-138 CHS
Los Angeles, CA 90095

Dear Dr. Levey:

I wish to commend and gratefully thank Marie Selig (Room 62-182 CHS), Administrative Assistant to Dr. Hillel Laks, for her prompt and continuous effort to insure that I had immediate medical attention for a life-threatening heart problem.

Although I was 130 miles from UCLA Medical Center, she arranged and coordinated my emergency appointment with Doctor Yeatman, Adult Catheterization Laboratory. Had she delayed her effort, even by a small margin, life-saving time would have been too short to be effective.

Marie Selig, by using her fine follow-through ability, was directly responsible for helping save my life.

Her fortitude reflects fine traditional UCLA Medical Center care.

Sincerely yours,

John David Porter
Lieutenant Colonel, U. S. Army (Ret.)

2214 VIA MONSERATE ROAD, FALLBROOK, CA 92028

259

In 1996, Marie and I started talking about where we would like to retire. I immediately thought about all the wonderful times we had in Carmel area. We would spend two to three days at Ventana Inn & Spa twice a year, and loved the area.

She agreed that Carmel would be nice, and the air would be better for her there. I found a real estate broker, and told him that we were looking for a two-bedroom, 2-bath condo with ocean views in the Carmel area. About two weeks later he called and had some places for us to look at. Marie and I planned to drive up the following weekend and look at them.

We made reservations at the Briarwood Inn in Carmel. On Saturday, the real estate person picked us up, and took us to lunch at the Pebble Beach Fitness and Tennis Club, and then showed us several places that had absolutely no ocean views. We were fairly frustrated. The last condo that he showed us was being built on the corner of Mission Street and Fourth Avenue. We told him that we would be interested in the second floor unit near Fourth Avenue, but we wanted to be able to make changes before construction was finished. He said he would let us know.

Since we were planning to downsize, we decided to sell our townhouse and find a one bedroom apartment, which would allow us to get used to something smaller. I was surprised that Marie was willing to do it, and she said she would ask if UCLA had any apartments for rent. She found that UCLA used the Oakwood Apartments in Marina Del Rey. We went to look, and they showed us one with a balcony with a view of the ocean, and it was furnished. All we had to do was bring our clothes and TV. We told them we had to sell our place first, and they agreed to hold the apartment for us. We were fortunate that our townhouse sold in two months. I found a place where I could store the stuff we could take to Carmel. Since we knew that our furniture would probably not work in our Carmel condo, I was fortunate to find a company that would buy everything. The day before they came, I went and got the City to put up "No Parking" signs, so they wouldn't block the street. I asked them to leave our bed, and they could pick it up the following day.

I told Marie that I would go to Oakwood and sign the rental agreement so I could bring our belongings there the following day. She was sorry that she couldn't help me, and I told her it was alright. That night I took her to Hamburger Henry's for dinner, and then back to our townhouse for our last night there. We watched television in our bed for the last time.

The following morning our bed was picked up, and I started making trips to our apartment at Oakwood. That evening, when I picked Marie up, I offered to take her to Islands Restaurant in the Marina, and she accepted. When we got back to Oakwood, she was surprised that I had done a good job putting everything away, and she then realized that we had downsized.

The following weekend we went to Carmel to look at some more places, including the new construction. The builder told us that we couldn't make any changes to the floor plan, and there was absolutely no view from the balcony.

After four trips to Carmel with no luck, we were not happy. On

Sunday, after going to Church at the Carmel Mission Basilica, we were having breakfast at the Briarwood Inn, and the manager, George, came over and asked how our hunt for a condo was going. Marie told him that we weren't happy with what we have seen over, and he asked if we were open to him talking to a friend of his that perhaps could help. We told him we didn't have an exclusivity deal with our existing realtor, but would be willing to talk to him. We gave George permission to give out our phone number.

On Monday evening we received a call from Earl Myers II, the realtor George referred us to, saying that a condo had just came on the market. Could we come up on Tuesday? I told him that Marie was working, but I could be there Wednesday morning. Earl said it could be gone by then, but I told him I would take the chance.

I called United Airlines, and booked a flight that would arrive in Monterey on Wednesday by 11:00 a.m. I also called our realtor, and told him that I was flying up to see the condo. He said he would pick me up, as he wanted to see the condo as well. I stopped by a drug store to get an instamatic camera so I could take pictures of the condo to show Marie.

On Wednesday, I flew to Carmel, not knowing what to expect. Earl was at the condo with some other potential buyers. I took a whole roll of pictures of the condo and the 180-degree view of the ocean. I told Earl that I was interested, and asked if I could call him that evening after Marie had seen the photos. When I showed Marie the photos, I told her not to look at the furniture, which was too big for the condo, but what we could do to put our stamp on it. She liked it, and I called

Earl, and said we wanted to submit a bid. He asked what our contingencies were, and I said none. I called our previous realtor and told him about our plans, and he was happy for us.

Earl called me on Thursday and said the condo was ours, because we had no contingencies. We agreed to that the move-in date could be whatever was convenient for the sellers. I called Marie, and gave her the GOOD news, and we asked Earl if we could drive up on Saturday so Marie could see it. Earl called back that afternoon and said we could see it on Saturday.

On Saturday, we left Marina Del Rey at 6:00 a.m., and drove up the coast, stopping in Summerland for breakfast at the Big Yellow House. From there, we drove to Carmel, and Earl was waiting in front of the building. We took the elevator up one flight, and Earl escorted us to the condo.

Marie agreed that the furniture overpowered the unit. But when she saw the view, she agreed it was unbelievable, and my pictures didn't do it justice. What Marie liked the best was that it a secure building, that there were only six units, and visitors had to be buzzed in.

Earl had made reservations for us at The Tradewinds across the street for us to spend the night. We asked Earl if George would be working that day at the Briarwood Inn, so we could thank him for recommending him. We stopped by and George was happy for us. Then Earl, Marie and I went to lunch, and signed the papers to make it official. We thanked him for making it so easy, and that he would let us know when the owners would be vacating. We went to Mission Ranch to celebrate. Marie had a steak, and I had prime rib.

On Sunday, we went to Carmel Mission Basilica for Mass, and thanked God for finding the condo for us. After Breakfast, we drove back to Marina Del Rey.

On the following Friday, Earl called and told me the condo would be vacated by June 26th. I called Marie at UCLA so she could let Dr. Laks know that her last day would be July 3rd.

I called David Sackeroff, who had helped us furnish our townhouse, and asked him if he could help us furnish the condo. He said he would. David agreed to fly up with us on Saturday, June 27th, the day after we took possession.

The only thing we had told David was about the view, and he agreed it was spectacular. David had brought his tape measure and pad, and started doing drawings and asking us a lot of questions. He made several suggestions, taking out doors and rearranging the flow of the rooms. He thought we should turn the second bedroom into an office, and replace many of the existing closet doors with bi-fold doors. He recommended recessed lighting for the living room, putting used brick around the fireplace. Since we wanted to spend a lot of time on the patio we asked about enclosing the iron railing to keep the wind out, and he liked the idea. He also suggested making the dining room into the den, and the den into the dining room. He also thought we should put another doorway to the kitchen for easier access to the dining room.

When David finished his measurements, we went to Pebble Beach for lunch, since our flight back to Los Angeles didn't leave until 4:00 p.m. David enjoyed seeing Pebble Beach, and then it was time to get to the airport.

Earl gave me recommendations for contractors to do the work we wanted to have done. I hired a contractor to start construction on July 13th, which would give us time to get our things out of storage, and pack up the apartment.

I found a local mover that was recommended to pack up our apartment and storage locker. He felt it would fit in a large van easily, and he would bring only one helper with him. His price was very reasonable, and I told him that we would put them up in a motel, and they could drive back the next day. We agreed on doing the move on July 8th.

We would need a place to stay in Carmel during the construction. We wanted to be on site while the work was being done. Earl put me in touch with a house rental person, and we found a house to stay in nearby.

Marie and I drove up on July 8th, and signed the rental agreement for the rental house. When we arrived at the house, we noticed a few things needed to be fixed. The rental company agreed to take care of it. The movers arrived that afternoon at our condo and unloaded our boxes in our storage room. We checked them into their motel and we showed them where to park the truck, and mentioned a few restaurants that they might like. Marie and I thanked them, and paid them. Marie and I treated ourselves to a dinner out.

The following morning some of the repairs to the rental house still hadn't been done. I called the rental company and told them that we would be leaving, and asked for a refund. I was surprised that they

ANDREW J. SELIG

agreed.

"Where will we go?" Marie asked. I said, let's see if I can make a deal at the Carmel Sands. Marie stayed outside, because she didn't want to hear the negotiations. They were very obliging, and rented us a room on a monthly basis. It didn't have a laundry, but the condo had a washer and dryer available for the owners. Marie asked if we were still going to install our own in our unit, and I said YES!

We took care of typical moving in details—getting a post office box since Carmel doesn't have mail deliver, opening a bank account, setting up utilities and telephone service.

We ordered appliances at B.I.D. (Built In Distributors) in Sand City, and Marie enjoyed choosing a refrigerator, stove, microwave oven, dishwasher, and washer & dryer. We arranged to have them delivered to our parking stall in the garage, to store them until they were installed. We also enjoyed shopping for a new mattress, and new cabinets for the kitchen.

While the cabinet makers were measuring the kitchen, Marie asked if it would be possible to get rid of the French Doors leading to the Patio, and put a slider instead. We asked the contractor about it, and he saw no problem. We also planned to install new wood floors.

That evening we went to dinner at Patisserie Boissiere Restaurant on Mission Street. It was a small intimate French restaurant, and we had gotten a coupon from the motel to use. The food was excellent, and we decided we would come back.

On our third visit to the restaurant, the hostess asked if we would like to take some pastries home for breakfast the next morning, and

266

Marie said yes. I took out my credit card, and she said they were on restaurant. Yes, we continued going there, and occasionally we would get pastries.

The other place we frequented was the Mediterranean Market on Ocean Avenue and Mission Street for sandwiches. Unfortunately, it has since closed and a furniture store is now there.

We kept in touch with David Sackeroff and let him know what choices we had made. He helped us pick out the wood flooring. He saw a couple of samples for the wood floors, and he said to look at Kahrs. We found a dealer in Carmel Valley, and we agreed with David that we would go with Kahrs. We called him and told him that we liked Ash Monterey, and got a price for the flooring with installation. David approved it, and he also recommended using Dunn-Edwards paints, and gave us what colors to use throughout the condo.

The next day when the contractor arrived, we informed him that we had purchased the flooring, and had the paint colors for the rooms. He was upset that he had had purchased the flooring, because he lost a commission on it. I then asked that, since we were going to use his painter, would he get some competitive bids on the painting. He told us he always uses the same one, and the same for the plumbing. Marie saw I was upset, but I went along with it, since we were getting close to having everything done.

The contractor decided to get out of his hair, and sent us to look at tile at Tileco for the bathrooms and kitchen counters, and to Monterey Tile and Marble to look at brick for the fireplace. We decided on white tile, and a natural brick. We were again lucky. The tile contractor was

Vandervort Tile, and they did an excellent job.

When the painters came to meet us, they were expecting to do all the walls in white. We told them that we were using different colors, and asked if they would put samples on the walls. They said yes, but they would charge a little more for doing the colors. Marie and I agreed. I also let them know that I knew a little about painting, because my Dad had been a painting contractor back in New York.

We informed David how things were progressing, and that we were ready to start looking for furniture. When could he come? He told us the following weekend would work.

David arrived and approved all the work, and agreed that the paint colors worked. Marie and I told David how happy we were with his designs. We then drove to Gregory's, a local furniture store, and David thought we would get most of our furniture there. We found a wood design that we liked for the bedroom, a round table with four chairs for the dining room, a cabinet that would work as a bar, and a mirror that would hang over it. David suggested a day bed in the den that would work for a sofa while we watched television, and could be used as a guest bed. We also asked his opinion of possibly putting two reclining chairs in the den, if the day bed didn't work. David picked one with plaid fabric that Marie liked, and a leather one for me. We told David how much we appreciated all his help and went to lunch before he left.

The following week the furniture started arriving, and the delivery men attached the headboard to the mattress in the Master, and the only piece we didn't like was the love seat for the den. It wasn't comfortable, and it was also damaged. I called Gregory's and told them, and they asked their delivery men to bring it back. So we opted for the chairs.

The next piece of furniture was for the office. We drove over to a furniture store in Salinas, and found an oak desk and an oak 2-drawer file cabinet.

About this time, we got a visit from a seagull that would come and sit on top of the wood patio enclosure. Marie started experimenting with what the seagull ate. Bread no, Cheerios no, salted peanuts no. After a week, she decided to call the seagull Charlie. She then got Planters unsalted peanuts, and that made Charlie happy. He came twice a day. About three months later, Charlie brought his wife to our patio, and Marie named her Mrs. Charlie. Sometimes Mrs. Charlie showed up before Charlie, and when he arrived he would give her a peck, and she would fly off until he was finished. Then it was safe to return. We were lucky that some stores had 2-for-1 sales on Planters, which helped.

Earl called and asked if we were interested in joining a health club where he was a member and offered to take us to see it. We wanted to continue exercising like we had in Marina Del Rey. We followed Earl in our car to Carmel Valley Athletic Club, which was about fifteen minutes away. He introduced us to Jill Shepherd, one of the owner's daughters, and she told us about the exercise room, tennis courts, swimming pool and café. She told us what the dues were. We took a walk with Earl to see the exercise equipment and look at the pool. Marie said she would exercise, and I would join her. I could also play tennis. We signed the paperwork with Jill, and got our membership cards. Earl thanked us, and said he would get a free month.

On the way out he introduced us to Ernie Saunders and Corleen Kretchmer at the front desk. I also asked about tennis lessons, because I hadn't played in a while, and I was told that there group lessons available from Kelly for $10 per session.

Finally it was time to move into our condo. We checked out of the Sands, after thanking them for all the coupons that they gave us. We went back to the condo, and brought up our bedding supplies, towels, glassware, and things from the storage unit. On one of our trips, we met one of our neighbors Tony, who lived on the second floor. He asked if we were into tennis, and I said I was. He asked if he could show us Carmel Valley Athletic Club. We told him that our realtor had already taken us there, and that we joined. Timing is everything.

I mentioned to Marie that I would like to have a stereo system in the den so we could listen to our records and compact discs. She said okay, if they were in a cabinet. I asked her if she wanted to join me, and she opted to keep putting things away.

I went to Monterey Stereo and met with John Bell the Owner. I told him what I was looking for, and I wanted it to be easy to operate. Everything he showed me was what we needed and not overly expensive. John told me that his son was into making furniture, and gave me his information. When I got home I called him, and made an appointment for him to come to the condo and measure. I wanted to make sure that Marie would like the piece of furniture. We showed him where in the den we wanted it, and he said he would have to build it in two sections, in order to deliver it, and put the base, and top on after they were connected. We gave him the go-ahead, and said he would talk to his father regarding the size of the equipment. Two weeks later he delivered it, and he even gave us more storage options. I called John at Monterey Stereo, and told him the cabinet had arrived, and that he would come by the next afternoon to do the installation. He saw the oak cabinet, and we told him how pleased we were.

The next morning Marie and I went CVAC to start exercising, and an instructor walked us through and explained how to the machines worked. When we were finished, I asked the front desk what days and times Kelly had her group tennis Lessons. Corleen said Mondays and Wednesdays at 10:00 a.m. I asked Corleen if they had any demo or loaner racquets to borrow, so I could decide on which one to purchase. They did. I asked Marie if I could go to the Club and start learning how to play Tennis again and she said yes.

Kelly couldn't have been nicer. She introduced me to everyone, and she really took her time to make sure we all understood what she was teaching. After forty-five minutes, we paired off and start playing, so she could tell what we needed to work on.

One of players was Jim Brauer and we would play together occasionally during the clinics. One day I asked him if he knew a handyman, because Marie wanted to have bookcases built in the office, and I wanted to have shelves in the storage room. He gave me that name of someone the he had used in the past. I contacted that person, and he came and measured the office space and the storage room in the garage. He said that he would build the bookcases, but asked me to get the shelving material and the bits to drill into the cinder block in the storage room. I went to Orchard Supply Hardware and purchased everything there. Two weeks later he came back and installed the bookcase and the storage room shelving. We were both extremely happy how everything looked.

I started unpacking all my LP's, and videotapes, and putting them on the shelves.

We invited Jim and his wife Beverly to come over to see the work that was done, and then go to dinner on us. They were surprised by the view that we had.

Marie was looking for something to do, and someone suggested going to the Red Cross Chapter in Carmel. She called them, and said she could come in for an interview that afternoon. She took the car, and when she came back, she said they could use her on the front desk answering telephones a couple of mornings. She asked if we could exercise a little earlier on those days, and I said yes.

While she was there she mentioned that we were looking for a physician to take care of us, and someone recommended Dr. Carl Bergstrom. Marie called and got appointments for both of us.

I enjoyed playing tennis. Jim and I would go to the CVAC and practice hitting the ball, hoping that someone would see us, and invite us to play with them.

I was fortunate, because a player named Leon Grandcolas recommended me for his group after someone left. He asked me to call Floyd Eisiminger and give him my phone number. He told me they played on Mondays, Wednesdays, and Fridays at 8:00 a.m. I was fortunate that when I met the other players, we were all around the same age.

Floyd oversaw scheduling, and asked me what days I played. After playing for two months, Floyd asked if I would schedule the tennis court times with the Front Desk, and I said yes, since I knew what court they liked to play on. I also found out that they played bridge on Wednesdays after tennis, and I started going to watch and learn. One Wednesday, a player didn't show up, and I was asked to sit in on the bridge game, and I was surprised I did so well. I finally did become a regular.

One day one of our regular tennis players couldn't make it, and I was introduced to Rabbi Bruce Greenbaum. He asked me to call him Bruce, and he played with us occasionally. One day, Bruce mentioned that his Temple, Congregation Beth Israel was having a Jewish Food Fair at the end of the August. When I got home, I told Marie, and she wanted to go. That Sunday, after going to Church, and having breakfast, we drove to Carmel Valley Middle School and parked the car, and took the shuttle to the Temple. When we dropped off we were handed a program of what events would take place during the day. We then went down the hill to where most of the festival took place. At the first booth we saw, we had to buy "gelt"—Jewish money. I used my credit card and was given a bag of chips used to buy items. Rabbi Bruce welcomed us, and then went to the stage and said an invocation prayer. The first booth we saw was the bakery, and we got a rye bread, and some other goodies. Then it was on to get corned beef, and some chicken liver pate. We decided to rest a bit, and listen to the entertainment. Alisa Fineman and Kimball Hurd performed. I found out that Alisa is also their Cantor. We then took a walk around and saw some of the arts & crafts booths, and then decided it was time to home and read the Sunday paper.

One year Bruce mentioned that the Temple was having a raffle, and the big prize was a wine refrigerator. Since Marie and I liked wine, I bought a few tickets. A couple of weeks later, he called and said I had won, and had it delivered. That summer at the Food Festival, one of the things up for auction was a case of good wine. Again I put my bid in, which I thought was reasonable. Again I won.

Marie was happy at the Red Cross, and was fitting into the group well. Andrea, one of the ladies there, mentioned to her that they had an opening in their Book Club, and would she be interested. She said yes. They met once a month on the fourth Monday. There were seven other ladies, and she fit in right away. She said the only problem was that no one did any research on the book they would read for the following month. I volunteered to do one, and see what they thought. Marie offered my services at the next meeting. When Marie came home, she said I had made her a hero. From then on, I showed Marie the different reports that I found about the books, and let her pick the one to take to the next meeting.

Marie still hadn't found a pulmonologist in Carmel for her lung condition. We still commuted to Los Angeles to see her doctor there. So, once a month we would leave at 6:00 a.m.. I would pick out the CD's that we would listen too, and Marie would usually take a nap. I usually started with the rainstorm CD, because it was so soothing, and she could sleep. She would bring a car blanket to keep her warm. We would have Breakfast at the Paso Robles Inn, and then take Route 46 to Route 5, and then the 405 to Westwood and UCLA.

After her appointment, we did the trip in reverse, stopping in Paso Robles. We found a restaurant on Route 46 called Big Bubba's Bad BBQ. It was a family style restaurant, and the sandwiches were delicious. From there getting back on Route 101 to Reservation Road, then to Highway 68, and then Route 1 to Carmel. We were on the road for ten hours.

I was fortunate to be asked to join another group of tennis players called the Snob-Nobs who played on Wednesdays and Fridays at noon. I only played on Wednesdays, and it cost me $2.00. This covered the drinks and food. Sam Balestari was in charge of scheduling this group.

One of the players, Ted Gold, said that he would talk to the pulmonologist he knew, to see if she was taking any new patients. As luck would have it, she was. Marie got an appointment with Dr. Gina Heal at the Cardio-Pulmonary Associates Medical Group in Monterey. Marie brought all her records, and gave her permission to talk to her doctors at UCLA. Dr. Heal recommended that Marie get "The Vest" to help her with her breathing, which she did. She was happy that we didn't have to make the trip to UCLA anymore. Still, if she hadn't found Dr. Heal, I had no complaints about making the trips if that's what we had to do.

Also through her friends at the Red Cross, Marie found out that the Carmel Art Association needed volunteers.. She called Janet, the director, and made an appointment to go in and talk to her. They needed someone to do the mailings once a month, and take them to the Pebble Beach Post Office to mail. They also said she could do them at home, and showed her the paperwork and how to code them for the different towns. Marie said that she was willing to try. She did the first one at the Gallery, so Janet could look it over, and make any corrections. She had done it correctly, and now she had gotten herself involved there.

Marie asked me to drive her to Pebble Beach Post Office to mail them, since they were heavy. Marie also mentioned that the Art Association was having an opening for the new exhibits on that coming Saturday and the artists would be there. I agreed to join her. I met Janet and her husband David, who also was one of the bartenders. They served white wine and cocktails, and finger food. One of the bartenders didn't show, and David asked me to fill in. When we finished bartending, David asked if I would like to do it again and I agreed, since Marie would be involved with the openings. After a couple of months, I recognized Dale, one of the artists, as he was coming to the bar, and by the time he got there, I had his martini waiting for him, which he appreciated.

I know this is going to sound strange, but growing up in New York City, and going to the Metropolitan Museum of Art on a regular basis, I didn't really appreciate the original artwork that I had seen there. At the Carmel Art Association, I realized what I had missed. Marie saw some pieces that she liked that were reasonably priced, and slowly we started buying some of these local works to put up on our walls. One of our favorites was Miquel Dominguez. We were also fortunate to purchase Pam Carroll, Anne Downs, Richard Tette, Mary Fitzgerald

Beach, Jan Wagstaff, Diane Wolcott and Will Bullas, just to name a few.

One of my tennis group asked if we had discovered the Gilroy Outlet Stores. He said it was about forty-five minute trip, and on Tuesdays they give seniors discounts. When I got home, I told Marie, and we decided to go the following Tuesday.

We could see the stores before we got off the highway. They had 145. I told Marie that we would drive around to see all the stores, and see if any interested her. We stopped to look at the Corningware store, where we bought things for the kitchen. Our next stop was at Ann Taylor Factory Store, where she was surprised by the great prices, and she found a few things there. We also stopped at Easy Spirit Shoes, Polo-Ralph Lauren and Jockey. I mentioned to Marie that there was another shopping center that I noticed about 5 minutes away, and she said let's look. Since it was about noon, and we were getting hungry, the first place we saw was Mimi's Café, and we stopped and ate. From there we visited Bath, Bath & Beyond, Home Goods, Pier One. There was also another restaurant to try at a later date, Famous Dave's for barbecue. All in all, it was worth the trip. And the best part we were home by 2:00 p.m., so Marie could watch General Hospital, which she was hooked on.

Another tennis player, Mac, asked if I would be available to play on a Tuesday afternoon, and I said yes. He told me to go to the Pebble Beach gate in Carmel, and tell the person that I was going to the Beach & Tennis Club to play tennis. I was wondering what I had gotten myself into. I had no idea what the guest fee was, and I didn't want to find out. So I just showed up and waited for Mac to arrive by the courts, so I wouldn't be asked any questions. Mac showed up, and I followed him to the court, where here introduced me to the other players. When we finished, I was invited to join them at the Beach Club to have a drink, and some finger food. When leaving I thanked them, and they asked me to play again the following week, and I accepted. One of the other players, Sebastian, lived at the Carmel Valley Ranch, and he invited me to play there with the group. When we finished, we went to the clubhouse to have refreshments, and I offered to pay for them, and they let me.

Dr. Heal recommended that Marie should consider going to the Cardio-Pulmonary Rehab Center at Hartnell Professional Center located in Monterey. I drove Marie over there, and she was introduced to Ida Corby, one of the team leaders. Ida told her that Dr. Heal had forwarded instructions to help her to strengthen her lungs. I told her that I would go for a walk, and be back in forty-five minutes, so she didn't have to worry about me. When I got back, she was finished, but exhausted. Ida said she was to come on Tuesdays and Thursdays at 8 a.m. We went twice a week. While Marie was exercising, I went for a long walk, and got back just as she was finishing. She appreciated not having me there watching her.

It was worth it. Marie started having more energy after exercising, and she really appreciated Ida going out of her way to give her pointers. She asked if we could take Ida out to dinner. We went to our favorite Patisserie Boissiere Restaurant on Mission Street, and Ida liked the restaurant.

At our Annual Homeowners Meeting in February, 2000, I was elected President, and Marie was named Secretary-Treasurer. One of the items discussed was putting double pane windows in the Condos, and the common areas. Each homeowner would be responsible for their windows.

I talked to three different window companies, and decided that Tom of Central Coast Window and Door Company had the best bid. I went to Carmel City Hall to find out about getting a permit to install the windows, and they informed me that the Planning and Building Department, would have to approve it, since we live in a Commercial-Residential zone. Tom went with me to the meeting, and they told us that our Building was Tudor and that we needed to install wooden windows instead of metal ones. I informed them that our building was designed by a Danish person. Our only recourse was going before the City Council to get it reversed.

I called City Hall and requested a meeting with Mayor Sue McCloud to find out what to do. She met with Tom and me, and told me to write a letter to the City Council in order to get it on the Agenda, which I did. I asked Tom to be there at the meeting to answer any questions they might have. After the discussion, Mayor McCloud stated that she had the same windows in her home, and the double-paned kept the heat in. It passed by one vote.

In 2002, Marie and I got into trouble with the Association. I forgot to read the CC&R's, and found out that they stated that only carpets were allowed on the floor. At the Annual Meeting I brought up changing the CC&R's to have either carpeting or hardwood floors. I stated that there is an air gap between the second and third floors, and that no one should hear anyone walking on them. We were fortunate, and it was approved. Stockman & Associates did the paperwork, and to save time and money, I went to Salinas City Hall to get it recorded.

To bring you up to date on the seagulls (Charlie & Mrs. Charlie), they have been having babies every year on our roof, which makes it easier for them to feed without going fishing. We never fed any of their offspring. We felt feeding Charlie and Mrs. Charlie was enough, and they didn't seem to complain about those arrangements.

Marie and I had made the adjustment to retirement in Carmel. We loved our condo. We had found new doctors and Marie's treatment seemed to be working. We made new friends, had activities to keep us busy, and the company of our feathered friends. We couldn't ask for more.

CHAPTER 16

CHALLENGES

It's amazing how everything can change in a day. Marie had scheduled a mammogram in February, 2007, and they found a lump in one of her breasts. One of her friends suggested going to Dr. Michael Stuntz for the surgery. Dr. Stuntz said the surgery would be done as an outpatient at Community Hospital. Marie consulted Dr. Heal about it, because her lung condition could be compromised by anesthesia. Dr. Heal agreed that she should do it, and would meet with Dr. Stuntz and the anesthesiologist prior to the surgery. Marie scheduled the operation for the beginning of March.

On the day of the surgery, I took Marie to the Outpatient Surgery Center. Before she went to surgery, I was able to see her, and give her a kiss for good luck. I waited in the reception area for two hours after the surgery. Afterwards, Dr. Stuntz found me in the waiting room and said everything went well, and that the biopsy didn't show any cancer. I thanked him for giving me the good news. Marie came out in a wheelchair at 3:30 p.m., and in her lap was a supply of what we would need to change her bandages at home.

When we got home, I told her that I would help her with changing the dressings, and she appreciated it. We had gotten makings for sandwiches, for a few days, because I didn't want to leave her to pick up meals. The following week she went to see Dr. Stuntz so he could see how she was healing, and he was pleased. The big question we had was when could she start having cocktails again, and he gave us the go ahead.

He recommended seeing Dr. John Hausdorff at Pacific Cancer Care for her follow-up examinations. Marie liked him. Dr. Hausdorff suggested she start getting Reclast infusions for bone density, which she did yearly after that.

Things got back to some regularity. Marie went back to exercising at Hartnell, and we walked two days a week, and I also went back to playing tennis.

In July, 2007, I was playing tennis at Carmel Valley Athletic Club, and my doubles partner Jack Anderson and I were leading in the third set. Then I told Jack we needed to finish it soon because I suddenly wasn't feeling good. We did!

I went into the men's locker room and changed my top for a dry one, left the club, and drove directly to Dr. Bergstrom's office. I told the receptionist that I thought I was having a heart attack. He told me to drive to the emergency room, but I didn't think I could get there. I knew Marie was at the Red Cross, so I drove there. As soon as I walked in the door, they knew I needed an ambulance and dialed 911. I gave Marie the keys to the car. Carmel Fire was there in two minutes, and drove me to the emergency room at Community Hospital.

I was fortunate that they had just hired Dr. Pir Shaw from Stanford.

I remember that the operating room was very cold, and I heard an intern say I think you should do it this way. Dr. Shaw told him to get out. That's the last thing that I remembered until I was wheeled out of the operating room and saw Marie standing there talking with Dr. Shaw. That's when I found out that they had put a stent in. They took me to the ICU, and Marie walked in five minutes later. I could tell that she was relieved, and I was glad to see her again. My room had no windows, so I had no idea what the outside world looked like. Marie stayed as long as she could before being asked to leave so I could get some rest, which was hard to do with two blood pressure cups on each arm.

The next morning she was there when Dr. Michael Galloway came in and introduced himself as my cardiologist, and said that I would be moved to a regular room in a day or so. The nurses in the ICU were not happy with me, because I could only use the urinal when I sat up on the edge of the bed. When I tried to do it myself, I guess I triggered something because they came running in and told me not to do that. The nurses wanted me out of their hair, and were happy to get me transferred to a regular room.

At least in my new room there was a window, phone and television. Dr. Galloway came in and told us that he wanted me to start walking the corridors at least twice a day tethered to my medicine pole. I asked Marie if she had called CVAC, and she had, and they wished me a speedy recovery. Finally they took the two blood pressure cups off, and I was allowed bathroom privileges. That Friday, Dr. Galloway said I could go home, and on Monday he said he wanted me to start exercising at the same Cardio-Pulmonary Rehab at Hartnell as Marie. I could tell that Marie was greatly relieved.

Monday, at Hartnell, I was introduced to Eric Coley, who instructed me on how to attach the leads to my chest so they could monitor my heart. I walked on the treadmill for ten minutes, and Eric came and checked my blood pressure and then showed me how to use the other machines. I think I went three days a week for a month, and Marie exercised on the same days.

We went to see Dr. Galloway, and he said it would be alright to start playing tennis again, but recommended I take the clinics for a month to see how I did. He would then re-evaluate to see if I could get back into playing sets. After the check-up, he gave me permission to start playing again, and I called Floyd Eisiminger, and Sam Balesteri to let them know that I could.

Looking back, one of the highlights of that time was the summer wedding of a tennis friend of mine, Steve. He and his bride Linda were married at the Hyatt Carmel Highlands. They had picked the perfect sunny day. After the ceremony, they served drinks and appetizers, followed by a sit-down dinner. We were fortunate to that we were seated next a couple that knew Linda, Sharon and Doug Clements. They were from Pulaski, Wisconsin, and Green Bay Packers supporters. I happened to be a Green Bay fan. We clicked, and before leaving we exchanged information, and began corresponding through e-mails.

A couple of weeks later, we received a book from them—*Green and Golden Moments*—about the Packers. I emailed them to say thank you.

What I found interesting is that the Packers is the only NFL team that is owned by the citizens of Green Bay. Sharon and Doug came back for a visit in September 2008, and we joined them for dinner at Steve and Linda's house that they had built in Carmel Valley with a terrific view. It was great to see them again and get caught up.

Andrea Thatcher, Marie's friend from the Red Cross, suggested that we look into joining The Carmel Foundation, because they had trips that might interest us. We liked what they had to offer, and became members. Our first trip was to San Jose to see a Broadway Musical. The bus picked us up at the Crossroads, where we parked our car. We boarded a chartered bus, and we took the *Monterey Herald* to read on the trip to San Jose. We stopped for lunch, and then the bus took us to the theatre and picked us up afterwards for the drive back to Carmel. It really was very relaxing, and we thought we would do it again. On one of the trips we saw *Jersey Boys*, and really enjoyed it.

Jim and Beverly Brauer invited us to join them for dinner at Vito's Italian Restaurant in Pacific Grove, and to meet their friends John and Mary Castagna. We found out that John played tennis and Mary was involved with the Bach Festival. The Festival was going to start in two weeks, and they asked if we would like to go to a concert at the Carmel Mission Basilica. We could sit with them. Marie and I both agreed to go. We enjoyed it, and said we wanted to go again the following year. When the schedule came out we decided to see the concerts at Sunset Center. John worked the ticket booth, and we were able to get seats on the aisle, because of my long legs. The first was a regular concert, and then we opted to go to closing night, where they perform the Best of the Fest. We did that for a couple of years.

After a couple of months, Carmel Valley Athletic Club raised the dues, and I went and asked if they had only a tennis membership, and they said that tennis and fitness was my only option. I said I would leave at the end of the month.

As fate would intervene, I got a call from Rick Theobald, whom I had met at CVAC, who asked if I would be interested in joining Mission Ranch. I could probably play on Tuesdays, Thursdays, and Sundays in the afternoon. I called Floyd, and told him that this would be my last week to play at CVAC and that I would be going to Mission Ranch.

That Wednesday, when Sam asked if I could play the following week, I informed him that I was leaving. After finishing playing tennis, we went up to the Café for refreshments as usual, and after everything had been ordered and delivered, I went inside and paid the bill. Sam wished me good luck at Mission Ranch. When I got home and told Marie what I had done, she approved.

On Monday I went to Mission Ranch and filled out the paperwork, and paid the initiation fee. I found out that Mission Ranch and the tennis facility were owned by Clint Eastwood. Rick called and said I could start the following month, and that was okay with me.

I was happy to get back to playing, and meeting the other members. At Mission Ranch, the winning team would move to another court, and be split up. I also learned that the group that played on Sundays would have a social gathering afterwards with wine and cheese, and that each Sunday it would rotate so everyone would participate.

I was having regular prostate exams, and my Doctor found that mine was enlarged. He called Comprehensive Cancer Center at Community Hospital and send them his report. A few days later, I set up an appointment with Dr. Bradley Tamler. On November 14th, Marie and I met with Dr. Tamler. He told me I had prostate cancer and that he wanted to do x-rays right away. After the X-Ray, Dr. Tamler suggested starting radiation treatments immediately.

I went straight to the treatment room. Ben, the technician would strap my feet to the table to make sure I didn't move. The treatment lasted about fifteen minutes. Dr. Tamler said I would have to have radiation treatments every day. I asked if I could still play tennis and exercise, and he said I could. On the drive home I told Marie I closed my eyes and thought about her.

On the second week while we were waiting for my treatment, we heard a bell ringing, and had no idea what it meant. When I went in for my session, I asked Ben about the bell. He told me it signifies that a patient had finished the treatments. I told Marie on our way home, and was looking forward to that day. That happened on January 16th, and I rang the BELL!!!!!!!! That night Marie and I went out to celebrate.

In 2009, Dr. Bergstrom our Physician got into trouble for felony sexual battery. His practice was taken over by Dr. Gregory Tapson. Marie called and got an appointment to see him. After examining her, he mentioned that he was sharing the office space with Dr. David Craig Wright, whose specialty was Infectious Diseases, and he might be able to help her. Marie wanted to meet him, and made an appointment.

On the day of the appointment, Dr. Wright's assistant Fergie showed us into the office. Dr. Wright had looked at Marie's chart from Dr. Tapson, and said that he did infusions that might help her. He wanted to start right away. He led us across the hall to a room that had eight reclining chairs. Marie sat in one, and he went over to the area that had a movable hood, where he would prepare the medicine for the infusions. He always made it up just before the patient showed up. The medicine was put on a pole so it would drip. The treatment lasted about forty-five minutes, and he said I could stay there, or go to the waiting room. I stayed.

Marie didn't have any reaction to the infusion, and looked forward to the next one.

She thought she should tell Dr. Heal about Dr. Wright at her next visit. Dr. Heal wasn't very enthusiastic about Dr. Wright's infusions, but her breathing had improved a little. She told Marie to keep getting the infusions and exercising. She also wanted Marie to cough up a sputum sample, and take it to CHOMP for the lab to analyze. When she coughed it up, it was dark, and Marie knew that it wasn't good.

On the next visit to Dr. Wright, Marie mentioned the sputum sample and Dr. Wright said he would try a different medicine to see if that would help.

Two months later we were at Dr. Heal's office, and something happened during Marie's breathing test. They called 911. The ambulance took her to the hospital. I followed behind the ambulance in my car. The doctor there said she needed to have a PICC Line put in her arm to receive the medicine. After receiving two days of treatments, and seeing improvement, Dr. Heal said she could continue getting the treatments at home, and would order the medicine for her. She gave us the number for the VNA (Visiting Nurses Association) so we could schedule a nurse to start administering the drug.

Marie was not happy with what was happening, and I tried to convince her everything would be fine. When we got home, I suggested she call Dr. Wright to let him know, and he said after the treatments started, he could infuse her through the PICC Line. That afternoon, the medicine and the other supplies arrived, and Marie called the VNA. They said someone would come the following morning.

The nurse showed up, and we took the medicine out of the refrigerator, and she checked inside the box to make sure everything was there that she would need. She said that she would come twice a day for three days, and demonstrated how to administer the drug. Marie thought that we could handle that. On the third day, the nurse wanted us to do it, so see could see if we could manage. I suggested that I make a list to follow, so it would be easier. The fact that Marie was a nurse also helped, and we did very well. The big question we asked the nurse was, could still have cocktails twice a week? She said yes.

To make things easier for Marie, I suggested that we get take-out for our dinners, and she agreed it would be better.

After finishing the treatments Dr. Heal scheduled blood tests and the results showed an improvement, and Marie asked if she could resume her regular infusions.

Marie's appointments were Monday, Wednesday and Friday

afternoons. On that Wednesday when we walked into Dr. Wright's office we could hear someone playing the piano. We were introduced to Jack, who liked playing the old songs. If Dr. Wright wasn't busy preparing infusion medications, he would sing along. Jack asked Marie if she would like to hear something, and she said "Moon River." He played, and Dr. Wright sang. It was very good. Some Wednesdays Jack tried to stump us by playing some really old songs. Marie was surprised that I knew some of them.

Marie was still going to Hartnell to exercise, and Ida mentioned to her that Chomp was going to open a gym in the Marina, and probably close Hartnell. They would probably move out there also. She asked if Marie would be interested in joining the gym. I could tell that Marie didn't want to drive out there, but I said let's visit, and then make a decision.

Ida introduced us to Kristine who was the General Manager for the Peninsula Wellness Center, and she explained what would be available there, and that in a few weeks they were going to have a walk through so people could see it. The best part was, since Marie was already exercising at Hartnell, we wouldn't have any initiation fee, and the dues for the two of us were reasonable. We visited two weeks later. It took us about fifteen minutes to get there, and they had ample parking. We were surprised by the size of the facility. It was still under construction, but we saw the exercise area, women's locker room, showers, steam room, massage rooms. The men's locker room, showers, steam room and massage rooms were still under construction. We saw where the therapy pool, regular pool, Jacuzzi would be.

I told Marie it would be worth the drive, and if she didn't like it, we could get out after a month. We decided to start on May 9th, after everything had been completed. They had instructors there to show you how to use the equipment. On the way home, I asked Marie her opinion, and she wanted to come back. About two months later Ida and her group arrived, and they had their own area and they brought some of their exercise equipment. Marie was happy because she had access to their portable oxygen tanks, because it would make it easier for her to exercise.

In September, 2011 I started having problems with my right hip. A friend of ours named Joan Hutton had just had hip surgery, and she felt that it helped her. Her surgeon was Dr. Christopher Meckel. I called and got an appointment. Marie came with me, and the first thing he did was take x-rays, and then he showed us that my hip joint was bone on bone. He said I had two options: (1) become a couch potato, or (2) have the surgery and stay active. I opted to stay active. I asked to be the first person on his schedule, and November 22 was available. I asked Marie if she would object to having Thanksgiving dinner in the Hospital, and she said that would be okay.

On that day, we arrived at the hospital at 7:00 a.m. After registering, we went to the surgery center, and were ushered into a cubicle. The anesthesiologist came in, looked at the chart that also had my medications listed, and told us what he was going to do. I looked at Marie for reassurance, and she saw no problems. I was then taken in to surgery. When I woke up, I could feel a little bit of pain. I was then transported to my room, and Marie was waiting there, and said everything went well.

When they brought my dinner, they also had a guest tray for Marie. After we watched the news, Marie went home, and came back the next morning. I told her that I had marked the menus through Friday, and I asked for a tray for her for Thanksgiving.

Dr. Meckel came in at 10:00. He said that everything had gone well, and that he did me a favor. He said my right leg was a half inch shorter than my left, and that when he replaced the hip, he was able to even it out. I thanked him, and was anxious to start walking on it.

Thursday morning, Marie and I were watching the Macy's Thanksgiving Parade from New York, when Dr. Meckel came in, and told me that I would be going to Westland House for physical therapy on Friday. Marie knew where it was because a friend had been there to recover from knee surgery. We were both happy to hear about Westland House. That evening we both enjoyed our turkey meals, and thanked God that everything turned out well.

The next day, I was anxious to get to Westland House. The nurse came with a wheelchair and I asked about a gurney. She said the gurney wouldn't fit in the transport vehicle. The driver secured the wheelchair and we started the trip to Westland House. As we approached the freeway, the driver said that he didn't get directions on how to get there. I told him to take the Monterey exit, get in the right lane, make a right turn at the traffic light, and stay in the right lane. Otherwise, he would have wound up on the freeway again. At the stop sign, I told him to turn left. I was starting to have pain in my right hip from the uneven road. I gave him enough warning for the Westland House turn.

I couldn't wait to get to my room and get into bed. After being put into bed, they brought in a machine called Cube Cold Therapy that they would put ice in, and placed the pad on the hip. It really worked well.

I started physical therapy the next day. I was very fortunate to find out that my therapist, Sherry Bettencourt, would take care of me during my stay. I told her I wanted to be able to play tennis again and she showed me the exercises to do.

On Monday, December 5th I was transported in a van to Dr. Meckel's office to have the staples in my hip removed. They told me to call the office if there were any problems. The trip back to Westland House went smoothly.

Sherry came, and said she wanted me to walk behind the wheelchair to see if I could. I stopped twice, but I made it to the exercise room without sitting down. On Wednesday, when Marie came, Sherry wanted to see if I could sit in the passenger seat of the SUV. I did, and she said that I would be able to go home on Thursday. She then ordered a walker for me, and when it was delivered, they couldn't adjust it to my height. Ordway Drugs came back with a walker that could accommodate my height. Sherry took a tennis ball and cut it in half and put it on the front legs of the walker to make it easier for me.

That night, I interviewed two physical therapy companies, and only one would guarantee the same therapist every time.

After being discharged from Westland House, Marie drove us back to the condo, and I told her not to worry, everything would be alright. There was a message on our phone from Jasmine from Alliance Home

Health, wanting to start therapy that afternoon. I called and gave her directions. She arrived along with a nurse to check the incision, to make sure it was healing properly, and check my vitals.

Jasmine brought elastic bands with her, that she put under the chair leg, and put the other end on my ankle. I would try to stretch it as far as I could, which wasn't very far. She then showed me exercises to perform to help strengthen the hip. On January 3rd, I asked when I would be able to drive again, because Jasmine would only be there for one more day. When we finished exercising, we took the elevator down to the garage, and I got into the driver's seat, and she asked me to start the engine, and try backing up, and then braking. She could tell that I didn't have any pain, and that it would be alright to drive. Friday was her last day, and I thanked her for pushing me. At that time, she suggested I find a physical therapy facility to continue my re-hab.

I looked for physical therapy close to home, and found Krpata Sports Therapy at Carmel Center Place. I got a letter from Dr. Meckel prescribing therapy in order to submit the bill to the insurance company. I started therapy on Wednesday, January 18th. Ryan was my therapist. The sessions lasted for a half hour, and included stretching exercises, and the stationary bike, and then ice packs on the hip for fifteen minutes. He also gave me exercises to do at home. My last treatment was on March 23rd, and I asked him if I could start playing tennis, and he suggested taking some lessons first, to get my timing back.

To make things easier for Marie, I suggested we should look into getting a cleaning service to come in and take care of the condo. It would be better for her health not to be dusting and vacuuming. Marie checked with her friends about their cleaning people, and she said two of them recommended the same person. Marie called her, and she was available. What made it better was that she would come at 7:30 a.m. every other Tuesday. I could tell Marie was relieved. While they were cleaning, we went to Pacific Grove and along Ocean View Boulevard looking for deer, and then stopped at The Bagel Bakery on Forest Avenue. From there we went to the Carmel Post Office for our mail, and then home. I could tell by the look on Marie's face that she was happy with her decision.

During my hip surgery and physical therapy, Marie stopped getting her infusions. She was worried about leaving me alone. She called Dr. Wrights office, and was put back on the schedule for Mondays, Wednesdays and Fridays. She looked forward to Wednesday afternoons, and the music.

She also scheduled an appointment with Dr. Heal, who wasn't pleased with Marie's breathing test. Dr. Heal suggested that she should start using oxygen at night to see if that would help. Marie wasn't happy, but said she would try it. The only problem was she couldn't get the right elevation from her pillows. The next day after exercising we went to Bath, Bath& Beyond, and found a wedge that would work. That night she had no trouble sleeping.

I went to Mission Ranch Tennis facility, and after getting a warm greeting, I asked Carolyn to see when I could get some lessons from their pro, Jeff Gilette. I said I wanted to start with some half hours. Jeff made it very easy to get back into it. After three weeks, he felt I was ready to start playing regularly. I notified the groups, and started playing again. After my time away, however, the games were a little uncomfortable. I asked Carolyn if any other groups were looking for players. There were, but I couldn't get regular games.

I started calling some of the other tennis players I knew, and Uli Siebeneick suggested I come to Meadowbrook Swim & Tennis, and check it out. I went there, and they had a nice facility. Jean Kracht, who was the manager, said I would have to be evaluated. She gave me the name and phone number of Kerry Neece. She had games on Wednesdays, Fridays and Saturdays from 9:00 a.m. to 11:00 a.m. I called her and told her I was interested in playing on Saturdays, and she had an opening that week. I showed up, and introduced myself, and she informed me which court I would be on, and that one of the other players would let her or Jean know if I would fit in.

It was strictly fun tennis, and that's what I was looking for. After finishing, I went to the office to see what the results were, and Muriel said I was a good player. Jean said I could become a member. She then she gave me the number for Murray Macdonald, who had groups that played on Tuesdays and Thursdays from 11:00 a.m. to 1:00 p.m. Uli said he would email the players who would be playing. The system worked very well. In case you forgot who you were playing with, he would post it on the bulletin board.

After all the health crises both Marie and I had weathered, it was great to be back out on the tennis court.

CHAPTER 17
SAYING GOODBYE

Everything was going very well until February, 2015 when Dr. Wright started increasing Marie's medications. In March during one of her sessions, Fergie noticed Marie shaking. He called for Dr. Wright, who came in and stopped the treatment, and said she had a TIA (Transient Ischemic Attack). After things settled down, they recommended going home.

Once at home, Marie didn't look good, and I told her we were going to the hospital. I drove her to the Emergency Room, and she told the nurse, that she had had a reaction to some medicine and had suffered a TIA. Marie was ushered into a cubicle, and a doctor came in to examined her, and promptly admitted her. Marie's pulmonologist, Dr. Koostra, was on call and came to see her, which made Marie feel better.

Dr. Koostra ordered a PICC line put in for medications, and came back to check on her after she was transferred to her hospital room. He came in and reassured her she would be alright. Marie asked me to go home. I kissed her and told her I would see her in the morning.

By the time I got there the next morning, she had been to x-ray, and was waiting to see Dr. Koostra. When he arrived, he said that they found a piece of her old lung hadn't been removed, and that was part of her problem. Although I didn't say anything, it bothered me that this hadn't this been discovered when she had other x-rays done.

Dr. Koostra suggested having arthroscopic surgery done, and he recommended a doctor to perform it. The surgeon came by about an hour later and said it would be an easy procedure, and gave us his card.

Later that afternoon, another doctor who specialized in infectious diseases, came by to consult about the operation. This came as a shock to both of us, since that was the first time we heard about needing an infectious diseases doctor involved. We questioned Dr. Koostra about it, who said the hospital didn't want to take any chances.

Two days later, Marie left the hospital with the PICC Line still in. She would continue getting medicine at home with the help of a VNA nurse. Marie called the VNA, and requested a nurse named Darcy because she had a good relationship with her. Darcy called and said she would come by later that afternoon, and start her treatments. Marie was relieved.

After her treatment, Darcy told Marie that the PICC Line needed to be flushed out and replaced, and that had to be done at the hospital. Marie got an appointment and we went back to the hospital for the replacement. We were home by 11 a.m. and Darcy showed up at noon to do her treatment. Darcy could tell that this had really taken a toll on Marie, but said she should be done the following week, and could have the PICC line removed.

After the line was removed, Marie wanted to see the infectious disease doctor to get more information. The Doctor really couldn't explain why Marie could now infect other people. She knew about the pending surgery, and suggested we go to Denver to have it done. My question was how we get there, since Marie couldn't fly in an airplane, and I said it was too long a trip by car. That ended that discussion.

In April Marie was notified that her next appointment at Pacific Cancer Care would be with Dr. Zach Koontz, and not with Dr. Hausdorff. Dr. Hausdorff was going to be doing Palliative Care. While we were waiting to see Dr. Koontz, Marie asked me if it would be alright to talk with Dr. Hausdorff about her upcoming operation. I said yes, and there was an opening after seeing Dr. Koontz. Dr. Hausdorff spent an hour with us, and said that she should have the operation, and that he would be at the hospital if she needed him. She felt better after that.

Marie had an appointment with her surgeon on May 13th, which was also her birthday. The surgeon said that it would be major surgery, and couldn't be done arthroscopically. We went to the front desk, and scheduled the operation for the following Monday, May 18th at 10:00 a.m. We were told to be at the hospital at 7:30 a.m. on the day of the surgery.

After the doctor appointment, we had scheduled to get our hair done by Kirsten, whose shop was in Salinas on Main Street. It took about half an hour to get there. Marie was glad for the break, and when we left to go home, I suggested that we stop at Tarpy's Roadhouse on Highway 68 to celebrate her birthday. I think she thought that I had forgotten, but with everything that took place on the 13th, I was looking for the right moment to do something. I insisted that she have their petite filet, and I had their meatloaf, which they were known for. She really enjoyed it.

On Sunday after Mass, we went to From Scratch for breakfast in the Barnyard Shopping Village, and then went home to read the Sunday paper.

We decided to have Chinese food for dinner. I put our glasses in the freezer to chill while I went to Tommy's Wok on Mission Street, in Carmel, and picked up appetizers, brown rice, and sweet and sour pork. When I got home, Marie got the appetizers ready, and I made her a gin martini with Beefeater's and 3 onions, and I had Tanqueray Gin on the rocks with 2 olives. That would be the last cocktails we ever had.

On Monday May 18th, we arrived at 7:30 a.m. Since she had pre-registered on Friday, we went directly to the surgery center. The nurse came and got us, and we went into a waiting cubicle, where she got Marie's vitals, and went over her medication list. She came back at 10:00 a.m., and said that the surgeon was running late, and Marie asked if we could turn on the television. The anesthesiologist came in at 11:00 a.m. and went over what Marie was allergic too. He told her what he was going to use, and she alright with it. At 11:30, they came to take her to the operating room. I kissed her and told her I loved her.

I wasn't sure how long the operation was going to be, so I stayed in the waiting area. At 2:30 p.m., the surgeon came out and said that he was successful, and that I could go to ICU in about an hour to see her. I went to the Garden Court Café at the hospital and had lunch. An hour later I took the elevator down to the ICU wing, and pressed the buzzer to enter. They were still getting her hooked up to machines, and asked that I wait in the waiting room down the hall. They would come and get me. Half an hour later they came, and took me to a room with sliding doors where Marie was sleeping. The nurse introduced herself, and said that I could sit there. Marie still had a tracheotomy in order to breath.

When she woke up, she was happy to see me, and I told her everything went well. One of the nurses came in and told her that she would be fed through the tube in her nose. She checked Marie's vitals, and said if I needed her to use the call button. At 6:00 p.m., they asked me to leave. I kissed Marie goodnight, and told her I would see her in the morning. I went to the outpatient waiting area, and made phone calls to our friends to let them know that the surgery went well, and that she was resting.

I was back at the hospital at 8:30 the next morning. At 9:00 a.m., a familiar person showed up whom we both knew from the Carmel Mission Basilica. Diana was a volunteer at the hospital, and she had brought Marie a get well wish from the Carmel Art Association. At 9:30 a.m., I was asked to leave so the doctors could do their rounds. Marie wanted to make sure I was going to play tennis, and sad she would see me later that afternoon.

Yet when I came back at 3:00 p.m., I was told that Marie's room was in isolation. They said she was contagious. I never learned why. I would have to put on a gown, face mask and gloves every time I entered her room. Since this was not like a private room, if I had to use a bathroom, I would take all the stuff off, and upon returning I would put on a fresh gown, face mask and gloves.

Marie wanted to watch *Judge Judy*, and then the News. Then it was time to leave, and I told I would see her the next morning after exercising. I kissed her goodnight, and went upstairs and made the same phone calls again.

When I got there Wednesday morning, Diana was on her way to the ICU, and asked if I needed to talk to someone. I said yes, and she gave me the number for Kevin, who was the chaplain at the hospital. We set a time to meet when I went to get lunch. He was very helpful, and asked if he could let the palliative team know if I needed someone to talk to. I said yes. The next day I met Kacie and John and they were very supportive. Also on Wednesday, Marie started both pulmonary and physical therapy.

This routine continued for about a month until I asked to have a meeting with Dr. Hausdorff, the surgeon, and the palliative team on Friday, June 19th. We discussed where Marie would go for rehab, and the surgeon suggested San Jose. I asked for a place nearer, and he said he would look into it and let me know. The doctors never told me how serious Marie's condition was. I was still expecting her to recover fully.

The following Tuesday, on June 23rd, the surgeon saw me in the hall, and said that Marie was not going to make it. This information came out of the blue, and I was shocked at this devastating news. I found the nearest place to sit, and started bawling. One of the nurses came over, and I told him what happened. He called the palliative team and they took me into the conference room, and told me that Dr. Hausdorff was on his way.

After I told Dr. Hausdorff what had just happened, he said that I would never have to ever see that surgeon again. After I quieted down, he wanted to go see Marie and let her know that he would be there if she needed him.

I left the conference room let the nurse know that Dr. Hausdorff would be replacing the surgeon as the person to contact. While Marie was distracted by the pulmonary therapist, I saw another nurse in the hall. I asked him to erase the surgeon's name on the white board and put Dr. Hausdorff's name there. Marie never noticed the name change. I never told Marie what had happened.

The next day, on Wednesday, June 24th, I received a sign from God that things were taking a turn for the worse. I asked Marie if there was anyone she wanted to see, and she wanted to see her best friend, Naomi Terman, whom she had met at the Carmel Red Cross Chapter. I called Naomi, and she came that afternoon. Naomi put on the gown, mask and gloves, and we had a good visit. When the visit was over, I walked her out and thanked her. On the way back to Marie's room, I stopped and called the Carmel Mission Basilica, and requested that a priest come and anoint Marie.

At about six o'clock, Father Paul, our Pastor, and Father Miquel both arrived. Father Paul said he would stay, and Father Miquel went on to help another parishioner. Father Paul performed the ritual of anointing the sick, and then we said some prayers. When he was finished, we looked at Marie, and there was a smile on her face. She knew that she would see God soon. I kissed her goodnight, and said I would see her the next day.

On Thursday, June 25th, I Got there at 8:30 a.m., kissed Marie, and stayed with her until 9:30 a.m. I tried to get back inside the ICU at 10:00, but they hadn't completed rounds yet. They said they would call the reception area, to let me know when I could go back in. When the phone rang, the receptionist said he would walk me to the door, and use his key to let me in. Marie was half awake, and I sat there holding her hand. I stayed by her side except for a quick trip at noon to grab a sandwich. The nurse pulled the curtain around her bed, and I sat there holding her hand. At 3:45 p.m., I gave Marie my last kiss, and the nurse came in and said she had passed. She was now with God, and finally getting the rest she deserved.

I don't know how long I sat there. It was hard to believe that this woman, my partner for 46 years, was gone. Eventually, the nurse came and said I had to leave. She helped me gather the cards and Marie's belongings, and walked me out of the ICU.

When I got home, I started calling everyone letting them know. Friday I called Naomi and asked her to come help me write Marie's obituary. I then called the Carmel Mission Basilica to see when I could schedule her Memorial Mass. We scheduled the Mass for July 2nd at 10:30 a.m.

After, Naomi arrived, I showed her what I had written. She made a few corrections, and I thanked her. I then called Andrea Thatcher to see who I could get to do Marie's eulogy, and she said she would let me know. Andrea called me on Monday and said that Sharon Crino, who had been the CEO of the American Red Cross in Carmel California, would do the eulogy. I then called Father Thomas Dove at

Old Saint Mary's Church in San Francisco, and asked him to say a Mass for Marie. He had married us in 1969. I then called the Neptune Society and informed them of Marie's passing, and told them that she was at Community Hospital.

On Monday, I went to the *Monterey Herald*, and met with Roberta Little, the Obituary Coordinator, and gave her Marie's picture, and obituary. She made a proof of it, and I approved it. I then went to Carmel Mission Basilica, and I met with Mary Kay from the Bereavement Ministry, and started discussing the Memorial Mass. She said that there would be the organist and soloist there, and that I should think about what music I would like to have. As we were discussing what readings to use, Father Paul came in and asked to sit in and give me guidance on what he thought would be appropriate. I told him which ones I would like, and he agreed. I asked him if it would be alright to have the organist and soloist do "Moon River" at the beginning of the Mass, and he didn't see a problem. I asked if, at the conclusion, the organist would play the Recessional from *Sound of Music*. He asked why, and I said that's what we had played after we were married, and leaving St. Paul the Apostle Church in Westwood, California. Both Father Paul and Mary Kay were a big help in preparing Marie's Memorial.

On Monday, June 29th, I called the Neptune Society to see if they had received Marie's remains, and they said they hadn't received the Death Certificate. I asked why someone hadn't called me, and they didn't have an answer. I called Dr. Koostra's office and was told to contact Dr. Hausdorff's office. They'd forgotten to do it. I called

Father Paul and told him, and he said to go ahead with the Memorial Mass. When I received her ashes, I could call him and he would bless them.

On July 2nd, I arrived at Carmel Mission Basilica, I went to the Church, and gave Mary Kay the picture of Marie that would sit on a table along with a bouquet of flowers from Caroline and Pauline from Canada. It was beautiful. She asked who I had picked to bring the gifts up to the Altar, and I said I hadn't. She suggested that the two of us would do that, and I thanked her.

When it was time for the guests to arrive, Mary Kay ushered me to my seat in the first pew, and the organist played incidental music. Some people came over an offered their condolences, and I thanked them. I looked up, and standing there was my godson Matthew Waterson, and I invited him to sit next to me. Then my nephew Stephen Prescott arrived with his girlfriend Ruby. Then the organist started playing the intro to "Moon River" and the soloist started to sing. Sharon Crino was introduced, and her eulogy to Marie was perfect. (A copy of her eulogy is included in Appendix B.) When she was finished, she sat in a chair in front of me, and gave me a copy of it. I thanked her.

Then the Mass started with the processional hymn, and then Father Paul welcomed everyone. I was fortunate that Mary Kay had selected people from the parish to do the first and second readings. Then Father Paul read from the Gospel, followed by his homily. I was happy that he remembered what I had told him about Marie, and he made it very personal by standing next to the pew where I was sitting.

Then the intercessions were said. I got up to meet Mary Kay and, as I was walking up the aisle, I noticed Rabbi Bruce Greenbaum sitting there. I gave him a nod, and then we brought the Gifts to Father Paul. After receiving Communion, Father Paul thanked everyone on my behalf for coming, and then I joined him, and we walked out together. The organist played the recessional from *The Sound of Music*.

When we got outside, I thanked him, and then the guests started coming out, and telling me how nice it was. Afterwards I went back inside the Basilica, and thanked Mary Kay, and gave her two envelopes, one for Father Paul, and the other for the Bereavement Ministry for all her help. I then took Marie's picture and the bouquet of flowers and left.

Matthew was waiting outside, and I asked him if he had time for lunch before getting back on the road to Los Angeles. He did, and I suggested going to Pebble Beach to one of our favorite places. We went to the Gallery Café, and got a window table, and could see the first tee. Afterwards we drove back to the Mission, and I told him again how much I appreciated him coming. I went home, and put the bouquet on the table, and Marie's picture back in the Den.

I decided that I didn't want to do anything over the Fourth of July weekend, except go to the 7:30 a.m. Mass on Sunday. Marie and I always sat in the last pew of the front section of the Basilica. About once a month the head usher Russ would ask us to bring up the Gifts for Communion.

On Wednesday, July 8th, I called the Neptune Society to see when they would deliver Marie's remains, and they had forgotten to do it. I told them I would drive up to San Jose the next day to get them. When

I got there, they handed me the death certificates, and said they would bring her remains to me. When they did, I reminded them that they were supposed to in an urn, and they showed me what they had, and I picked one that I thought Marie would like.

On Friday, I called Carmel Mission Basilica to see if Father Paul had any time to bless the urn. I arrived at 11:00 a.m., and I was shown to his office. He then proceeded to bless the urn, and then I went home and put it on top of a cabinet, so Marie would be able to see me feeding the seagulls, and see the sunsets.

I had promised Marie that I would continue exercising and playing tennis, which I am doing.

I went to a few meetings on how to deal with grief, and they really didn't help. At one of the meetings in November, they said there would be a symposium on how cope during the holidays. It was held at Shoreline Community Church in Monterey. They had six speakers, but only one had a solution, and his name was Mick Erickson. He recommended a book by Judy Tatelbaum, called *The Courage to Grieve*. I went to the public library, and they didn't have it. Then I remembered that Yellow Brick Road had a library. I went and they had a copy, and I bought it. It really helped me, so I bought Tatelbaum's second book, *You Don't Have to Suffer*. In my opinion, reading "The Courage to Grieve" first worked for me. Then I found out that Mick also did group counseling for The Carmel Foundation on the 2nd and 4th Wednesdays. I went for a month, and I told him how much he had helped me.

ACKNOWLEDGEMENTS

I have had so many interesting jobs in my life, have had great adventures. Many of my opportunities, however, came through relationships with some very special people. I would like to acknowledge their roles in my life.

Meeting **Marie** while she was a private duty nurse taking care of Frank Wilcox, and **Frank Wilcox** for asking me to take her lunch. We dated for 5 years. Through her, I decided to become a Catholic. Being married for 46 years was the icing on the cake. Every time the opportunity to move on to a new job, she was very supportive, and I grew as a person with each new challenge.

Kyle Faber was the Treasurer of EPI, and interviewed me and thirty-five other applicants for the position of Office Boy, and he picked me, giving me my very first job in television. Being recommended by Ronald Dubin probably didn't hurt.

I was very fortunate that I met a lot of people along the way that cared about what I was doing. The first was **Lou Cowan**, who was a Vice President at CBS. In December, 1955 he left Louis G. Cowan Productions and sold the company to join CBS, and they changed the name to Entertainment Productions Inc. (EPI). I think he requested me to bring papers that he had to sign so we could talk. He taught me to always take the time to listen and then help if I could. His wife Polly, who was also very creative in creating "Down You Go" and the NBC Radio show "Conversation," was also very kind to me. Unfortunately they died together in a house fire on November 24, 1976.

Gay Taylor was influential in having me selected to be interviewed for an article in the *World Telegram & Sun* newspaper about Television Production.

Bill Egan and I remained lifelong friends, even though he was in New York. We would talk, and he would give me good advice.

George Habib, Director of Unit Managers, took a chance on me, and he kept giving me challenges after I was made a permanent Unit Manager.

Senator George Murphy invited me into his family when Marie was a nurse for Mrs. Murphy. When she passed away on September 30, 1973, I drove the Senator to the funeral home to select her casket, and Marie and I were there at the house after the funeral. Senator Murphy asked me to take care of answering the doorbell for him and greeting their friends. Senator Murphy passed away on May 5th, 1992 in Palm Beach, Florida. A week later a Memorial Mass was held at the Church of the Good Shepherd in Beverly Hills, California. Bob Hope gave the eulogy, and thanked George for introducing him to his wife Delores.

Harry Waterson really didn't know me very well, but thought enough of me to get me an interview for *SOAP* and then mentored me on preparing the budget.

Bill Fisher took a gamble on hiring me, but found out I was a team player. He also let me continue doing some post-production work as a DGA (Directors Guild of America) member.

Jay Sandrich was instrumental in getting me an interview at GTG (Grant Tinker/Gannett) Studios, formerly known as The Culver Studios where *Gone With The Wind* was filmed.

Deborah Aal suggested I get an agent near the end of *Raising Miranda* and recommended **Beth Uffner**. Beth had enough confidence in me to recommend me to Steve Papazian at Warner Brothers Television. Steve had me meet Grant Rosenberg, Executive Producer, and was hired as a producer on *Molloy*. Beth also put me in touch with KTMB at Walt Disney Studios. I knew Kathy & Terry from *Benson*.

Erwin Stoff (Deborah Aal's husband) called and asked me to do *Down The Shore* for HBO Independent Productions, and I was hired.

Ida Corby has been there for me when Marie was in the ICU, and after her passing, she has been a true friend.

Barbara Allen Burke made this a true labor of love for me. I told her that my wife Marie had wanted me to write this book. It took two years. When I met Barbara, I knew she and I would work well together. Thank you for making *Would You Believe!* happen.

In closing, I'm going to use Bob Hope's sign off on his television shows:

"Thanks for the Memories."

APPENDIX A
RATE CARDS

I wanted to include two additional items here. So much of my job as a producer involved working with the studios and including their costs into the budgets of the shows. I have included a sample of the rate cards from both NBC and ABC to record this little-known aspect of television history.

ABC

Rate Manual Number 10
Facilities and Services
Effective November 1, 1970

ABC Television Network

Facilities

Studios:

The rates apply to the use of a studio or theatre with its regular complement of lighting and technical equipment. All equipment in excess of basic complement must be specified on Request for Facilities and Personnel form. Basic studio complement will be furnished on request.

The studio or theatre rate will be charged from the start of dry rehearsal and/or technical set-up through end of air or tape time, pro-rated to the next ½ hour with a six-hour minimum charge per day.

All personnel and extra equipment will be charged for at their applicable rates in addition to the studio or theatre charge.

Orchestra rehearsal and pre-recording studio rates furnished on request.

New York	Net Hourly	Cameras
TV-1	450	4
TV-2	400	4
TV-1 & 2	850	8
TV-7	300	3
TV-11	300	4
TV-14	450	4
TV-15	400	4
TV-16	400	4
TV-18	450	4
TV-19	450	4

Hollywood		
A	400	4
B	400	3
D	450	4
E	450	4
Palace	450	4
Vine St. Theatre	450	4

Washington		
B	300	3

Control rooms — 100
(No Stage Activity) (1 hour minimum)

Extra Cameras — 400 per day

Color Mobile Unit Facilities
(Exclusive of Personnel)

Usage and rehearsal -- For each color camera or video tape machine -- $1,000.00 per day

Travel Day -- $1,000.00 per day

Set, strike or other non usage days -- $2,000.00 per day

Notes:

Daily rate computed on maximum of 10 hours total elapsed time beginning from engineering set up to end of rehearsal, air and/or tape.

Travel day charge includes one driver per vehicle, driver expenses and mileage.

Technical survey personnel will be charged at applicable rates in addition to per diem and travel expenses.

Cost of tape, audio and video lines, loops, electrical installations, generators, lighting equipment and other equipment and services will be quoted on request.

Basic remote truck complement furnished on request. Additional equipment on request.

Film Projection Facilities
(Including Personnel)

Film, Slide or Telechain -- $90.00 per hour

The charge will be pro-rated to the next quarter hour with a one half hour minimum charge. Charges will be based on total elapsed time ordered or used, whichever is greater for rehearsal, air and/or record time. Breaks of ½ hour or more will not be charged. Projection print must be supplied to ABC.

Technical Personnel Chart

hours	Number of men																			
	1	2	3	4	5	6	7	8	9	10	11	12	13	14	15	16	17	18	19	20
3	40	80	120	160	200	240	280	320	360	400	440	480	520	560	600	640	680	720	760	800
4	51	102	153	204	255	306	357	408	459	510	561	612	663	714	765	816	867	918	969	1020
5	62	124	186	248	310	372	434	496	558	620	682	744	806	868	930	992	1054	1116	1178	1240
6	73	146	219	292	365	438	511	584	657	730	803	876	949	1022	1095	1168	1241	1314	1387	1460
7	84	168	252	336	420	504	588	672	756	840	924	1008	1092	1176	1260	1344	1428	1512	1596	1680
8	96	192	288	384	480	576	672	768	864	960	1056	1152	1248	1344	1440	1536	1632	1728	1824	1920
9	116	232	348	464	580	696	812	928	1044	1160	1276	1392	1508	1624	1740	1856	1972	2088	2204	2320
10	136	272	408	544	680	816	952	1088	1224	1360	1496	1632	1768	1904	2040	2176	2312	2448	2584	2720
11	161	322	483	644	805	966	1127	1288	1449	1610	1771	1932	2093	2254	2415	2576	2737	2898	3059	3220
12	186	372	558	744	930	1116	1302	1488	1674	1860	2046	2232	2418	2604	2790	2976	3162	3348	3534	3720
13	221	442	663	884	1105	1326	1547	1768	1989	2210	2431	2652	2873	3094	3315	3536	3757	3978	4199	4420
14	256	512	768	1024	1280	1536	1792	2048	2304	2560	2816	3072	3328	3584	3840	4096	4352	4608	4864	5120
15	291	582	873	1164	1455	1746	2037	2328	2619	2910	3201	3492	3783	4074	4365	4656	4947	5238	5529	5820
16	326	652	978	1304	1630	1956	2282	2608	2934	3260	3586	3912	4238	4564	4890	5216	5542	5868	6194	6520
17	361	722	1083	1444	1805	2166	2527	2888	3249	3610	3971	4332	4693	5054	5415	5776	6137	6498	6859	7220
18	396	792	1188	1584	1980	2376	2772	3168	3564	3960	4356	4752	5148	5544	5940	6336	6732	7128	7524	7920
19	431	862	1293	1724	2155	2586	3017	3448	3879	4310	4741	5172	5603	6034	6465	6896	7327	7758	8189	8620
20	466	932	1398	1864	2330	2796	3262	3728	4194	4660	5126	5592	6058	6524	6990	7456	7922	8388	8854	9320

Beyond 20 hours technical personnel will be charged at the maximum rate indicated on the chart.
This rate will be charged until there is a 12 hour break on the same show.
All rates are pro-rated to the next full hour.

Production and Technical Services

The following rates will be charged for the entire period of assignment. All expenses incurred will be additional. The first meal period for engineers where required will not be charged. Engineering manpower will be charged from engineering set-up through and including engineering knockdown. Pre calls when required by the production will be charged. Additional penalties and cost incurred by ABC for personnel requested by name will be charged to user. All rates, unless otherwise specified, will be pro-rated to the next ½ hour. Rates on the technical personnel chart will be pro-rated to the next hour.

Survey when required will be charged on the basis of personnel rates plus applicable per diem and travel expense.

	Net Hourly Rate	Minimums
Announcer	on request	
Associate Director	see technical personnel chart	6 hours
Carpenter Scenic (materials not included)	10.00 (N.Y.) 6.50 (Hollywood)	1 hour
Costumer	on request (N.Y.) 10.00 (Hollywood)	8 hours
Drape Fabricator (materials not included)	10.00	1 hour
Electric Shop Personnel	10.00	1 hour
Engineer	see technical personnel chart	
Engineer (other than days of studio usage)	per 7½ hr. day 115.00 after 7½ hrs. 15.00 per hr.	7½ hours
Engineer (pre calls only)	15.00	
Film Editing Services	15.00	1 hour
Graphic Artist	9.00	1 hour
Hair Stylist	9.00	8 hours
Lighting Equip. Additional	on request	
Makeup Artist (includes normal materials)	9.00	8 hours
Mimeographing & Typing	on request	

	Net Hourly Rate	Minimums
Musician	applicable single engagement rates	
Cue Card Holder (staff personnel)	4.00 (Hollywood) on request (N.Y.)	8 hours
Prop Shopping and Delivery	8.50	1 hour
Rehearsal Halls	on request	
Scenery Delivery	8.50	1 hour
Scenic Designer	14.00	8 hours
Scenic Artist	12.00 (N.Y.) 11.00 (Hollywood)	1 hour
Screening Rooms	on request	
Sound Effects Personnel	see technical personnel chart	3 hours
Sound Effects (crack) (maximum charge per day $30.00)	7.50	2 hours
Special Effects	10.00 (Hollywood) on request (N.Y.)	1 hour
*Stagehands	8.00 (N.Y.) 8.00 (Hollywood)	4 & 8 hour minimums 8 hours
(effective June 1, 1971)	8.50 (N.Y.) 8.50 (Hollywood)	4 & 8 hour minimums 8 hours
Stage Manager	see technical personnel chart	6 hours
Storage (when available)	on request	
Technical Director	see technical personnel chart	
Technical Director (other than on days of studio usage)	per 7½ hr. day 115.00 after 7½ hrs. 15.00 per hr.	7½ hours
Technical Director (pre calls only)	15.00	
Technical Supervisor	150.00	per day
Trucking	30.00 (N.Y.) 15.00 (Hollywood)	½ hour ½ hour
Wardrobe Handler	7.50	8 hours

*pro-rated to the next full hour.

Kinescope Recording
On Request

Video Tape

Recording, Playback, Rehearsal, Screening, Editing, Dubbing

| Per Machine | $100.00 1st hour |
| Per Machine | 90.00 each additional hour |

Minimum, ½ Hour Per Machine
Charges will be based on time ordered or used, whichever is greater.
Breaks of less than ½ hour will be charged.
Rate does not include cost of tape.

Raw Material Cost

$75/15 min. pgm segment for tape purchased, stored or otherwise made unavailable for normal ABC use.

Technically acceptable tapes previously purchased from ABC may be redeemed at $200.00 per hour reel. The rate does not include the cost of tape check.

Storage

| First Week | No charge |
| Per reel, after first week | $5.00 per month |

ABC assumes no responsibility for storage of tape.

NBC

RATE MANUAL NUMBER 8
EFFECTIVE APRIL 1, 1967
NBC TELEVISION NETWORK
PRODUCTION FACILITIES

GENERAL INFORMATION

1 Except for Integrated Networking charges, all rates included in this manual become effective April 1, 1967, with one month's protection to programs scheduled or to time periods contracted for on or before this date. Integrated Networking charges to advertisers become effective September 9, 1967 with protection under the prior rate manual lasting until this date.

2 All rates included herein are quoted net except for Integrated Networking charges which are quoted gross.

3 The rates apply in all Network locations and for all Network TV programs. Locations not covered by these rates will be quoted on request.

4 All materials, designs, sketches and floor plans supplied, constructed, or purchased by NBC remain the property of NBC, unless otherwise agreed to by NBC in writing prior to show presentation.

5 The usage of all personnel must be in accordance with current labor union contracts and operating conditions.

6 The furnishing of facilities, services and materials covered by this manual is not guaranteed. All orders for them will be subject to availability.

7 All orders for production facilities and services that cause NBC additional expense due to their lateness will be subject to an additional charge as compensation for these costs.

8 All rates are subject to City and State taxes where applicable.

9 All data herein are subject to change without notice.

FACILITIES

STUDIOS: (NOT INCLUDING MANPOWER) The rates apply to the use of a studio with its regular lighting and technical equipment complement as posted at each location. All items ordered over and above these will be charged. All manpower will be charged additionally at appropriate rates. The charge for studio usage will be on a clock-hour basis from the time the studio is ordered for dry rehearsal and/or technical setup until the end of air or tape time. Studio charges will be prorated to the next full half hour. On usage of two or more days, there will be a six-hour minimum per day.

	HOURLY RATE	CAMERAS
N.Y. 3B	$300	3
N.Y. 6A	300	3
N.Y. 6B	300	3
N.Y. 8G	300	3
N.Y. 8H*	400	4
N.Y. Brooklyn I*	400	4
N.Y. Brooklyn II*	400	4
Burbank I*	400	4
Burbank II*	400	4
Burbank III*	400	4
Burbank IV*	400	4

*6-hour minimum per day.

Rates quoted on request for non-audience usages of audience facilities.

2

3

315

EXTRA CAMERAS AND MONITORS:
(NOT INCLUDING MANPOWER)

Camera	$250 per day
Monitor	20 per day

Rates for all other technical equipment including Special Effects quoted on request.

COLOR MOBILE UNIT

Color Mobile Unit including five color cameras, one black and white camera, and two video tape machines . . . . $750 per hour.

An eight hour minimum will apply on all Color Mobile Unit usage. The hourly rate applies to camera usage commencing at dry rehearsal, or technical setup, prorated to the next half hour. All manpower used will be charged separately at appropriate rates.

Travel days . . . $500 per day plus $.50 per mile.

Set, Strike, or other
Non-Usage days . . . . $1,500 per day.

Technical surveys when requested will be performed by NBC assigned technical personnel at a daily rate of $100 plus transportation and living expenses.

Estimates of additional charges for transportation of manpower, administration travel expenses, lighting equipment, micro-wave, audio and video lines, electrical installations and other services quoted on request.

Rates for other Mobile Unit equipment quoted on request.

4

VIDEO TAPE FACILITIES
(INCLUDING MANPOWER)
RECORDING, PRODUCTION PLAYBACK, DUBBING, MACHINE EDITING, AND VIEWING

Per machine	$100 1st hour
Per machine	$80 for additional hours
Minimum ¼ hr. per machine	

A minimum of two machines required for recording, production playback, and dubbing.

These rates will be charged on the basis of total elapsed time ordered or used, whichever is greater. Breaktimes equivalent to fifteen minutes per elapsed hour may be taken at no charge if ordered in advance. Breaks may be taken in one or more fifteen minute segments.

SALES AND/OR BREAKAGE

60 minutes	$250
30 minutes	150
15 minutes	75
5 minutes	30

The above rates include reels. Breakage is determined to be the total minutes of tape used less nonspliced lengths (34 and 64 minute lengths).

Technically acceptable tapes previously purchased from NBC may be redeemed at $200 per hour reel.

STORAGE: Storage will be charged at the rate of $5 a month per reel commencing 14 days after air or use date. Arrangements may be made with NBC Video Tape Operations. NBC accepts no responsibility for storage of program or commercial tapes.

5

FILM FACILITIES (INCLUDING MANPOWER)

Per film chain . . . . $90 per clock hour per program. Minimum of one clock quarter hour. These rates will be charged on the basis of total elapsed time ordered or used, whichever is greater, for rehearsal, air, or recording time. Control rooms, when required, are $80 per hour with a one hour minimum.

ANNOUNCE FACILITIES
(INCLUDING MANPOWER)

	HOURLY CHARGE
5 HN N.Y. Color Announce Studio (two cameras)	$180
Audio Announce Booth	80

A one hour minimum will apply to Announce Facilities with additional usage prorated to the next half hour. These rates include the use of a control room.

VIEWING ROOMS

System viewing rooms and non-system viewing (screening rooms) . . . . . $15 per hour.

Minimum of one half hour required. Charges will be prorated to the next half hour.

Film chains or video tape machines used in conjunction with system viewings will be charged separately at the appropriate rates.

KINESCOPE RECORDING
(INCLUDING MANPOWER)

Rates for NBC's Kinescope Recording and print services quoted on request.

6

PRODUCTION SERVICES

STAGING SERVICES: The following rates will be charged for the total period of assignment. All hourly rates will be prorated to the next half-hour, unless otherwise indicated.

	HOURLY RATE	MINIMUM
Associate Director	$9.00	—
Stage Manager	9.00	—
Associate Director	9.00	6 hrs.
Stage Manager additional or on other than show day	9.00	6 hrs.
Stagehands, basic crew*	7.00	—
Stagehands, extra*	7.00	4 hrs.
Stagehands, Hollywood*	7.00	5 hrs.
Wardrobe Handlers & Dressers	6.00	4 hrs.
Hairstylist	8.00	6 hrs.
Makeup Artist including normal materials First Artist	8.00	2 hrs.
Each Additional Artist	8.00	6 hrs.

*Prorated to the next full hour.

SOUND EFFECTS: (NOT INCLUDING MANPOWER) Technical stock sound equipment will be charged at 1-hour intervals at $7.50 per hour, with a minimum charge of $15.00 per day and a maximum charge of $30.00 per day. Manpower will be charged in accordance with the Technical Personnel Chart.

7

STORAGE: NBC will supply storage facilities on request if and when available. Prices quoted on request. NBC reserves the right to change location without notice.

SCENIC SERVICES: All manpower charges listed below are prorated to the next half-hour, with a half-hour minimum for each service. Charges for material including scenery, props, or other elements will be quoted on request.

Rates apply to NBC staff personnel. Weekly rates for Scenic and Costume Designers supplied on request.

	HOURLY RATE
Scenic Designer	$13.00
Costume Designer (N. Y.)	9.00
Graphic Artist	8.00
Prop Handler (N. Y.)	7.50
Drape Constructionist (N. Y.)	7.50
Scenic Carpenter	7.50
Scenic Artist	9.50

Trucking Services (New York) will be charged at $180 per full load per round trip.

Minimum of one eighth load will be charged at $40 per round trip. Hollywood trucking services will be quoted on request.

8

TECHNICAL SERVICES: The following rates will be charged for the total period of assignment. The hours charged for all Basic Engineering Calls will be based on the time the crew is ordered until end of air or tape, on a consecutive clock-hour basis. The first meal period, where required, will not be included in the total number of hours charged for engineering manpower. All charges will be prorated to the next half-hour, unless otherwise indicated.

	HOURLY RATE	MINIMUM
Engineers, Basic Crew Calls	See Technical Personnel Chart	
Non-Studio Usage Days up to 8 hours: Engineers (including Technical Director)	$100.00	
After 8 Hours	$12.00	—
Studio Usage Days: Engineers (including Technical Director) on prior/post calls	12.00	—
Sound Effects manpower and Projectionists when called at times other than basic engineering crew	12.00	2 hrs.
Film Editing	15.00	1 hr.

9

TECHNICAL PERSONNEL CHART*

NUMBER OF MEN	2	3	4	5	6	7	8	9	10	11	12	13	14	15	16	17	18	19	20
3	66	95	123	154	185	205	234	270	315	380	450	527	609	675	744	816	891	969	1050
4	88	126	164	205	246	273	312	360	420	506	600	702	812	900	992	1088	1188	1292	1400
5	110	158	205	256	308	341	390	450	525	633	750	878	1015	1125	1240	1360	1485	1615	1750
6	132	189	246	308	369	410	468	540	630	759	900	1053	1218	1350	1488	1632	1782	1938	2100
7	154	221	287	359	431	478	546	630	735	886	1050	1229	1421	1575	1736	1904	2079	2261	2450
8	176	252	328	410	492	546	624	720	840	1012	1200	1404	1624	1800	1984	2176	2376	2584	2800
9	198	284	369	461	554	614	702	810	945	1139	1350	1580	1827	2025	2232	2448	2673	2907	3150
10	220	315	410	513	615	683	780	900	1050	1265	1500	1755	2030	2250	2480	2720	2970	3230	3500
11	242	347	451	554	677	751	858	990	1155	1392	1650	1931	2233	2475	2728	2992	3267	3553	3850
12	264	378	492	615	738	819	936	1080	1260	1518	1800	2106	2436	2700	2976	3264	3564	3876	4200
13	286	410	533	666	800	887	1014	1170	1365	1645	1950	2282	2639	2925	3224	3536	3861	4199	4550
14	308	441	574	718	861	956	1092	1260	1470	1771	2100	2457	2842	3150	3472	3808	4158	4522	4900
15	330	473	615	769	923	1024	1170	1350	1575	1898	2250	2633	3045	3375	3720	4080	4455	4845	5250
16	352	504	656	820	984	1092	1248	1440	1680	2024	2400	2808	3248	3600	3968	4352	4752	5168	5600
17	374	536	697	871	1046	1160	1326	1530	1785	2151	2550	2984	3451	3825	4216	4624	5049	5491	5950
18	396	567	738	923	1107	1229	1404	1620	1890	2277	2700	3159	3654	4050	4464	4896	5346	5814	6300
19	418	599	779	974	1169	1297	1482	1710	1995	2404	2850	3335	3857	4275	4712	5168	5643	6137	6650
20	440	630	820	1025	1230	1365	1560	1800	2100	2530	3000	3510	4060	4500	4960	5440	5940	6460	7000

*Prorated to the next full hour.

10   11

317

APPENDIX B
MARIE'S EULOGY

Delivered by Sharon Crino

July 2, 2015

Good Morning.

Thank you all so much for attending this service today to pay tribute to our Marie, wife, sister and great friend to all of us in this room.

For many of you who know me, you know that I am a "from the heart" speaker. Sometimes it is difficult to do that. But today, speaking from the heart is the easiest and most natural way I can express my thoughts about Marie, and I am sure yours as well.

My time with Marie has not been as long as many of you in the room. But I can tell you that it has been one of the most meaningful relationships that I have had. I first met Marie in 2008 when I became the CEO of the American Red Cross in Carmel. She was our front desk volunteer. On our first meeting, we became fast friends and felt like we had known each other for years. Marie was kind, gentle and always there to lend a helping hand. She was at the office before I was on the mornings she was working. She looked for my car and when she saw me pull up, she immediately had a cup of coffee ready for me. She knew exactly how to make it—a little coffee in my milk.

Over the years we came to talk about everything from shared stories about our families to what we liked to do and our passions in life. If you did not know this already, Marie was a special duty nurse. One of her assignments in Los Angeles was for the wife of George Murphy. (It is the first time I can say this in a long time. I am too young to know who George Murphy was) so I did what everyone does—I Googled him. I urge you to do the same. He had quite the Hollywood career and then moved on to be a California State senator.

During this time, she met and began courting Andy Selig. So after the courtship, it was only fitting that on May 31, 1969, George Murphy gave away Marie LeVasseur to Andy Selig. That handing over resulted in a 46-year love affair between the two.

At the Red Cross I observed Marie's kindness, dedication, compassion, empathy and work ethic. For example, during Hurricane Katrina and 9/11 our Red Cross Chapter was receiving hundreds of dollars in *coin* donations daily from schools and school children all over the country. This money was all in coins. Marie would diligently work single-handed at the office, not only counting, but rolling the coins so they could be deposited in their respective funds. That work resulted in thousands of dollars in coins being counted. Now, the Red Cross policy was that only a board member could handle money, but due to Marie's character, calmness and capability, we bent the rules and were much better for it.

When she could not come into the office she would call me and ask me to get all my donor thank you notes (sometimes upward of 200 at one time) written and she would pick them up, take them home to address, stamp and mail. She did that for all four years that I was at the

Red Cross.

Marie had a great love for the Carmel Art Association. In speaking to the executive director of the association, Nikki Erlich, she stated, "To say she will be missed is an understatement. She was a tireless advocate of the CAA and helped to keep the gallery in top shape and running smoothly for the last 13 years. She was a thoughtful and loving person and a dear friend. She will be remembered always."

She was an avid participant and one of the original founders of the Peninsula Readers Book Club since its inception in 2001. The club membership is mainly made up of members of the Church in the Forest. Marie was not a member of that church as she was a Roman Catholic. So, she was affectionately known as the "token Catholic." Since 2001 Marie was the administrative guru of the book club handling all of the details that go along with it.

In all of the conversations that I have had with people about Marie there was one common theme that described her over and over—it was her kindness, gentleness, compassion and positive attitude about people and situations.

It was too soon for us to say goodbye to Marie as she had much more to do and much more to give. Since the Lord felt that it was Marie's time, there are three things that we should remember about her.

1. She loved Andy second to none.
2. She gave in abundance to all those around her, and
3. I know that heaven is on its way to greeting the best cheerleader they could ever dream of having in its midst.

She would not want us to be sad, or to cry for her. She would want us to celebrate her life, as we should. We will miss her greatly, think of her often and love her forever.

Thank you for being here today and celebrating our Marie.

ABOUT THE AUTHOR

Andrew J. Selig, a New York native, started his career in the Golden Age of Television. Moving his way up from office boy to associate producer, and relocating to Hollywood, he worked on different productions, from *The $64,000 Question* to the ground-breaking sit-com *SOAP,* from sports to television specials. He retired with his wife Marie to Carmel, California, where they stayed active with tennis and volunteer work, and enjoyed beach walks, ocean sunsets, and hosting a pair of local seagulls until Marie's death in 2015.

Made in the USA
San Bernardino, CA
25 January 2018